Catholic Life in the Church of England

Good News for Every Body

Edited by

Simon Cuff

CANTERBURY
PRESS

© Simon Cuff 2025

Published in 2025 by Canterbury Press

Editorial office
3rd Floor, Invicta House
110 Golden Lane
London EC1Y 0TG, UK
www.canterburypress.co.uk

Canterbury Press is an imprint of Hymns Ancient & Modern Ltd
(a registered charity)

Hymns Ancient & Modern® is a registered trademark of
Hymns Ancient & Modern Ltd
13A Hellesdon Park Road, Norwich,
Norfolk NR6 5DR, UK

All rights reserved. No part of this publication may be reproduced,
stored in a retrieval system, or transmitted,
in any form or by any means, electronic, mechanical,
photocopying or otherwise, without the prior permission of
the publisher, Canterbury Press.

The editor and contributors have asserted their right under the Copyright,
Designs and Patents Act 1988 to be identified as the Authors of this Work

British Library Cataloguing in Publication data

A catalogue record for this book is available
from the British Library

ISBN: 978-1-78622-672-3

EU GPSR Authorised Representative
LOGOS EUROPE, 9 rue Nicolas Poussin, 17000, LA ROCHELLE, France
E-mail: Contact@logoseurope.eu

Typeset by Regent Typesetting

Contents

Biographies vii
Foreword by Archbishop Stephen Cottrell xv

Introduction 1
Simon Cuff

1 Eucharist 10
  Rowan Williams

2 Living Eucharistically: The Sacrament and Christian Ethics 19
  Michael J. Leyden

  Sermon: 'Invited by Name' 32
  Arwen Folkes

3 The Catholic Life: Radical Dependence 35
  Mel Marshall

4 Visual Theology of the Eucharist: Altarpieces in London, 1880–2024 47
  Ayla Lepine

  Sermon: 'How Are You?' 62
  Peter Allan

5 Discernment 67
  Ben Kerridge

6 Scripture 81
  Steffan Mathias

  Sermon: 'Hannah's Prayer: Testimony, Thanksgiving and Action' 98
  Joanne Woolway Grenfell

7   Prayer   103
    Nicolas Stebbing CR

8   Community   113
    Mitzi James

    Sermon: 'The Love of God Lived Out'   121
    Peter Groves

9   Baptism   124
    Christina Beardsley

    Sermon: 'Singing the Lord's Song'   139
    Kathryn Fleming

10 The Bridegroom and His Bride: Learning about Celibacy
    from Early Christian Fathers and Mothers   142
    Morwenna Ludlow

11 Marriage   156
    Charlie Bell

12 Children and Young People   169
    Sally Jones and Jack Noble

    Sermon: 'Mass and Motherhood'   181
    Esther Lay

Index of Names and Subjects   185

Biographies

Fr Peter Allan

Fr Peter's love of Catholic Christianity and its distinctive Anglican expression took shape through participation in the liturgy and life of Pusey House as an undergraduate. As a brother in the monastic Community of the Resurrection for the last 40 years he has been further grounded in the tradition through the study and practice of western chant and through teaching systematic and moral theology and guiding ordinands in formation at the College of the Resurrection at Mirfield. Arrival at Mirfield as a novice in the early 1980s coincided with one of those times of liturgical renewal. The monks of Solesmes were producing the new Latin editions of the chant for the post-Vatican II liturgy and the parallel task of making the whole Office available in English has proved the richest possible theological and spiritual inspiration.

Mthr Christina Beardsley

Christina (Tina) Beardsley SMMS, a Church of England priest, is a member of the dispersed Anglican community, The Sodality of Mary, Mother of Priests. Born in West Yorkshire, Tina moved first to Brighton – where she met her husband, Rob – to read Religious Studies at Sussex University, and then to St John's College, Cambridge, where her doctoral studies were on the Victorian Romantic preacher, Robertson of Brighton. Her focus was Robertson's theology and she subsequently wrote a biography, *Unutterable Love: The Passionate Life and Preaching of F.W. Robertson*. During ordination training at Westcott House, Cambridge, Tina was part of a student exchange with the Venerable English College in Rome. Ordained in Portsmouth Diocese, she served first in the Parish of St Mark, North End, Portsea, and then as Vicar of All Saints, Catherington, and St James, Clanfield. Afterwards Tina was a healthcare chaplain for 15 years, mostly at the Chelsea and Westminster Hospital, where she was Head of Multi-faith Chaplaincy from 2008 to 2016. Now retired and helping in London churches, north and south of the Thames, Tina is a Visiting Scholar at Sarum College, and co-author of a trilogy of books about the spiritual care of trans people.

Fr Charlie Bell

Fr Charlie Bell is a priest and a doctor. He practises as a forensic psychiatrist in South London, and is a Fellow in Medicine and Public Theology at Girton College, Cambridge. He is a priest at St John the Divine, Kennington, in the Diocese of Southwark in South London, a Research Fellow and Associate Tutor at St Augustine's College of Theology, Visiting Scholar at Sarum College and Scholar in Residence at the Cathedral of St John the Divine in New York City. He has written a number of books in the medico-theological interface, including two addressing the contribution of queer people to the life and doctrine of the Church. He doesn't really do spare time.

Fr Simon Cuff

Fr Simon Cuff is Vicar of St Peter de Beauvoir Town in the Diocese of London, Vice-Chair of the Just Money Movement and trustee of Migrants Organise, a charity organizing for justice in asylum and refugee communities, and of London Catalyst, a public health charity. He has recently completed a short series of reflections on priestly life, *Waiting Upon the Lord*, to be published soon, and is the author of three books: *Love in Action*, *Only God Will Save Us* and *Priesthood for All Believers: Clericalism and How to Avoid It*, on catholic social teaching, divine impassibility and responses to suffering, and the particularity of Christian vocation respectively. His current project is on the theological consequences of mortality and human limitation, exploring how theologies of baptism and creaturely limit, rather than being taboos to be avoided, are the grounds for creative response to God's call and an invitation to live life in all its fullness.

Mthr Kathryn Fleming

Given that she sang before she spoke and was reared on a diet of Radio 3 and poetry, it is perhaps unsurprising that Kathryn found her way to cathedral ministry after some years as a parish priest in Gloucester diocese. Serving first as Canon Pastor and latterly as Canon for Worship and Community at Coventry, she arrived at Southwark as Canon Precentor in 2023 and is committed to enabling liturgy to flex to accommodate all those who find their way into our wonderful buildings.

Mthr Arwen Folkes

Mthr Arwen Folkes is the Vicar of Eastbourne in Chichester Diocese. Having been sent from Truro Diocese to train at Westcott House, Cambridge, Arwen moved to be made Rector of East Blatchington and Bishopstone in 2019 after serving her title post in St Just in Roseland and St Mawes in Cornwall. A member of General Synod, with a continuing academic interest in St Augustine of Hippo, Arwen is also chair and co-founder of The College of Catholic Anglican Women. Her interests include her children, her dogs, the literary critical study of Scripture and a quite ridiculous amount of crochet.

Bishop Joanne Woolway Grenfell

Joanne Woolway Grenfell has served as the Bishop of Stepney in the Diocese of London since July 2019, having previously served as Archdeacon in the Diocese of Portsmouth, Residentiary Canon and Director of Ordinands in the Diocese of Sheffield and as an inner-city parish priest in Sheffield and Liverpool. In London, her diocesan responsibilities involve oversight of safeguarding and chairing the London Diocesan Board of Schools. In the Church of England she is the national lead bishop for safeguarding. She is a trustee of the Woodard Corporation. Joanne's forthcoming book, *Who Do You Say That I Am? Reflections for a Holy City*, written with Adam Atkinson and illustrated by Ali Mulroy, uses poetry, prayers, art and Scripture meditations to explore discipleship in today's world.

Fr Peter Groves

Fr Peter Groves has been at St Mary Magdalen, Oxford, for almost 20 years, having previously been a college chaplain. 'Mary Mags' is a busy city-centre Anglo-Catholic church celebrated for its liturgical tradition and well known for nurturing vocations in men and women. Fr Peter is also Associate Archdeacon of Oxford and a Senior Research Fellow at Worcester College, where he teaches theology. He is married to Beatrice, who teaches English at Trinity College, and they have two sons, Michael and Edward. Fr Peter's vices include wine, quizzing and Queens Park Rangers football club.

Fr Ben Kerridge

Ben is Vicar of Holy Innocents, Hornsey, in North London. He grew up in Bodmin, Cornwall, and lived in Italy, working as an English teacher, before returning to this country to train for the priesthood at the College of the Resurrection, Mirfield. He practises as a Spiritual Director and Supervisor, as well as training Spiritual Directors on the third year of the Ignatian Spirituality Course at the London Jesuit Centre. He enjoys wild swimming and improvisation.

Mthr Mitzi James

Mthr Mitzi is the Vicar of St John and St Luke, Clay Hill, in the Diocese of London. Before this she was curate of Hornsey Parish Church, after training for the priesthood at the College of the Resurrection, Mirfield. Mthr Mitzi has a background working with those who have experienced homelessness and domestic abuse, and was also a volunteer with the Samaritans and at Pentonville Prison. She is a newly qualified Spiritual Director and member of a dispersed international Community – The Sodality of Mary, Mother of Priests.

Mthr Sally Jones

Mthr Sally is Vicar of St Mary Magdalene, Munster Square, Regent's Park Estate – a Victorian Tractarian Church set in a working-class, inner-city parish between Camden and Euston in the Diocese of London. She is also Assistant Superior of The Sodality of Mary, Mother of Priests. She was previously Minor Canon Youth Chaplain of St Albans Cathedral, following a curacy in rural Wales.

Mthr Esther Lay

Mthr Esther was born in the USA, brought up in East Asia and has been based in the UK for nearly 20 years. She read Philosophy and Theology at Queen's, Oxford, before training as a classical singer at the Royal Academy of Music. After a ten-year career as a concert soloist specializing in baroque repertoire under the name Esther Brazil, she worked for two years as Ministerial Assistant at the University Church in Oxford, and trained for ministry at Ripon College Cuddesdon. She served her curacy at St Mary Magdalen, Oxford, where she was the first woman to hold the post; she is now the first female Rector of Wootton, Glympton and Kiddington. She is married to Ben, a serving naval officer, and they have two small children. She can be found reading and writing poetry in any available spare time.

Mthr Ayla Lepine

Ayla is a Church of England priest, art historian and theologian. She has been the Associate Rector at St James's Piccadilly since 2022. She was the 2021–22 Ahmanson Fellow in Art and Religion at the National Gallery, where she co-curated the exhibition *Fruits of the Spirit: Art from the Heart* with community partners across the UK. Following her PhD in Victorian sacred architecture at the Courtauld Institute of Art in 2011, she held fellowships at Yale's Institute of Sacred Music and the Courtauld Research Forum, and was lecturer and fellow in Art History at the University of Essex. She was ordained in the Diocese of London in 2018. Her publications have appeared in *British Art Studies*, *Theology and Sexuality*, in the Tate's 'In Focus' series, and she has co-edited books including *Modern Architecture and Religious Communities* and *Gothic Legacies*. She is a trustee of Art and Christianity, a Visiting Scholar at Sarum College, a member of the Church of England's Contested Heritage Committee and a member of the St Paul's Cathedral Visual Arts Committee.

Professor Morwenna Ludlow

The Revd Canon Professor Morwenna Ludlow is Professor of Christian History and Theology at the University of Exeter and Canon Theologian at Exeter Cathedral. Morwenna researches and teaches the history of the early Church, especially focused on fourth-century theologians writing in Greek, such as Gregory of Nyssa. She has published, among other books, *The Early Church*. Her current project, 'God and Good Speech', aims to identify the models and theological foundations for ethical and godly speech in Early Christianity.

Mthr Mel Marshall

Mthr Mel is a classicist by training and was a curate in a lovely London diocese. She lives in Oxford and has worked in university chaplaincy for the last eight years. She loves opera and knitting and poetry and writing sermons and singing the Mass and helping her friends with their renaissance Latin, but above all she loves hanging out with people.

Fr Steffan Mathias

Fr Steffan Mathias is Vicar of St Peter's, Streatham, in the Diocese of Southwark. His doctoral research was in Old Testament/Hebrew Bible studies, specializing in texts that respond to childlessness and death. He is passionate about teaching Old Testament, from trainee priests to parish groups. He loves St Ignatius of Loyola, his garden and hearing people's stories.

Canon Jack Noble

Fr Jack is Rector of St Giles Cripplegate in the City of London, one of two City parishes with a large residential population, and Canon for International Relations in the Diocese of Kagera, Tanzania. He was previously school chaplain of The St Marylebone School and The St Marylebone Bridge School (an SEN school), and Assistant Priest at St Marylebone Parish Church. He served a curacy in a large suburban parish in outer London.

Fr Nicolas Stebbing CR

Fr Nicolas Stebbing is a monk of the Community of the Resurrection, Mirfield. He was born and grew up in Zimbabwe and is still proud of his Zimbabwean identity. He studied in Zimbabwe, England and South Africa and was involved in the action and politics of the struggle against apartheid. He worked on missions in Zimbabwe for some years before joining the Community of the Resurrection. Since joining the Community he has lived in Johannesburg and in England and has travelled widely in Europe in the course of ecumenical work with other monks and nuns. He has had a ministry of retreat work, chiefly within the Ignatian tradition, and has taught seminarians at the College at Mirfield. His work now, apart from the central part of it, living the monastic life, revolves around teaching the novices the Greek New Testament, raising money for Zimbabwe and travelling to Zimbabwe to work with the Church there, and the charity Tariro for Young People, of which he is a founder.

Bishop Rowan Williams

Dr Rowan Williams' career began as a lecturer at Mirfield (1975–77). In 1984 he was elected a Fellow and Dean of Clare College, Cambridge. During his time at Clare he was arrested and fined for singing psalms as part of the CND protest at Lakenheath airbase. Then, still only 36, it was back to Oxford as Lady Margaret Professor of Divinity for six years, before becoming Bishop of Monmouth and, from 2000, Archbishop of Wales. In 2002 he became the 104th Archbishop of Canterbury.

Acknowledgements

Scripture quotations marked RSV are from the Revised Standard Version of the Bible, copyright 1946, 1952 and 1971 by the Division of Christian Education of the National Council of the Churches of Christ in the USA. Used by permission. All rights reserved.

Scripture quotations marked NRSV are from New Revised Standard Version Bible: Anglicized Edition, copyright © 1989, 1995 National Council of the Churches of Christ in the United States of America. Used by permission. All rights reserved worldwide.

Bible extracts marked KJV are from the Authorized Version of the Bible (The King James Bible), the rights in which are vested in the Crown, are reproduced by permission of the Crown's Patentee, Cambridge University Press.

Scripture marked NKJV is taken from the New King James Version®. Copyright © 1982 by Thomas Nelson. Used by permission. All rights reserved.

Bible extracts marked NJB are taken from The Jerusalem Bible, published and copyright © 1966, 1967 and 1968 by Darton, Longman and Todd Ltd and Doubleday, a division of Random House, Inc. and used by permission.

Scripture quotations marked ESV are from The ESV® Bible (The Holy Bible, English Standard Version®), copyright © 2001 by Crossway, a publishing ministry of Good News Publishers. Used by permission. All rights reserved.

Foreword

Always refreshing and sometimes bracing, this collection opens a much welcome window into what it means to be Catholic *and* Anglican, particularly with its sharp focus on good news for everybody and the reminder that Catholicism is first about the universal rather than the particular. That said, Anglo-Catholic spirituality, with its focus on the sacramental, is also very particular, and it is the particularity of sacramental life that leads to the universal. Or to put it plainly: you have to find God *somewhere* before you can find God *everywhere*; and once you have discovered that this is good news for *your* life, then it must be good news for *everyone else's life too*. Hence the trajectory of Anglo-Catholic renewal in the Church of England, starting as a kind of theological corrective and challenge, a movement for academics and theologians, then becoming a more widespread movement of renewal, evangelization and church planting.

At the root of a sacramental understanding of Christian faith is the Incarnation, and the very particular kenosis of God in the womb of the Virgin Mary. The sacramental and incarnational theology that then feeds Anglo-Catholic spirituality and practice is capacious and beautiful, with a universal vision that is forever being worked out in the particularity of people's lives and contexts and, following the sacramental principle, always looking and expecting to find God in the world God has made. Therefore Anglo-Catholicism has always been concerned with the beauty of worship, the converting power of the sacramental life, a deep care for the poor and a missionary zeal to serve God in the poorest and most deprived places. And a paradox: Christ is there already; our task is to make him known; to point to him; to lift high the cross and declare and embody the beauty of the gospel in the holiness of our own lives and ministry.

This is Anglo-Catholicism at its world-facing, missionary best, but like all good things it has its shadow. Sometimes it has become precious, preoccupied with the minutiae of liturgical ritual, self-serving, just another 'party' rather than a progressive movement charged with an absolutely essential gospel truth that is needed by the whole Church, namely that if Christ is – as it were – the sacrament of God, God's presence with us, then this sacramental pattern will be found in all of our life in Christ; that we need this in our discipleship and mission; and that without it we are in danger of losing that universal revelation of God in Christ. Moreover, because this is about our belonging to Christ and being welcomed and nourished by him, then catholic witness also holds on to the important but often neglected truth that you can't actually find Jesus without also finding his Church; and even though his church on earth may be battered and compromised, it remains a thing of exquisite beauty because it is the body and the bride of Christ. It really is a life of faith offered with angels and archangels and with the whole company of heaven.

For me, as someone shaped by this tradition, the Eucharist itself is the place where all this comes together, and the contributions in this encouraging book keep coming back to the eucharistic heart of Anglo-Catholic theology and spirituality. In the Eucharist we encounter God in word and sacrament. In the Eucharist we are re-membered. In the Eucharist we are sent out to minister to the same Jesus we have received in bread and wine, to celebrate his presence in the world and work for the establishment of his kingdom. In the Eucharist we come as equals to the place where everyone is welcome. It really is for *every body*.

Something that I remember Ken Leech saying years ago is that the literal meaning of the word 'catholic' is 'that which accords to wholeness'. The awesomely universal and the scandalously particular life of the Anglo-Catholic tradition within the Church of England, the wonderfully diverse and the essential unity of belonging, has saved the Church of England from becoming just another protestant denomination. It holds on to a vision of what the Church is meant to be in that place where all our current divisions are transcended. God is at the centre. God has a vision for all things and all people and for integration and wholeness. God's heart is for those who are excluded and left behind. That should be our heart too. For if we see and receive God in a broken piece of bread, we may also have eyes to see God in the world and love God in one another.

Years ago I remember turning up to say the Wednesday evening Mass at the church where I was serving. It was winter. It had snowed that evening. We never got a large congregation, but on this Wednesday evening there was just one person there. As the clock ticked round to 7.30 and this startled person realized they were the only one in the congregation, they made a beeline for the sacristy to stop me in my tracks. 'Don't worry, just for me', she said.

I smiled in return. 'Whatever makes you think I am doing this for you?' I replied.

This too is the Catholic faith. It is *my* faith. But more importantly, it is *ours*. We receive Holy Communion for ourselves but never only for ourselves. I preside at the altar but it is Christ who speaks and serves in me.

The offering of our worship is first for God and second for the world and – I suppose – only incidentally for ourselves, though I'm sure God would see it differently, because God's very particular love for each one of us is unequivocal, unconditional and absolute. God is certainly doing it for us. And what we *call* prayer and what we *call* worship is simply our response to this, our offering of praise and prayer to God. This is the paradox of faith. We put God at the centre of our lives and God puts us at the centre of God's.

And with God at the centre, and with the world on our hearts, and seeking to participate in that mission of God which is to bring all things together in Christ, it is this Catholic and Anglican way of being Christian that has helped me to serve and follow Christ. The renewal of this witness is urgently needed in the Church of England today. This book will help us.

+Stephen Cottrell
Archbishop of York

Introduction

FR SIMON CUFF

One, holy, Catholic and apostolic

Any attempt to explore the catholic life in the Church of England has to wrestle with two contested notions: Anglicanism and catholicity. What it means to be a catholic in the Church of England today depends both on what we mean by catholic *and* what we mean by the Church of England. In other words, we can't explore Anglo-Catholicism without also exploring Anglicanism *and* catholicism. It is important to note that a central claim of Anglo-Catholicism is that these two concepts are decidedly not at odds. Anglo-Catholicism is first and foremost the claim that Anglicanism (in all its forms) entails catholicism.

Anglo-Catholicism as a distinct phenomenon within the history and tribal make-up of the Anglican Communion and Church of England began as a reminder that to be Anglican is to be catholic. The earliest days of the Oxford Movement saw its central claim to be the reaffirmation that to be a member of the Church of England is to be a member of the one, holy, catholic and apostolic Church throughout the world and to share in the threefold order of ordained ministry of bishop, priest and deacon in a line of succession that can be traced back to the earliest history of the Church. It was in the reassertion of this claim that Anglo-Catholicism became a movement of reform and revival.

The reform and revival that would flow through the Oxford Movement into the wider Church of England and the nascent Anglican Communion and beyond stems from intellectual efforts and liturgical practices intended to make this natural catholicity more clear. From those first days of the catholic movement there has been division within the movement about where to look to make this natural catholicity most obviously felt. For some, reconstructions of medieval Christianity, when the catholicity of the Church of England was never in doubt, were the best means of making this catholicity apparent. For others, sharing in the liturgical and ecclesiological traditions of the contemporary Roman Catholic Church made this case more strongly. As time went on, commitment to these distinct Anglo-Catholic attempts to make this membership of the universal Church real has given rise to the variety of iterations of liturgical practice and ecclesiological thought that we encounter within catholic Anglicanism today.

The problem for all of us who are catholics in the Church of England comes when we mistake these practices and ecclesiological understandings for our commitment to catholicity itself. Anglo-Catholicism make a particular set of ecclesiological claims about all Anglicans, not just those who identify as Anglo-Catholics or do a particular set of things or pray in a particular set of ways. As catholic Anglicans we get ourselves in trouble when we say that to be a 'catholic' is first and foremost to do this set of things or pray in this set of ways, celebrating the Eucharist in this particular way or wearing this particular set of things when we do. We also get ourselves in trouble when we forget that we are first and foremost a reforming and revivalist movement, dedicated to reinvigorating the catholicity of the whole. We get ourselves in most trouble when we reduce ourselves to the role of custodians or museum guardians for catholic practices of generations past.

Because of this, at the end of the last millennium Fr Ken Leech bemoaned the state of Anglican Catholicism: 'the movement has become more precious and effete ... the fetish of correctness, the delight in fuss, the neurotic clinging to ceremonial trivia – these are well-known signs of pathology, of serious spiritual illness.'[1]

In his chapter below, Rowan Williams reminds us that recollecting the primary claim of the Anglo-Catholic movement to be about the catholicity of the whole Church is a powerful antidote to this ever-present danger within Anglo-Catholicism:

> Remembering that that word 'catholic' has to do to with wholeness is one of the things that should prevent our catholicism becoming what Ken Leech and others were so anxious about – a sectarian, inward-looking and partisan movement that provided the rather ambiguous pleasure of being able to say, in the name of catholic 'wholeness', 'We are so much more whole than you are.'[2]

However, for most members of the Church of England, Anglo-Catholicism is known by its fruits. Parishes or individuals are known as 'catholics' within the contemporary Church of England because their clergy tend to wear a certain colour of clerical shirt (black), their clergy tend to wear a certain kind of vestment (chasuble), they tend to refer to the Eucharist in a certain kind of way (Mass) and so on. This is not to denigrate any or all of these as part and parcel of the catholic life in the Church of England. Vestments, incense, the liturgical year and so on situate us as a worshipping community in continuity with the long history of Western and Orthodox Christianity, as we worship in a way that has been Spirit-led and -formed for centuries. These practices take us outside of ourselves and into a community formed in response to God's action in the world for generations. However, it's important to note that as catholics our devotion to these is not because of the importance of the practices themselves but because by adopting these particular practices we are making a claim that we are part of a wider whole. All of these things situate us within Western catholic Christianity and in more or less continuity with those forms of Christianity, including Orthodox and Lutheran, that retain the historic episcopate in which we share.

All of these practices help us to make clear the underlying claim to catholicity that is at the heart of Anglo-Catholicism. Too much focus on these things in themselves risks undermining this claim to catholicity, especially when particular liturgical practices or ways of expressing catholicity become devoid from the theological foundation of catholicity itself. There is an increasing tendency to regard Anglo-Catholicism as a particular aesthetic or particular worship style within a range of available worship styles. It's important to bear in mind that the varying aesthetics and ways of worship within catholicism and catholic Anglicanism are catholic in so far as they have as their basis this claim in relation to the catholicity of the whole, and serve to make this catholicity real in the life of the worshipper and wider community. It's this that provides the theological and ecclesiological basis of catholicism as it is lived out in the lives of catholic Anglicans and Anglo-Catholic churches and communities.

The chapters that follow represent the responses of different contemporary catholic voices in the Church of England on a variety of topics as they work out this commitment in the life of the Church of England and in the catholic life as it's been received by catholic Anglicans reflecting and ministering today. While there are admittedly elements of Leech's diagnosis of the state of Anglo-Catholicism at the end of the twentieth century that continue to have some semblance of truth ('Today, Anglican Catholics are more divided, fragmented and confused than they have been for a long time'[3]), it is also the case that the note of hope with which Leech concluded his essay was well founded: 'There are signs of hope, and I would not be surprised if the coming decades saw a new mutant within Anglican Catholicism which was more positive, unfussy, thoughtful, and more healthy in its handling of matters of sex and gender.'[4]

Leech's fear at the end of the millennium was that 'Anglican Catholicism manifests itself today as an example of a tradition which seems to have fossilised.'[5] He is unsure whether the Anglican Catholicism of his day was able to escape this fossilization, even as he recognized: 'traditions can be renewed and reinvigorated. I am not sure whether this particular tradition is open to such a process. Time will tell.'[6]

The chapters in this book are, I think, a sign that the kind of Catholicism for which Leech longed is alive and well in the Church of England. In his chapter, Rowan Williams unpacks catholicity as a commitment to an integrated wholeness and explores the centrality of, and our dependence on, the Eucharist as a response to that primary wholeness. Melanie Marshall explores the catholic life via the theme of dependence and the God-givenness of our identity in Christ. Ayla Lepine interrogates the physical witness to the impact of the Oxford Movement that changed church architecture and aesthetics, and the underlying visual theology of the Eucharist that this artistic legacy of the catholic revival betrays. Ben Kerridge offers a wonderful reflection on the crucial but often unexplored daily task of discernment, drawing especially on the teaching of Ignatius of Loyola. Steffan Mathias explores the role of Scripture in the life of catholic Anglicanism today and what it means that for Christianity the fullness of revelation is contained not in a book or set of books but in the person of Jesus. Nicolas Stebbing CR writes honestly about making prayer the heart of our Christian lives, and the real difficulties all of us face as we try to take seriously our command to pray. Mitzi James unpacks a vision of catholic ministry as a commitment to the task of beloved community, grounded in the sacraments to serve the whole of a local context.

In chapters exploring particular sacraments, Christina Beardsley considers the importance of catechesis in relation to baptism and the nature of baptism as foundational for the Christian life. Charlie Bell explores what the sacramentality of marriage means for our understanding of marriage as catholic Christians and some important questions about the role of marriage in the catholic life, given recent focus on who may and may not participate in marriage. Finally, Sally Jones and Jack Noble draw on their experience as expert practitioners in catholic ministry among children and young people to explore what the catholic vision of Christianity offers to future generations and what catholic Anglicanism has to offer children's ministry and ministry with and alongside young people.

INTRODUCTION

Part of the catholic life is the attempt to practise what we preach. This book takes this rather literally as our chapters are interspersed throughout with sermons that were offered as part of the study days that formed the inspiration for this text. Peter Allan, Kathryn Fleming and Esther Lay each explore the centrality of music and song in the catholic life and what it means for us as we strive to be human beings who inhabit the wholeness to which catholicity invites us. Joanne Woolway Grenfell and Arwen Folkes reflect on what the catholic life means in the life of individuals and as part of our commitment to mission and evangelism. An additional sermon from Peter Groves offered at the requiem Mass of Fr Michael Farthing – an inspirational priest to dozens of women and men in the catholic life – is a reflection on the catholic life generally, and the catholic life of the priesthood in particular as one way of inhabiting 'the love of God lived out in our world and in our lives, lived out in the ministry of the church which is the Body of Christ'.[7]

The study days that inspired this book were organized precisely because of my sense that there is a vibrant form of catholic spirituality and practice alive in the Church of England, exactly of the sort for which Leech longed. Moreover, this form of catholic Anglicanism has an essential role to play in the life of the Church of England now and in the years to come. All of the theologians and practitioners who participated in the study days, and in the book that follows, reflect in varying ways the kind of robust Anglo-Catholicism whose commitment to catholicity expresses itself as 'positive, unfussy, thoughtful, and more healthy in its handling of matters of sex and gender'. Such a form of Christian witness is sorely needed in the Church and the world today.

The voices in these chapters and sermons each help us to explore and resource a particular snapshot in the history of the catholic movement in the Church of England that has been, and continues to be, life-giving for so many in their own discipleship. This is one of the benefits of the resolute commitment to catholicity at the heart of Anglo-Catholicism. In these voices, a commitment to the wholeness and catholicity of the Church also leads to a commitment to the wholeness or catholicity of the person. This in turns leads to the kind of robust and hope-filled version of Anglo-Catholicism for which Leech longed.

This focus on genuine wholeness has meant that for many, Anglo-Catholicism is first encountered as a place of healing following an encounter with other forms of Christianity. This is true also for many of those in other traditions (both within and beyond the Church of England) who come to rely on some aspect or other of catholic Anglicanism to sustain them in their Christian witness and ministry – whether through spiritual direction, liturgical prayer, sacramental confession or times of silent and eucharistic adoration. It is important to note that to highlight the essential pastoral role the catholic life often plays in the contemporary life of the Church of England is decidedly not to say that Anglo-Catholicism has not itself been a place of harm and abuse, particularly in terms of misogyny, structural racism and to a lesser extent closeted homophobia. While Leech noted the presence of 'sexual confusion and dishonesty' in Anglo-Catholicism, he also noted that 'for a long time, many Anglican Catholic parishes provided a way in which gay people were able to be themselves in an oblique way'.[8] Nonetheless, it is the case that entry into Anglo-Catholicism is often through the space that the catholic life enables for restoration and pastoral care after having experienced a difficult or harmful Christian encounter elsewhere. Part of the vital contribution catholic Anglicanism has made, and continues to make, is providing a safe space where Christians can learn afresh what an integrated wholeness means both ecclesiologically and pastorally in terms of genuine human flourishing.

Within the contemporary Church of England this means that there are clergy and Christians who sometimes find themselves worshipping in catholic contexts and catholic ways because these are the safest Christian communities they have encountered. For some this becomes a conversion to Anglo-Catholicism. However, for many others this sojourn in Anglo-Catholicism becomes a destination when they really only require a harbour from a particular storm. The rise and increased visibility of inclusive forms of Evangelicalism that can themselves provide the kind of safe spaces that catholic Anglican churches have otherwise been can only be a positive for those for whom forms of catholic Anglicanism itself have been spiritually stultifying in other ways. Any rise in the commitment to wholeness in any part of the Church is something at which Anglo-Catholicism in its commitment to genuine wholeness can only rejoice.

To say that there are those for whom catholic Anglican churches have provided a haven, and yet for whom Anglo-Catholicism is not or perhaps should not itself become a destination, may seem to be at odds with the whole thrust of this Introduction, which is that Anglo-Catholicism is a commitment to defending the claim that each and every Anglican is a catholic simply by virtue of their being Anglican. This is partly because of the contested nature of Anglicanism. Anglicanism is at once catholic and reformed. It is made up of those of us who are catholics, whose vocation it is to remind the whole that we too are a part, and those who stand in the Reformation tradition of holding that wider 'whole' to account, ensuring that the whole is not adrift from its foundation in Christ and the articulation of that foundation in Scripture. To say this is simply to reaffirm the argument of Michael Ramsey in *The Gospel and the Catholic Church* that catholicism and protestantism as distinct forms of Christianity need each other; indeed this is a prerequisite of the catholic 'whole'.[9]

To push this point further, if it is the case that there are those who find in Anglo-Catholicism a haven but whose vocation is to remain the Protestants that the wholeness of the Church needs them to be, then there must be something that Anglo-Catholicism *is*, beyond simply an articulation of the claim that all Anglicans are catholics by virtue of their membership as Anglicans of the one, holy, catholic, apostolic Church. If it's not, as we've been setting out, simply an aesthetic, a worship style or a particular set of habits or practices, what then is it that distinguishes a genuinely catholic Anglicanism? What does it mean to be a catholic in the reforming and revivalist sense of which Anglo-Catholicism is an expression? How are those whose vocation is to more Protestant forms of accountability for the sake of the whole distinct from those of us whose vocation is to the catholicism to which Anglo-Catholicism points? What is the catholic life as those of us who see ourselves as catholics are called to live it?

Many of the chapters and sermons below are an attempt to demonstrate an answer to this question. However, as the study days on which this book is based went on, a more positive account of the 'catholicism' in which these authors share became apparent. Catholicism, as a theological foundation – to be a catholic, to live out a catholic life – is to live in a certain relationship to the fact of our utter dependence on God as our shared foundation. Catholicism is a life lived in the knowledge of our utter dependence on God for all that we think and say and do. This dependency finds its ultimate expression in obedience to the command: 'Do this in remembrance of me.' As Rowan Williams writes below: 'we keep on coming back to the table, coming back to the recognition of our hunger and dependence as if our lives depended on it – because they do.'[10] This is not to say that Protestantism doesn't also acknowledge this radical dependency, but it draws different conclusions from this acknowledgement. Whereas Catholicism's acknowledgement throws us into a shared togetherness based upon our dependence, Protestantism cultivates a more individual response to that dependence, based in part on a suspicion that a shared togetherness results in a dependence on others that takes the place of the radical dependence on God at the heart of the gospel.

Catholicism as a way of life and system of thought begins and ends in the recognition that all we have and all we are depends on God and therefore we are bound together in a shared dependence that is vital because it is called together and cultivated by God.[11] This called-togetherness is what it is to be church, to be those God has assembled together into and out of the world. Michael Ramsey is right to note that this is open to 'distortion', just as Protestantism is open to opposite and equal distortions.[12] Ramsey notes that distortions enter particular Christian traditions when they cling to some elements in their original charism and witness to the wider whole and yet have distorted 'those elements by severing them from others. The result is that the inner unity of the Christian tradition is divided, and all our systems represent sadly battered versions of the fullness of the Gospel and the Church.'[13]

As catholics we can all too easily slip from the theological truth of radical dependency on God to a human aberration that distorts not only this theological truth but the lives of those individuals whom this truth destines to flourish, as Protestantism's vocation is to remind us. The reason catholics in the Church of England need their protestant siblings is that we need to be reminded that the individual and Scripture cannot be sacrificed at the altar of a system that pretends to mediate God's will to them but is in fact offering the will of a majority rather than the radical dependence on God that is the essence of catholicism.

For those of us who are catholics, this grounding in radical dependence is the source of the theology that undergirds our commitment to the whole. It's this which determines our theological framework and indeed all the practices, or fruits, that make us known as catholics to the wider Church of England. The realization of our radical dependence on God means that we are thrown to the Eucharist, to the communion of the Saints. The catholic life as lived in the Church of England and in every denomination is the realization that we are part of a wider whole that needs to be fed on Christ in the Mass, a wider whole that encompasses not only the entirety of the Church catholic with its bishops, priest and deacons but also our departed siblings and the Saints, as real and present Christians praying for us even now, on whose prayers we rely as much as we rely on those of the people we ask to pray for us each and every day. We are part of a Christian family throughout history and yet to come, but which is already ever present and alive to God.

As catholics, our foundational commitment means that we recognize that our protestant siblings, not least in the Church of England, are as much members of the catholic Church as we are. This means that we are open to the gift of Protestantism, which is the reminder of the potential site of creativity that is the individual, and that Scripture is intended to nourish the individual as much as provide a deposit of doctrine for the whole. However, we also insist that there is a greater fruit from the dependency on God which is at the heart of our catholic faith, that we are part of a greater whole, and that the Eucharist and the prayers of the Saints and Our Lady, our membership of the entire Body of Christ, are part of a wider whole which itself discerned the content and canon of Scripture and in which every Christian is invited to share. We believe that a Christian life grounded in this dependence, shaped by the Scriptures, nourished in the Mass, surrounded by the Saints and focused on a genuine wholeness and flourishing of each and every individual in relationship, is a way of Christian life that is life-giving and enables an encounter with the love of God that is life-long.

The invitation at the heart of the Catholic life finds its realization in daily life in the reception of the Eucharist, a foretaste of that heavenly banquet in which the wholeness of the Church will one day be fully realized, free from the distortions and troubles we make for ourselves, as we see Christ face to face. Until then, for those of us who have seen a glimpse of this in the catholic life lived out in the Church of England today, this book attempts in various ways to unpack why this matters to us, and why we want each and every Christian to share a little of that glimpse in these pages and in churches in this country and across the world, and to get caught up with us in that shared heavenly gaze.

Notes

1 Kenneth Leech, 'The Church in the Back Streets', in Michael Farrer and Michael Young (eds), *Faithful Cross: A History of Holy Cross Church, Cromer Street* (London: Cromer Street Productions, 1999), pp. 111–15, p. 114.
2 Rowan Williams, below, p. 10.
3 Leech, 'Back Streets', p. 113.
4 Leech, 'Back Streets', p. 115.
5 Leech, 'Back Streets', p. 115.
6 Leech, 'Back Streets', p. 115.
7 Peter Groves, below, p. 123.
8 Leech, 'Back Streets', p. 115.
9 See further Simon Cuff, 'The "Difficult Adventure": Michael Ramsey's Church Catholic & Beyond', available at: https://www.theschooloftheology.org/posts/essay/michael-ramsey-church-catholic-beyond, accessed 31.10.2023.
10 Rowan Williams, below, p. 14.
11 On the radicality of this dependence, see Mel Marshall in Chapter 3 below.
12 Michael Ramsey, 'The Healing of Our Divisions. A Sermon Preached before the University of Oxford on 27 April 1947' (Westminster: Dacre Press, 1947).
13 Ramsey, 'The Healing of Our Divisions', p. 7.

I

Eucharist

BISHOP ROWAN WILLIAMS

It's a very particular personal pleasure for Ken Leech to be quoted at the beginning of this volume. It's now some 50 years since Ken and a few other people, including myself, established what became the 'Jubilee Group' in the 1970s, in an attempt to revive both theological and political witness within the catholic wing of the Church of England. I gladly dedicate what follows to Ken's memory, with affection and admiration.

In speaking of the role of the Eucharist in the catholic identity of the Church, it may help to begin with a few thoughts about the word 'catholic' itself. In spite of the still very prevalent misunderstanding that 'catholic' just means 'universal', there is also a sense of the word that denotes 'wholeness', 'integrity'. In the fourth century Cyril of Jerusalem, speaking about the meaning of the word, insisted that the adjective 'catholic' essentially referred to a Church that witnessed to the 'wholeness' of faith and spoke to the 'wholeness' of human experience.

If that is indeed part of what 'catholic' means, the Eucharist clearly has a very significant place in filling out this sense of the word, since the Eucharist is precisely the moment when the wholeness of our human experience is taken into the movement of Christ's humanity towards God the Father. And it is also the moment at which we remember that the work, the prayer, the eternal reality that is Christ's life on earth and in heaven opens itself to the entirety of the human world, without exception or reservation.

Remembering that that word 'catholic' has to do with wholeness is one of the things that should prevent our catholicism becoming what Ken Leech and others were so anxious about – a sectarian, inward-looking and partisan movement that provided the rather ambiguous pleasure of being able to say, in the name of catholic 'wholeness', 'We are so much more whole than you are.'

We should bear this in mind as we reflect that, from the very beginning, what marked out Christianity as a new moment in the history of the world was the promise of a divine realm, a divinely shaped community, that extended beyond the available and conventional boundaries. That new reality is not primarily a religion called 'Christianity'; it is the catholic Church. This needs emphasizing: nobody in the first Christian century thought that there were things called 'religions', separate, self-contained systems of belief. They didn't have comparative religion in their schools or interfaith councils. People believed that they experienced relation to divine power in various ways, that they could relate to 'gods', that they should practise rituals in order to consolidate those relations; and quite often these rituals and relations were closely bound up with the dominant forms of political power in society.

The growing Christian community was, for a long time, a fragile body of people, fragile largely because their practices did not have official political endorsement. Quite the contrary; their rituals were regarded with suspicion or loathing by the authorities. But they were fragile also because they didn't have a single, given ethnic identity: they believed they were a pilot project for the restoration of the entire human race, in which the whole history of human reality and of each particular person could in principle find fulfilment in relationship with God through Jesus Christ. That was and is the catholic Church; it did not begin as a scheme of ideas among other schemes from which someone might choose, a religion among other religions, but as a form of belonging together in common habits and language.

Christian Scripture – especially Paul's letters – show it starting with people gathering to eat and to argue and to study – not in study groups armed with neat, black-covered Bibles but in sometimes rather chaotic evening meals in houses. The first descriptions of Christian worship in Paul's First Letter to Corinth present a noisy and diverse gathering very unlike our idea of an ordered ritual. Yet Paul is struggling to disentangle the heart of this activity from all that surrounds it; that here is the moment when this community affirms that it exists simply in virtue of the invitation of the risen Jesus of Nazareth. In that moment of invitation and affirmation, it becomes also a moment of encounter, where the dependence of the believer on Jesus of Nazareth is so close that the only way in which it can be spoken of and imagined is in the bodily act of eating. The life that comes to us from our ordinary food and drink is a routine element in our humanity, entering into who we are from outside, becoming the energy that keeps us alive. And so in the life of this new humanity, the food and drink that keeps us alive and keeps us human is Jesus Christ. In the food and drink, the bread and wine, that we bless in the power of the Spirit of Jesus, the very life of Jesus, what lives in the flesh and blood of Jesus, becomes ours. In this bread, in this wine, the living Word is as present and as active as in Jesus of Nazareth on the streets of Galilee or on the cross.

It's clear enough from the way that St Paul writes about the church in Corinth that getting this clear in theological bullet points was not very near the top of most people's agenda at these community meals. But Paul insists that when we meet in this vision and in this Spirit, when we meet as the pilot project of new humanity, what we do that is new and distinctive to us as a group is to 'feed' on Jesus. If we turn from St Paul to St John, we see in the famous sixth chapter of John's Gospel just how shocking and startling a claim that was. For Paul and John alike, there is no way of expressing our openness to and dependence on the crucified and risen Jesus of Nazareth without using this imagery of food and drink, without the practice of identifying the food and drink shared in the Spirit of Jesus as being, in some profound and abiding sense, the material place where the risen Christ 'happens' and once again enters into our humanity.

Out of this comes, ultimately, everything else in our theological world. Out of those chaotic, overcrowded, Saturday evening meals come the New Testament, the Church's hierarchy, the Nicene Creed, the World Council of Churches and the local PCC. It starts with this encounter at the table, because this is where believers affirm what most deeply holds them together as a new human community. We belong together because of a shared dependence on the gift that is Jesus Christ; a shared awareness that, because of this feeding on Jesus, we grow further into the life that is his, the life of unconditional commitment to and freedom with God the source of all, the 'Abba' to whom Jesus prays. We grow into the wholeness, the maturity and authority that belongs to full humanity by letting ourselves be fed. It is the great central Christian paradox – the more dependent we are, the more free we become. In the familiar language of the old Prayer Book, borrowed from St Augustine, we recognize that God's 'service is perfect freedom'. Jesus the eternally free and sovereign divine Word, is eternally also the human 'slave' to our need, the one who lets himself be defined by our need for healing.

In this context, we can see how a Church without the Eucharist, without the invitation and encounter of the Lord's Supper, is a Church that is somehow selling us short, a Church that is not promising the fullness of a restored humanity. It is a church that is still unhappily vague or unhelpfully abstract about what our human destiny is in terms of intimacy with God the source of all things. This is why, from the very beginning, the Church has held to the belief that this is what Jesus wanted his friends to do and that's why he told to them to do it: 'Do this in remembrance of me.'

So there is the first key point about how Christianity begins, not as a 'religion' but as the catholic Church, as the community of humans released into a new fullness, a new intimacy with God, a new confidence in relation to each other, a new generosity in the mutual creativity that exists within the worshipping community. When Paul writes about this in his letters to Corinth, he constantly seeks to evoke this sense of an overflow of generosity arising from the sense of gratitude that motivates all who gather for the meal. To understand how we are now to relate to one another, we must grasp what happens if you live in radical dependence on the self-giving love of Jesus, if you are entering into Jesus' own relation with God the Father. What happens is the overflow of creativity with and towards one another, each person now endowed by the Holy Spirit with the gifts of the Spirit to make their neighbour more deeply alive.

St Paul is clearly profoundly engaged by this vision, returning to it repeatedly in his letters. As a Christian community we are not simply an assembly of individuals; we are in 'communion' through the Spirit with Jesus of Nazareth, our existence is deeply and comprehensively 'in common', because we are praying Jesus' prayer and living in his life, and so living within the creativity that is in God which has been embodied in Jesus. This is the life that becomes in some degree our own way of life. We are assembled here at the table as human children of God so as to 'create' one another in and through the Spirit of Jesus; the gifts given to each are given for all. Each one of us becomes a self, a reality, a person in Christ through the gift of the neighbour and through our gift to the neighbour. 'The communion of the Holy Spirit' is this movement of mutual creative engagement and commitment.

Here then is a second dimension in our thinking about the Eucharist. First of all, we have reflected on how we are brought to be in Christ by feeding on the life that is his, to such a degree that, just as food becomes part of our physical reality, so this sacramental food becomes part of our humanity, uniting us in Christ's own relation with God the Father. But second, and because of this, the creative interaction with others that Christ sets in motion, the capacity of the Spirit to bring one another alive in love and hope and generosity, becomes ours. And this of course is why the eucharistic community is already a social vision, not in the sense that we are a group of people who agree on a 'programme' of things that we all want (this is manifestly not a very credible description of the Church), but as an organism in which we are dependent on one another, whether we like or it not – as a Russian Orthodox friend of mine liked to say, going to heaven (or elsewhere) 'in each other's pockets'. This is a level of unity, a level both of creativity and of risk, that is deeper than simple human consensus. And yet – precisely because the stakes are so high – this is the distinctiveness of the newness of life in Christ that is embodied in the Eucharist. As the great Anglican theologian of liturgy Gregory Dix liked to say, we are a new species, we are *homo eucharisticus* not just *homo sapiens*. We are eucharistic human beings because we are renewed in mutual creativity. To stand where Christ stands as we pray the Eucharist is to be involved in Christ's creation of new life through the Spirit; this is the 'social programme' of the Eucharist, a programme that, in its own way, presses us to recognize a particular kind of equality among ourselves.

Once again St Paul gives us the clue here. In this eucharistic community there is no one who has a privileged place, because each person shares the same level of dependence. We all urgently need the same healing, we need to be drawn out of darkness into light and from death into life. We all need to be fed, we are all hungry. And to stand alongside each other as human beings, recognizing this universal hunger for truth, for growth and healing, is to recognize our human equality and mutual involvement at a very profound level.

Translating all this into the structures of human society, even translating it into the way the Church itself operates, has not exactly been straightforward across the centuries. Yet we keep on coming back to the table, coming back to the recognition of our hunger and dependence as if our lives depended on it – because they do. And this opens up a third dimension of thinking about the Eucharist and our catholic identity. In the tradition of how the Lord's Supper was established on the night before Jesus died, Jesus was remembered as having said that the cup we share was 'the cup of the new covenant'. Just as the first covenant was marked with the sacrificial shedding of blood, so too with this new covenant. The death of Jesus on the cross was to be seen as a moment in which God's faithful promise to God's people was reiterated, reinforced, newly imagined in more radical form. It's worth remembering in passing that to talk about 'new' and 'old' covenants has some pitfalls. We have so regularly seen 'new' and 'old' as mutually exclusive. But think about the ways we use the words 'new' and 'old' in ordinary discourse:

'We've just bought a *new* car.'
'What have you done with the *old* one?'

'We've just had a *new* baby.'
'What have you done with the *old* one?'

I suspect that the language of 'new' and 'old', where covenants or Testaments are concerned, is rather closer to the latter than the former. After all, the 'Old Testament' itself talks about a new covenant that will be made to anchor and enhance the first, looking to a renewal of promise and a new affirmation and discovery of God's faithfulness.

Here we are then, sharing bread and wine as a sign of the new rooting and affirmation of the same covenant promise of God to be with us, the eternal, unchanging, unshakeable commitment of God to God's world, which the entire story of Scripture tells us about. We keep returning to the table because we know that God has promised, 'covenanted', to be here, to put it in the simplest terms. One of the most important things we can ever say about the Eucharist in the language and practice of the Church is that, whoever else turns up, God does. God's promise to be Emmanuel, to be God with us, is here affirmed in the most straightforwardly embodied way possible. God has promised to welcome us and share life with us, and here we are indeed welcomed and given a share in God's food, in what makes God alive, which is God's own delight in the divine life and love. In the unforgettable image of George Herbert's great poem 'Love': '"You must sit down," says Love, "and taste my meat."/ So I did sit and eat.'

Covenant love, committed love, does not turn away; and the Eucharist crucially is the sign of that in the Church, which does not turn away or fade away or walk away. The eucharistic presence of the God who has made covenant with us is one of the things that ought to enable us as Church to be signs of God's faithfulness, to be a community that doesn't fade away or walk away; to be a community that is faithful to the communities in which it is set, a sign of stability and hope for all those around. There is a very great deal to be said about the implications of this in our polity and practice as a Church these days. One of the things people most rightly and reasonably expect from the Christian Church is that it won't walk away; and one of the greatest tragedies generated by the variegated pressures afflicting the Church of England and other Churches these days is the message that is often given to communities, urban and rural alike, that the Church is comfortable with 'walking away' from them in terms of resourcing or sympathy or hopefulness.

No one should make light of the practical challenges here, and there are no magic-bullet solutions; but it is crucial to remember that people in communities that may already feel forgotten need the Church to let them know in whatever ways are possible that they matter. The new covenant affirmed in the Eucharist is not only something that tells about the fidelity of God to us but – because of our involvement in the divine life, the divine promise and the divine action – tells us what sort of community we are to be in terms of faithfulness, in terms of commitment to one another and to our world, not least these days to the non-human world as much as the human, a theme that needs more attention than I have space to give it here.

We are a covenant community, not first because we have made a lot of serious promises to one another – though that is not a bad start – but because we are here to embody the promise of God in the communities and in the world in which we are set. We are here to say to a world of profound brokenness, hopelessness, forgottenness or, indeed, indifference that, in the name of God, we are not going away. If the Eucharist is what we say it is, a celebration of the new covenant in Christ's blood, here we are, because here is God.

A brief digression but perhaps a significant one. Those forms of devotion to the Blessed Sacrament of the Eucharist that have grown up in catholic practice over the centuries are perhaps best understood in terms of this affirmation of faithfulness. Of course, the focal eucharistic action is our gathering for Holy Communion, our gathering to eat, and nothing should obscure this (as has sometimes threatened to happen in Christian history). But the Sacrament reserved on our altars, the Sacrament contemplated and adored in Exposition and Benediction, is a very powerful sign of the fidelity of a God who doesn't just turn up on Sunday mornings for Mass but remains committed, remains there as our food, our drink, our life, whether we're here or not. This is why I believe that devotion to the reserved Sacrament is an intrinsic part of embodying our belief in a God who is faithful, a God who has made covenant. For so many people, the presence of the Sacramental Christ on our altars is in all sorts of ways and degrees an assurance of hope, of not being forgotten. The person who casually drops in to – that rarity – an open church and finds the Sacrament on the altar, is likely to discover or rediscover something of this transforming faithfulness, this not-walking-away, that is part of the Christian gospel, whether or not they have the words for it. And I'd venture to guess that a significant number of people hearing or reading these words will have experience of such a discovery for themselves.

All of these themes could be explored at greater length and far greater depth; but if we're thinking about the role of the Eucharist within the identity of a catholic Church, these seem to me the most generative, the most constructive elements on which to build our understanding and our practice. We are here, invited to feed, to absorb into our souls and bodies the reality of Christ's filial love for the everlasting source of all things. We are here to bear to and for one another the created gift of Christ bringing us alive out of that death of isolation and self-preoccupation from which we need to be delivered. We are here to renew our awareness of God's promise to us and to commit ourselves afresh to that commitment in relation to God's world. And we're here not least to model a way of being together as human beings, recognizing a shared hunger and vulnerability, recognizing an equality at the level of our human fragility that everyone needs to be fed, recognizing the dynamics of that which is the way we can be food to one another. We can grow in a creative relationship.

Let me conclude by picking up one further aspect of classical theological eucharistic thought and liturgical imagery. It sometimes helps to remember that the Eucharist is a genuine foretaste of heaven, a theme illustrated by the old story about how the Russians were converted to Christianity in the tenth century by the experience of attending the liturgy at Constantinople, 'not knowing whether they were in heaven or on earth', so we are told. It's possibly not what everybody would feel on Sunday in the average Anglican parish church; and yet what is going on in that moment is indeed a share in heaven. St Paul likes to talk about the gift of the Spirit in the Church as the 'down payment', the anticipated experience of a future reality, and this language is especially apt for that experience of the Spirit that occurs in the eucharistic action. Here we are what we ought to be and by the grace of God shall be; here we are absolutely equal before God as beloved children and as hungry creatures. Here we remind ourselves of our created responsibility to one another and our whole world in the fellowship of the Holy Spirit. Here we are modelling the radically new community that is the Body of Christ. Here we are promising faithfulness to the world. All of which is 'heaven' – our future in full harmony with God.

I remember as a choirboy being deeply struck by words from one of the great patristic and mediaeval hymns in the old, unabridged *English Hymnal*: 'Alpha and Omega, to whom shall bow / All nations at the Doom, is with us now.' The end of all things is here. What happens in the Eucharist is in a very important sense the end of the world. When we emerge from Mass we are living for a brief moment on the far side of the end of the world. We are where we ought to be in relation to God, to one another, to the world around us. We are in a right and just (*dignum et justum*) relation with a material creation which, for this short time, we have treasured and adored and valued as it delivers the incarnate God to us. We are at peace with creator and creation; we are on the far side of the end of all things, because this is where everything converges and comes together, the 'end' that is goal rather than simply conclusion.

And then, of course, it all falls apart again as we return to our history of hurting and being hurt. We shall need to be reminded all over again of the commitment of God, and come back and do it all over again, and again, and again, and again. Eternally in heaven, Christ the everlasting Son made flesh holds before the eternal Father the world he loves, laying it bare to that endless fount of life. The Father breathes into it the Spirit, brings Christ himself alive again in it, and we are created afresh. So it goes on, day by day, world without end. As we pray the Eucharist, we pray in Christ's everlasting prayer; as we invoke the Spirit over the bread and wine of the Sacrament, we once again recall the God who breathes the Spirit in all its bewildering and revolutionary power over the chaos at the start of creation. We stand not only at the end but at the beginning of all things: Alpha and Omega, with us now. As Gregory Dix says at the end of one of his most wonderful passages, 'All that going with you daily to the altar!'

An ambitious view of what the Eucharist means in the Church? Well, yes; because the mystery into which we are caught up, the mystery of the newness of Christ in the life of the Spirit of Christ, is something that never comes to an end and about which we can always afford to be as imaginatively and intellectually ambitious as we can. But also, alongside all the imaginative and intellectual ambition, nothing is as important as to begin with open hands and open mouths, with the need and the hunger, and the invitation from everlasting love. '"You must sit down," says Love, "and taste my meat."/ So I did sit and eat.'[1]

Note

1 This final sentence is taken from George Herbert's poem, 'Love (III)'.

2

Living Eucharistically: The Sacrament and Christian Ethics

MICHAEL J. LEYDEN

While there is overall agreement about the purpose and goal of Christian ethics, there are many and varied approaches to the task. The discipline principally concerns ways of thinking-towards-action. That is to say, it concerns the work of reflection, deliberation and moral discernment that are the necessary a priori activities underpinning morally responsible actions. In this regard it has much in common with its counterparts in philosophy or other world religions, where thinking is reckoned necessary if actions are to be intentional and meaningful rather than random and worthless. The challenging part is identifying the distinctively *Christian* substance of Christian ethics. Determining this is the subject of much methodological disagreement. What does it mean to think as a Christian? Or perhaps better, what does it mean to do ethical deliberation Christianly? Does a Christian world view bind its adherents to a particular way of doing ethical discernment? There are a variety of different, and sometimes competing, answers to these questions.

For example, some theologians will say that what is distinctly Christian about Christian ethics is its fundamental commitment to biblical exegesis and explication. Thus often in such traditions, ethics takes the form of contemporary application of biblical precepts and commandments. Other theologians will emphasize the life and teachings of Jesus as holding distinctive moral force within the canon of Scripture, and the emphasis on divine love, justice and liberation that he both embodied and preached should be the beating heart of Christian decision-making. When viewed thus, actions are definitively Christian when they lead to the liberation of oppressed people and/or deconstruct oppressive structures. Others still will resist the dangers of ethical colonialism or moral superiority that can be inherent in holding to an absolute world view (as many Christians do) by arguing that Christian ethics is best understood as a participant in a wider cultural and societal discourse. The subject of this discourse is the question of what constitutes human flourishing, and Christian ethics has a seat at the table as both contributor to and recipient of moral knowledge.

By contrast to these approaches to Christian ethics, one of the great gifts of the catholic tradition has been its contention that the universal, identity-conferring elements of Christian faith should be basic to moral reasoning. By this I mean that the catholic Anglican tradition (as I have experienced it) does ethical deliberation and moral reasoning by consistently directing the discourse towards those habits of thought and practice that immerse us more deeply in the definitive Christian narrative: the story of God at work in the life, death, resurrection and ascension of the specific, nameable, narratable, historical person Jesus of Nazareth. In so doing it locates moral reasoning within the global fellowship of faithful people who practise those habits.

The tools the Anglican catholic tradition uses to draw us into Christianity's defining narrative are the joint ministries of Word and Sacrament that the Spirit enlivens for the good health of that global fellowship. In so doing, the tradition aims to direct the Church and all humanity towards a truer understanding of our identity and purpose as objects of divine love and grace.

As an ethicist and a Christian, I think this approach to moral reasoning is deeply inviting. It reveals a backdrop for thinking-towards-action that is bigger than simply the application of rules or contextualization of moral themes and demonstrates confidence in the content of the Church's proclamation. The approach frames the Christian life in such a way that the purpose of ethical deliberation is not the performance of moral goodness and righteousness for their own sakes, but that Christians learn to inhabit the identity given to us by God in Christ through baptism. In practice this means learning to align our daily decisions and actions with the vision of human flourishing that is revealed in Christ. The shape is thus vocational and the aim is an integrated and consistent self. As Gregory Dix has put it: 'It is by the sacraments that you receive what you are, your true Christian being; it is by your life that you must become what the sacraments convey.'[1]

Dix is typically generous and inviting here: enacting our true selves in all areas of our lives takes a lifetime of practice and the formation of holy habits that keep us attentive to Christ's call and nurtured by the grace and freedom he brings – prayer, worship, contemplation, Bible study and so on. Even the apostle Paul knew the personal conflict of becoming fully oneself in Christ as he tried and failed and tried some more to align his life in the way I'm suggesting: 'I delight in the law of God in my inmost self, but I see in my members another law at war with the law of my mind, making me captive to the law of sin ... Who will rescue me from this body of death? Thanks be to God through Jesus Christ our Lord!' (Romans 7.22–25 NRSV). That this confession is epistolary suggests that, like the apostle, we practise and are formed in community with others on the same journey, hence the ministries of Word and Sacrament are given to the people of God to perform together.[2]

In what follows I want to begin to explore what I regard as the ethical contours of eucharistic theology as I have understood them in fellowship with catholic Anglicans, and highlight some implications for discipleship and ethics. The nature of a piece like this can be only indicative rather than exhaustive, so there will be lacunas in my approach for which I beg the reader's patience. I begin by thinking about orientation and how the Eucharist may be understood as a supratemporal event that directs us towards the past-present-future of God's saving activity, before turning to outline, in dialogue with Alexander Schmemann, the (future-facing) transformational impact of eucharistic worship. I finish with a brief examination of selected elements of the eucharistic, suggesting how it might be ethically formational for Christians today.

The Eucharist as a supratemporal event

O sacred banquet in which Christ is received;
The remembrance of his passion is renewed;
The soul is filled with grace;
And a pledge of future glory is given to us!

Written by Thomas Aquinas as an antiphon for the Solemnity of Corpus Christi, this prayer also forms part of the liturgy for the adoration of the sacrament and part of the daily cycle of prayers for Dominican nuns. It is powerful and widely referenced among catholic liturgists because of the way it depicts both the temporal and supratemporal dimensions of the eucharistic event. I want to outline these dimensions before turning to consider the implications of that duality for our thinking-towards-action.

The Eucharist's temporality is evidenced in that each celebration happens in a spatiotemporal context that we can describe and experience, and in which we may participate. Something sensory happens. There are liturgical prayers and ritual actions, sacred spaces and gathered congregants, vestments, a priest and the creaturely elements of bread and wine that come together in place and time in a configuration that equates to an *event* – 'Christ is received'. Of course, theologically speaking, reception is an act of faith by the community. But it's a mistake to think this is simply a human activity. The agent whose work it is that all these parts of the celebration function together to their stated goal is the Holy Spirit.[3] In *Common Worship*, the pneumatological aspect has been made more explicit with the recovery of the *epiclesis* during the eucharistic prayer. The sacrament is a miracle, wrought by the Spirit's making Christ really present in the creaturely elements. Thus we might say that at each Eucharist the triune God is the celebrant; and the triune God is celebrated. The congregants gather in obedience to Christ's command and receive Christ afresh; and because of this event, the people continue to receive the grace that moves from God to humanity, which is the heartbeat of the gospel.

The supratemporality of the eucharistic event consists in knowing that when all those same temporal ingredients come together, they move us beyond the present moment and draw us into a much bigger narrative. We are existentially relocated within a wider spiritual reality in which – by the Holy Spirit's work – we are made at once present to the past and the future as well as remaining contemporaries of the world in which we live. Aquinas demarcates this as three distinct clauses, but they should be understood as happening simultaneously and coterminously in each celebration of the Eucharist.

First, Aquinas calls attention to the past as we remember the historical events of Holy Week. We must recall the passion narratives and the suffering of Jesus of Nazareth in Roman-occupied Jerusalem in the early decades of the first century CE. This roots the good news of redemption in a specific historical identity rather than an ethereal or amorphous image of the divine. But this rootedness does not relegate remembrance to the past: *anamnesis* is an active remembering because by it we know that the God who saves is the one who was incarnate and dwelt among us (John 1.14), who has been revealed to the world in Jesus by the Spirit (Ephesians 3.2–6) and who is now present among us in this ritual act. The people whom the triune God saves are real people – historical figures like us – capable of tremendous good and unspeakable evil, both of which Jesus knew and experienced in his ministry. Looking backwards gives clarity about who God is and what God does to whom in the present.

Second, Aquinas recalls us to the present work of God as we physically, emotionally and spiritually participate in the ritual activity of this gathered community. In so doing we, here and now, receive the benefits of this historical sufferer's passion with such immediacy that there seems to be no distance between us here and him there: the soul of each recipient 'is filled with grace'. The gospel of Christ is not confined to its historical circumstances. It is not a celebration of a past occurrence. Rather, it is happening now. It is a counternarrative showing that what God did in the past in the face of sin, hatred, oppression and violence has present and future consequences. It is intended to alert us to what this self-same God is doing *among* us and *through* us in a world that continues to be marred by sin, suffering and oppression. The eucharistic event is a making-present of that once-for-all historical act of injustice that is the death of Christ, understood from the light of his resurrection. The crucified and risen Christ is present to us and we are made present to him, and as we share in his feast, our current circumstances are opened to the possibility of transformation: the crucified Christ is here in resurrection power, he is sufficient, our souls are nourished, grace is bestowed.

Third, Aquinas invites us through the Eucharist to look to the future and what will be given to the people of God in Christ. Sometimes called 'the eschatological character' of the Eucharist, the idea is that it anticipates the heavenly banquet that is the marriage supper of the lamb and is part of the bigger eschatological hope of the kingdom of God (Revelation 19.6–9, cf. Isaiah 25.6).[4] Viewed from this perspective, the Christ who is made present by the Spirit's activity is not principally the historical persona Jesus of Nazareth – he does not come to his people as an artefact of the past (despite the importance of the historical narrative!). Rather, this Christ is the one who has gone ahead to prepare a place for his people in his Kingdom and who therefore meets us in the Eucharist from the future (John 14.3–5). The crucified and resurrected Christ is simultaneously the ascended and glorified Christ, now ahead of us and calling us forward to meet him. Aquinas describes this aspect of the feast as a 'pledge' or solemn promise, orientating the participants towards God's horizon and all that it means to find our end in God. In my thinking, this also provides the orientation for Christian ethical deliberation.

The temporal and supratemporal overlap in every celebration of the Eucharist, but the supratemporal narrative provides context and continuity for each episodic celebration of the Eucharist. It is my contention that each temporal celebration of the Eucharist therefore maps the spiritual terrain of ethical deliberation: those who here and now receive the grace of God in the sacrament are also commissioned by that same grace to live in a way that aligns with the eschatological hope to which this God calls us in Christ (cf. Philippians 3.14). And furthermore, the liturgical content of the Eucharist trains us to live it. Therefore, to receive Christ in the bread and wine into our own bodies is to say 'yes' to that divine commission. It is, simultaneously, to acknowledge our need of God's help and to receive resources for what lies ahead. As with the sacrament itself, the lives of its recipients take on a *proleptic* quality in this paradigm, as thinking-towards-action produces concrete decisions that instantiate the future kingdom in the present. Herein, each instance of ethical deliberation and its subsequent decision and action carries the weight of moving an agent closer to or further from embodying something of the eschatological glory pledged in the sacrament.

Participation and ongoing transformation

One theologian who has fired my own thinking on the ethical dimension of the past-present-future paradigm in the Eucharist is Alexander Schmemann (1921–83). Much of his body of work focuses on worship and liturgical theology. Key to Schmemann's constructive theology is that liturgical worship is not an event that a congregation attends but rather one that the congregation co-creates with the priests in the power of the Holy Spirit as they enact the script in a particular time and space. It is something the whole Church *does*; the congregation is a liturgical actor playing an active part:

> The nature of this action is both *corporate* and *personal*. It is *corporate* because through the unity and faith of its participants it realizes and fulfils the reality of the Church, i.e. the presence of Christ among those who believe in Him. It is *personal* because this reality is every time conveyed to *me*, given to *me* for *my* personal edification, for my own growth in grace. Thus, in worship I am an active builder of the Church – and to be so is my Christian duty – and I am also its 'beneficiary' – for the whole of the Church's treasure is offered to me, is a Divine gift to me.[5]

Worshippers participate in the spatiotemporal event as they pray, sing, proclaim, listen, receive and attend to Christ in their hearts. The ritual activities form a scaffolding for this more important work. Those who put in 'spiritual effort' in worship find that they also participate in the bigger supratemporal reality of God's saving grace in Christ – 'the

Church's treasure'.[6] Worship thus functions as 'a door leading us into the wonderful reality of new life in Christ'.[7]

It would be easy to see Schmemann as advocating for a Christian withdrawal from the world around us – through 'the door' into the comfort and security of the 'new reality' – and thus to see church attendance as a form of escapism. But this would be a mistake because it denies the purpose of the edification and growth in grace that worship of the triune God gives to its participants. This is especially so regarding the Eucharist. Schmemann describes each episodic celebration of the Eucharist as a movement or journey:

> The journey begins when Christians leave their homes and beds. They leave, indeed, their life in this present and concrete world, and whether they have to drive fifteen miles or walk a few blocks, a sacramental act is already taking place, an act which is the very condition of everything else that is to happen. For they are now on their way to *constitute the Church*, or to be more exact, to be transformed into the Church of God. They have been individuals, some white, some black, some poor, some rich, they have been the 'natural' world and a natural community. And now they have been called to 'come together in one place,' to bring their lives, their very 'world' with them and to be more than what they were: a new community with a new life.[8]

Here, as before, the sacrament involves a transition from one state to another enacted in the movement from house to church building. Those who gather will become more than they were by participating in it (again, personally and corporately). And this newness is to be reflected in their way of life. It is an identity-conferring event for the Church by which it is located spiritually, mentally and emotionally within the grand narrative of God's salvific activity; a story in which people from all backgrounds and identities may find their place, though perhaps not without having their 'natural' identities reconfigured and renewed in the light of Christ. The same event commissions Christians to exit the gathering to live in the newness of life they have received.

We can begin to see how the spatiotemporal celebration of the Eucharist is an important feature of its purpose and intent. The separation from the world is not permanent. We are not really *escaping* at all, because our celebration of the Christ's saving work really happens within the world; we are not escaping because the purpose of the celebration is to equip Christians to live well within it – to make decisions and to act in ways that move towards God's future for all people. The Eucharist might best be understood as a temporary stepping out from the usual busyness and distraction to get a better vantage point on what really matters, on who we are as Church, and what we're for by encountering afresh the living God as we rehearse and participate in the story of Jesus Christ.

For Schmemann, there's also a missional dimension to this that is ontically significant for the Church. Christians carry the good news of the kingdom of God with them and others see and experience it through their decisions and actions. Rather than withdrawal and advance, Schmemann uses the biblical language of ascent and return:

> The early Christians realized that … they must ascend to heaven where Christ has ascended. They realized also that this ascension was the very condition of their mission in the world, of their ministry to the world. For there – in heaven – they were immersed in the new life of the Kingdom; and when, after this 'liturgy of ascension,' they returned into the world, their faces reflected the light, the 'joy and peace' of that Kingdom and they were truly its witnesses. They brought no programs and no theories; but wherever they went, the seeds of the Kingdom sprouted, faith was kindled, life was transfigured, things impossible were made possible. They were witnesses, and when they were asked, 'Whence shines this light, where is the source of this power?' they knew what to answer and where to lead men. In church today, we so often find we meet only the same old world, not Christ and His Kingdom. We do not realize that we never get anywhere because we never leave any place behind us.[9]

To participate in the Eucharist is to continue to be immersed in and remade by the gospel. Anything else is spectatorship. Transformed lives are inspiring and provocative and they make a difference to others in society. And this, Schemman argues, is why the Eucharist is essential for learning to live Christianly and why regular participation should not be compromised. To extend his metaphor, our faces reflect the light we receive.

Schmemann's summary of the lived impact of the sacrament might be a bit vague for some. But by the application of the ethical imagination, we can begin to explore what participating in each constitutive element of the eucharistic *liturgy* might mean within the concrete reality of our daily existence.

Some ethical implications of the eucharistic liturgy

In a standard *Common Worship* service of Holy Communion there are several constituent elements that form the liturgical journey: the gathering, the penitential rite, the Word (including preaching), intercessions, the peace, the eucharistic rite, and the blessing and dismissal. Though clearly the Eucharist is a single event comprised of these various parts, it is reasonable to assume that the Holy Spirit is distinctly at work in each of the elements of the liturgy for our edification and growth in grace. My interest here is the way that these distinctive parts frame our thinking-towards-action. By way of example, I limit my observations here to just two constitutive parts of the *Common Worship* liturgy – *the gathering* and *the peace* – but the same principle can be applied across the liturgy.

The Gathering

At the point of gathering the congregants together the president will normally invoke the triune name before extending a greeting to the faithful,

> In the name of the Father
> And of the Son,
> And of the Holy Spirit
> **Amen.**
>
> The Lord be with you
> **And also with you**

Though a simple enough liturgical piece, the greeting has profound implications both for our understanding of what's going on and for who is included. It does more than indicate that the ritual has begun. The invocation of the triune name informs both the president and the congregants that something is happening and it belongs to neither of them: it is the triune God's event.

Gathering is more than welcoming. The president is not acting as host for a members' event. The president is leading the liturgical performance as actor and director. Welcome is certainly a feature of gathering people together, but gathering is more purposeful. It is more than tolerating. The president is not indicating that the regulars must put up with the visitors for the duration of this service. Toleration of this kind is such a diminished form of welcome that it does violence to the dignity of those with whom we disagree or find it hard to love! By contrast, gathering is a great leveller. It informs all the people that they can and may participate in the life of the triune God mediated to us through the eucharistic liturgy because the basis of our participation is God's grace enacted in Jesus of Nazareth. Thus the Church is reminded that all those who are gathered are within the purview of God's salvific purpose and we must be very careful about excluding any. The cue for this is the content of the supratemporal narrative, Jesus 'who fed the crowds and who regularly ate with those on the margins of society like prostitutes, tax collectors, and sinners' in the past, now summons the Church to live today and tomorrow as a fellowship of those who 'no longer admit distinctions based on age or sex or race or wealth or class or caste or disability'.[10] We are to resist the temptations to create silos and echo-chambers and to embrace our calling to be the Body of Christ in all its diversity (see 1 Corinthians 12.12–27).

Gathering assures those who do not know that they belong, and are not sure that they may participate, of the generous hospitality of the God-host.[11] It also challenges those who would try to police the boundaries of participation too rigidly. This is where I think there is value for ethics. In a world (and Church!) that can so often be siloed and tribal in its approach to difference, the liturgy of gathering calls us to live towards the future for which Christ has called us and to think-towards-actions that reinforce the value and status that God accords to each person we meet.

The Peace

The liturgy of the peace normally comes after the intercessions and before the eucharistic prayer. It usually begins with a declaration of God's peaceful intent towards humanity before inviting the congregants to make peace with one another. It is an important ground-clearing activity that mirrors the biblical call to interrupt worship and be reconciled to enemies before we can presume to continue (Matthew 5.23–24). Where the penitential rite seeks to fix the vertical relationship between the penitent and God, the peace is designed to bring reconciliation on the horizontal plane: we shake hands and embrace those around us as a sign and symbol of our intent towards them. How can we expect to receive Christ afresh in the sacrament if we will not pursue peace with those for whom Christ died and now lives? It is an outward demonstration of our inward determination to live in love and peace with all (Romans 12.18).

This social dimension of the Eucharist is a gift and a discipline. The gift of sharing in the global fellowship of those who participate in the supratemporal narrative comes with the discipline of living peacefully with those fellow disciples who are our immediate neighbours and may, from time to time, test the depth of our Christlike formation! The presence of the liturgy of the peace should alert us to the reality that we need both to give and receive forgiveness regularly:

> The eucharist ... is a catalyst for forgiveness and reconciliation, an alternative to anger and violence, an antidote to the fostering of hate and revenge. The alternative that the eucharist offers is by no means easy ... It often involves a struggle not to give in to anger but rather to love one's enemy.[12]

A simplistic application of eucharistic peace could encourage the kind of ethical deliberation that measures its success by a shallow social concept – namely, the absence of obvious conflict; that is, that we're not clamouring or fighting one another. But such an approach does not go deep enough: it runs the risk of colluding with injustice because it fails to name when something is wrong by not seeking accountability and thus not putting things right. Peace without justice is incredulous and will not last.

By contrast, the presence of the liturgical peace in the Eucharist shares in the supratemporal narrative by directing worshippers' attention backwards to God's response to the great injustices incurred by Christ in his passion. What happened to Jesus in the first Holy Week is flooded with injustices: his friends and family denied him, the courts lied about him, the powerful abused him, the guilty mocked him and the elite murdered him. But Christ willed to endure the cross and its shame for a greater purpose (Hebrews 12.2–3) and now the resurrected and ascended Christ calls all humanity forward to his peaceable kingdom. The liturgy demonstrates that genuine peace requires people to move towards their enemies and embrace them, and on a weekly basis trains Christians to do that work. While one could perform the liturgy in a perfunctory way, for a participant in the Eucharist the physical embrace symbolizes the deeper work of reconciliation that necessarily involves both truth-telling ('This person has been my enemy because ...') and hope ('We can be reconciled to one another as we ...').

Sharing the peace summons us to a life of justice and inclusion, resourced by Christ's own life mediated to us in the sacrament. For the task of thinking-towards-action it means preferring truth-telling and justice as the essential ingredients of social cohesion and justice as basic to our life together. This is true not only for the Church but through the Church for a world that desperately needs peace. A peaceable Church is a just Church, enabling others to anticipate the kingdom in which all things shall be made new.

Notes

1 Gregory Dix, 1982, *The Shape of the Liturgy*, London: Adam & Charles Black, p. 267.
2 See Justo González and Catherine Gunsalus González, 2022, *Worship in the Early Church*, Louisville, KY: Westminster John Knox Press, chapter 6.
3 Alexander Schmemann, 1987, *The Eucharist*, New York: St Vladimir's Seminary Press, p. 216.
4 Dix, *Liturgy*, p. 263.
5 Alexander Schmemann, 1993, *Liturgy and Life: Christian Development through Liturgical Experience*, New York: Orthodox Church in America, p. 23; emphases original.
6 Schmemann, *Liturgy and Life*, p. 24.
7 Schmemann, *Liturgy and Life*, p. 25.
8 Alexander Schmemann, 1998, *For the Life of the World: Sacraments and Orthodoxy*, New York: St Vladimir's Seminary Press, p. 27; emphasis original.
9 Schmemann, *Life of the World*, p. 28.
10 Margaret Scott, 2008, *The Eucharist and Social Justice*, New York: Paulist Press, p. 6 (see also Galatians 3.28).
11 See Scott, *Social Justice*, pp. 5–7.
12 Scott, *Social Justice*, p. 27.

Bibliography

Balasuriya, Tissa, 2004, *The Eucharist and Human Liberation*, Eugene, OR: Wipf & Stock.
Conway, Stephen (ed.), 2001, *Living the Eucharist: Affirming Catholicism and the Liturgy*, London: Darton, Longman, & Todd.
Dix, Gregory, 1982, *The Shape of the Liturgy*, London: Adam & Charles Black.
González, Justo and Catherine Gunsalus González, 2022, *Worship in the Early Church*, Louisville, KY: Westminster John Knox Press.
GS Misc 632, 2001, *The Eucharist: Sacrament of Unity. An Occasional Paper of the House of Bishops of the Church of England*, London: Church House Publishing.
Leyden, Michael, 2019, *Living Faithfully: Discipleship, Creed, and Christian Ethics*, London: SCM Press.
Lysaught, M. Therese, 2000, 'Eucharist as Basic Training: Liturgy, Ethics, and the Body', in David Hammond (ed.), *Theology and Lived Christianity*, Waterford, CT: Twenty-Third Press.

Meyers, Ruth and Paul Gibson (eds), 2010, *Worship-Shaped Life: Liturgical Formation and the People of God*, Norwich: Canterbury Press.
Schmemann, Alexander, 1987, *The Eucharist*, New York: St Vladimir's Seminary Press.
Schmemann, Alexander, 1993, *Liturgy and Life: Christian Development through Liturgical Experience*, New York: Orthodox Church in America.
Schmemann, Alexander, 1998, *For the Life of the World: Sacraments and Orthodoxy*, New York: St Vladimir's Seminary Press.
Scott, Margaret, 2008, *The Eucharist and Social Justice*, New York: Paulist Press.

Sermon

'Invited by Name'

Preached at Evensong and Benediction at
St Peter de Beauvoir Town on 18 May 2024

Mthr Arwen Folkes

Deuteronomy 16.9–15; John 7.37–39

Let anyone who is thirsty come to me.

Over the last month I have been preparing ten candidates for confirmation. The group is diverse, ranging from the ages of 19 to 79, from a professor to one of life's rough diamonds, a former Unitarian to a former orthodox. As we have explored who Jesus was and is, how Church and creeds came to be, and the formation of character through the sacraments, we have had all the forms to fill in, honouring the Anglican preoccupation with paperwork. Within them was the one from our confirming Bishop asking for each candidate's testimony.

Reading, as I scanned and sent them to the Bishop's Office, I was taken by a striking and startling similarity between them all. Each spoke warmly and passionately of the moment they were invited to join in, to be confirmed, to come and see. They described, by name, who had invited them and how this invitation had been the sign to say the 'yes' carried on their hearts, in some cases for many years.

'Let anyone who is thirsty come to me' underlines the centrality of invitation to Christ's ministry. Again and again we witness our Lord in the Gospels 'closing the deal' as a salesperson might say; not leaving an open-ended conversation hoping it might stick, but giving tangible opportunity to transform words into action, thought into deed.

At the heart of our faith in the Eucharist we regularly see words being transformed into action. From the Gospels, Paul's letters, even the *Didache*, covenant words are brought to life in human hands, in speech, in gesture and in liturgy. Scripture jumps from the past into the present and lives in the hands of today's generation. The sacrament manifests God to dance in the hands and hearts of our people, who take that dance into the world and the interior life of the Trinity expands and expands like ripples upon water.

To abundantly invite others into the full life of Christ is to mirror and magnify the essence of the gospel itself. Joyful invitation is the basis of evangelism. But I wonder if we have lost that art, of joyfully inviting others. I wonder whether a crisis of confidence prevents us from inviting? An overstatement of the secular imagination? An unconsciously gnostic view of our inner ecclesial life? Witnessing our nervousness and numbers, I find myself asking: How have we misunderstood the assignment?

I am sure that we all know priests, churchwardens and Christians who view themselves as gatekeepers of church life and guardians of the sacraments – guardians in a military sense rather than angelic. Standing as sentry at the altar rail or porch door studying who and how participates. What a terrible theological problem this presents, betraying a diminished sense of God because it beggars belief that anything of God could ever be, or even need to be, protected by a mere human being.

Yet hoops, huddles and hurdles remain and people walk by oblivious to the deep well that awaits them inside. I find myself saying with some regularity, whether at General Synod or the PCC: 'The church door is not the narrow gate.'

Evangelism begins with holding open the door and singing of the joy of this place; it is to beckon and point towards the great promise of Christ that can and will be found in this sanctuary, this well of living waters. It is to allow the very presence of God to so shape us that we can do nothing but invite others to come and be shaped too.

Isn't it wonderful that Christ says 'Let anyone' just as Deuteronomy declares the covenant invitation extended right across social and economic divides, across ethnic divisions. 'Allow them all, bring them in, do not keep them away.' Both the earliest and the newest establishment of God's covenant includes all – all are to worship together. So important is this that we hear the invitation given twice for the slaves, the sons, the daughters, the Levites, the strangers and the orphans. God yearns to be equally present to all, and displays his power through a straight and simple 'let them come', because these three words hold up a mirror to structural and social injustice. Every human name is written on the door-list and they await their invitation.

Isn't it remarkable how Christ says 'Let anyone who is thirsty', knowing full well that the whole of humanity cries out in drought for the living waters – whether known yet or not. All are thirsty. Sometimes we forget this and fruitlessly wait to be invited to invite. And yet, Christ showed us, we all labour under the great burden of sin. We all lament and tear our garments at the terrible evil in the world. We all increasingly recognize, deny or fight the frailty, fallibility and fragility of our humanity. We all thirst.

Souls longing to be fed and watered, baptized and nurtured yet living without such invitation, stray towards the dry, dangerous and diabolical wells miraging as an oasis.

Isn't it joyful that the one who said 'Let everyone who is thirsty come to me' makes himself present before us and calls us to himself again. He stands by his word by being present at the altar, daily, weekly, eternally. Our Lord beckons, shows the way, encourages and inspires; he literally places himself into our clay hands and loves us, deeply, madly and richly. Our evangelism to others has to be rooted in this miraculous fact. 'God is here, God is with us, God wants you here too.'

Blow me if even that word 'catholic' (uncapitalized, of course), the focus of this book, isn't itself an invitation. Because to be a Church catholic is to be a Church that is universal, embracing and all-encompassing. It is to be a Church in which the whole of us have been welcomed, claimed and changed. And it is to be a Church that won't rest until every living person has been looked in the eye and invited by name to come and see, to come and drink, to come and live.

When Our Lord says, 'Let anyone who is thirsty come to me', let the Church say, 'Everyone is thirsty, let them come.' Amen.

3

The Catholic Life: Radical Dependence

MTHR MEL MARSHALL

A number of years ago a friend of mine announced the end of an era had come: she had felt compelled to give up reading *The Guardian*. She was tired of getting the message from its pages that her occupation was an embarrassing waste of time. Her occupation at that time was looking after her two small children. A journalist for *The Times* identified the same trend. The parenting columnist of *The Guardian*, she said, 'writes about new motherhood as if she's an inmate in Abu Ghraib'.[1]

Readers of *The Times* needn't feel complacent. Our whole society teaches parents to resent their small children, just as it teaches adult children to resent the claims of elderly parents. It tells us more generally that freedom consists in unfettered autonomy and that independence must be prized at any price – even at the price of people's lives. Multiple casualties are caused on our roads each year by dangerously geriatric drivers, and always with the same justification: 'He wanted to keep his independence.' To enjoy some solitude and spontaneity is not in itself an evil. But how quickly these natural inclinations are enfolded in the bleak rhetoric of personal independence, elevated to sacred status and treated as though no other form of value or freedom or dignity could be entertained.

As Christians of any tradition we are committed to the view that independence is a myth at best. At worst it is a lie, whose pernicious effects can be seen all around us. It is seen in the widespread demonization of the poor as somehow at fault for their condition. It is seen in high rates of mental ill-health and suicide, especially among men because they are less likely to feel comfortable asking for help. It is seen in the collective contempt and boredom we habitually exhibit towards the most dependent among us – the very young and very old and those who are sick, frail or differently abled.

And yet every one of us has proceeded from conception to birth, from infancy to childhood to adolescence, only with the care of others. Even at our fittest, not one of us could survive a single day without a vast network of mostly unseen others on whom we depend for every kind of sustenance. Each of us has been loved into existence and is held in existence by love. The catholic life – the way of life implied and promoted by the practices of catholic Christianity – calls us first to embrace the basic truth of human sociality and relationship. It is a counter-cultural movement whose adherents are learning both to accept and to rejoice in living a life of radical dependence. And our guide and model in this way of life is the person Jesus Christ. All that we know about being human we learn from him.

In John's Gospel there is a powerful moment at the Last Supper when the Beloved Disciple is described as 'leaning on Jesus' bosom' (John 13.23 KJV). This is a reference back to the only-begotten Son who is 'in the bosom of the Father' at the very beginning of the Gospel (John 1.18 KJV). It's a shame that modern translations often disguise the verbal link between these passages. The link is not just a verbal similarity but a theological analogy. The Beloved Disciple stands for us all. Our dependence on Christ is an analogue of Christ's dependence on God the Father. The icon of that divine–human dependence, the visible sign in the world of that new reality, is the mutual dependence of the Church. That's how the truth of human dependence on God can be made known – through Christians visibly depending on each other.

This dependence can take many forms, and the Christian tradition has sometimes emphasized some of these at the expense of others. It's no longer fashionable to use the image of Christ the Bridegroom that we find in Revelation and elsewhere (though Jesus himself used it).[2] Feminist and other critiques have pointed out the sexist implications of a metaphor that treats Christ as the husband and the Church as the wife. But, dare one suggest it, the theological shape of the thought may be less to do with sex and more to do with dependence. The mutuality of God and Christ is seen as extending itself to encompass a new mutuality between God-in-Christ and humankind. Those mutualities are made visible in the world through the mutuality between spouse and spouse. Now, this is far from the only kind of human mutuality, and different strands of theological thinking have focused on others (friendship, for instance). But if the Bridegroom image has any mileage left in it, it will be because of the generative dimension of marriage. It is new life that is at stake here. And for new life to come about – in any of its forms, the spiritual and emotional even more than the parturitional – there must first be mutual dependence. At its best, that's what this metaphor might suggest.

Of course, it's worth saying that dependence comes in unhealthy forms as well. It shouldn't surprise us when a culture that lionizes personal achievement produces achievement addicts. Toxic independence breeds toxic dependence, whether on drugs and other kinds of chemical hits or on individual relationships that can't possibly offer the sense of total fulfilment that is sometimes expected of them. This tension is part of the life of the Church as well. The European Reformations of the fifteenth to seventeenth centuries were nothing less than successive crises of dependence. The stupidity and cruelty of human institutions led even some Christians to reject the forms of dependence that Christ came to inaugurate. Many people are still drawn to a purely private and personal vision of knowing Christ. But as the patristic formula goes, *unus Christianus nullus Christianus*: the sole Christian is no Christian at all. Radical dependence, as frightening and off-putting as it may sometimes be, can't be sidelined. It is at the very heart of the risen life we are called to instantiate and show forth.

Just as Christ's life was and is a life of dependence on God the Father, so through Christ's Spirit all aspects of our lives – first our existence, then our identity, our formation and our salvation – are forms of radical dependence as well. We'll look at these in turn, each section depending on the ones before and so (you'll be glad to hear) becoming progressively shorter. Let us begin by considering our very existence as sheer gift.

Existence as radical dependence

Our being has no independence. Existence itself is participation in the being of the one who is Being. That is the beginning of Christian metaphysics. God is. We are, because God willed that we should be and because God goes on willing it. The gift of 'being' that is bestowed on us is bestowed out of un-forced love. 'Does God exist?' is a much-asked question (usually by those who are eager to answer in the negative). The theologian John Macquarrie had a better way to phrase it. He suggests that we ask not 'Does God exist?' but rather 'Is Being gracious?'[3] Our answer, our faith and the *kerugma* (proclamation) of the Church universal, is Yes. Yes, Being is unfathomably gracious. And the sign and reality of that Yes is the person of Christ.

So what does this mean for us? Here is the psalmist pondering that question:

> O LORD, my heart is not lifted up;
>   my eyes are not raised too high;
> I do not occupy myself with things
>   too great and too marvelous for me.
> But I have calmed and quieted my soul,
>   like a weaned child with its mother;
>   like a weaned child is my soul within me.
> O Israel, hope in the LORD
>   from this time on and for evermore. (Psalm 131 ESV)

'O Israel, hope in the LORD' ends the song. The image of the child on its mother is a metaphor then, perhaps for the spiritual experience of the psalmist himself but certainly for the whole people of God. All of Israel (and the Church is part of God's chosen family by adoption) has in common its dependence. The psalmist reminds us that this dependence is a basic biological reality, from which we can infer the spiritual reality. The Church indulges many theological disputes about female bodies, what they can and cannot – and may and may not – do. We forget that bearing Christ into the world was first of all the privilege and burden of an ordinary female body. Every birth is the result of the cooperation between God's will and the will of a woman. We all, no less than our Lord, owe our existence to the Yes of our mothers.

There is not enough of the Hebrew language for us to be enormously precise when it comes to the meaning of the word for 'a weaned child'. We do know that the word is derived from the verb *gamal*, meaning 'to deal bountifully'. So whatever else we know, we know that this is a child who has received lavishly. (As St Paul puts it, God gives 'abundantly far more than all we can ask or imagine' (Eph. 3.20 NRSV), and Paul too employs the image of a milk-weaned child to describe Christian dependence (1 Cor. 3.2; cf. 1 Peter 2.2)). Is this child a nursling, full to the brim and lying milk-drunk on its mother? Or is the implication that this child has passed the age of breastfeeding and is reclining in the bosom of its mother simply to revel in the comfort of dependence?

What it must be to rest in God as that infant rests! To sit lightly to our sense of our own capacities and choose instead to rest in the abundance of our Maker. But our ambivalence begins early. Developmental psychologists describe how babies and children have to learn how to inhabit the powerful contradictory feelings that dependence awakens in us. If someone can satisfy us, they can frustrate us. If they can frustrate us, they can satisfy us. It is frightening to discover that the fulfilment or frustration of our deepest and most vital needs are ones we cannot

THE CATHOLIC LIFE: RADICAL DEPENDENCE

supply for ourselves. Our very lives depend on others. Consumer culture works by disguising this primitive fear and feeding off it. We fantasize that by becoming masters of our own boundless consumption we become immortal. If we are to be unshackled from the consumerist lie of self-sufficiency, a completely different orientation of life is needed. That re-orientation we call prayer.

There is no bad way to pray. Pray as you can, not as you can't. Singing hymns is prayer. Reading the Scriptures is prayer. Holding a cross is prayer. Every moment spent in any kind of prayer is a moment not spent buying something or killing someone. It is re-training us in another, more truthful way of being human. The Dominican friar Simon Tugwell has a good exercise for practising this re-orientation. In his short two-volume book *Prayer*, he suggests the following: 'Lie down flat on the floor ... shut your eyes, and just become aware of your whole bodily situation.' He goes on: 'You will be making a real, if primitive, act of faith: you entrust your body to the floor and the floor holds it up.' And he adds 'How efficiently [your body] runs itself – all without your permission.'[4]

Tugwell is careful to specify that this is not prayer but that it tells us something about prayer. It tells us something about existence too. It is not us 'doing' existence (or prayer). We do not own it or control it. Existence, like prayer, is pure gift. (If his exercise should fail to convince you there is always the option to get a cat. Nothing in this world knows how to rest in the sheer givenness of its existence like a domestic shorthair.)

Existence and prayer are the breathing in and out of the Church's life, and they are an exercise in dependence. First, in acknowledging that it is God who exists (and prays) in each of us. And second, in coming to see that it is the Church who prays. Catholic Christians are committed to the universal dimension of the Church's life, shared through time as well as space. We are often challenged on the cult of the saints, fielding questions about why prayer should be mediated through other people. The saints on earth provide the answer. When we can't or won't or simply don't pray ourselves, the Church is still praying. Catholic Christians are often challenged on formal prayer too – isn't it rather rigid and impersonal? But we delight to join our prayers to the prayers of the whole Church. We rejoice in the privilege of using the same words at the same times as our brethren across the world. In prayer we show how we uphold one another as a gloriously indiscriminate whole. Prayer is no respecter of persons, thank God, any more than existence is. Participation in the divine knows no hierarchy, as though with amoeba at the bottom and the Oxbridge educated at the top. The Lord has hidden many of his secrets from the wise and learned. Instead he invites us to rest. To rest on the bosom of the Church, which rests on the bosom of the Lord, who rests on the bosom of the Father. He calls us to embrace our dependence like a little child.

Identity as radical dependence

A phrase much found in our media at present is 'self-identity'. It is used both with a specific application (concerning how sex should be verified in transgender individuals) and to express a wider idea that identity is partly or wholly something we choose for ourselves.

As Christians, our identity is given to us by Christ. More particularly, it arises from our witness to the risen Christ, our belief in a historical moment when the world of beings is broken into and inhabited by Being itself. The resurrection appearances in the Gospels are all powerfully communal: on the Road to Emmaus in Luke, on the hilltop at the end of Matthew. The moving moment when the risen Lord calls Mary Magdalen by name is highly personal, but culminates in the instruction 'Go and tell my brethren …' (John 20.17). Thomas can only believe when he is back within his community of belief (John 20.28). Peter can receive his threefold absolution only within and for that community (John 21.15–19).

What it means to live out this communally bestowed risen identity has never been a matter of simple agreement. If the modern world of identity politics seems factious, it is nothing to some of the Church's controversies. From the birth of the Church onwards there have been anxieties about how this new identity is to be forged and inhabited and bodily expressed. Through keeping the Jewish law or not keeping it? Through recognizing schismatic baptism or not recognizing it? And who gets to decide? The sacraments in particular can easily become emblems of disunity precisely because of their totemic status as symbols of unity.

Perhaps we would benefit from viewing the catholic life as a commitment to common identity in practice rather than theory. The Acts of the Apostles repeatedly describes the powerful communal urge of the newest Christians, as for instance at 4.32ff.: 'Now the whole group of those who believed were of one heart and soul, and no one claimed private ownership of any possessions, but everything they owned was held in common' (NRSV). Acts goes on to relate how lands, houses, fields were sold by their owners and the money 'laid at the apostles' feet'.

Any spiritual director will tell you that many Christians will happily talk about their prayer life and even their sex life, but ask them how they spend their money and a wall goes up. Yet there is nothing more expressive of our identity than those with whom we share money spontaneously. Monasteries and marriages hold funds in common. Friends do not hesitate to help friends. The Church of England aims to distribute clergy and other goods as they are needed, not according to a congregation's ability to pay.

Declines in church attendance and income now endanger the parish system, a truly catholic institution that guarantees to everyone living in England, regardless of faith, a church or churches to call their own. Advocates of the parish have pointed out that church is one of the few places where we will encounter people who are not like us in important respects, whether age, income or attitudes. This identifying catholicity is central to the Church's life, joy and vocation. It is certainly imperilled by a lack of money. But it is imperilled by too much money as well. Churches that accrue wealth and aim to attract the wealthy (and aspirationally wealthy) can grow at the expense of other churches. A more mixed community will face challenges of various kinds – of resources, of differences in perspective on important matters. But these are not optional parts of being Christian. God calls us into the Church with the aim of introducing us to human beings, in all their variety, and helping us to recognize them as fully human. Not objects of charity or envy but partners in the shared endeavour of being fully alive.

That is how the Roman Catholic Church has become and remained the most successful instantiation of catholic Christianity in history. It knows how to cultivate and value diversity – the local practice here, the cultural difference there – and to do it on a truly global and millennial scale. Every catholic Anglican who has walked into a Roman church knows the pang of longing that arises when you see there a whole world at prayer, people of every tribe and language and people and nation. The totalizing pronouncements of the Vatican can blind us to another universal: the wholesale tolerance and delight in difference that underpins that truly international institution. We can call ourselves catholic only in so far as we desire communion with places and people who lie staggering distances away.

To desire and inhabit that communion is never easy, and it is made even harder by the power gradients that still scar our relationships across the globe. At the end of her time in a college choir I asked a singer what piece of music had brought her most joy. With stutters of apology and embarrassment she admitted 'A West African Magnificat'. Her worry was of course about so-called cultural appropriation. We have a long way to go before we are accustomed to accepting an identity given by a huge and disparate whole. A long way before we can say with joy that if it is a Magnificat, then it is of and for the whole Church. Those strange rhythms and new melodies are part of us too.

To do that we would need to see ourselves as dependent on the whole Church, not just our part of it, to make us who we are. It's a natural temptation to want to be defined by our allegiance to those who are like us and by our opposition to those who are not. In matters where the Church experiences grave divisions, we struggle not to identify ourselves by who is in and who is out. And that is precisely why the Lord Jesus died and rose again. To bring the inside out – God himself, cast out to a squalid rubbish dump beyond the city walls. And to bring the outside in – that executed slave coming back to claim the lives and hearts of his traitors and conquer them with love. After Christ, there is no more inside and outside. Those are fictions of our insecurities. After Christ, there is only the whole.

How would it feel, then, to say, 'I depend radically on those who oppose me'? To depend on them not to give me an identity forged in opposition, but as those who as part of Christ's body are part of my own? Who pay for the church I pray in? To believe is to live as though something were true. Have we faith enough to live as though God's embrace is capacious enough for all kinds of confusion and error to be held and forgiven – our own included – and for all kinds of conflicting truths and assumptions to form a part? This world is a school for love. I depend radically on the love and devotion of the whole Church to remind me that love and devotion are not just what I (in my inevitable blindness and folly) say they are.

The challenge facing the truly catholic Christian is to embrace these differences without neutralizing or assimilating them. This is crucial. If you have ever had a good psychotherapist or ever known the gift of true prayer, you will know that it is the very fact that the other voice is not us, that it is instead the radically other on which we radically depend, that gives it such transforming power.[5] The philosopher Simone Weil said: 'I cannot conceive of the necessity for God to love me [...]. But I can easily believe that he loves that perspective of creation which can only be seen from the point where I am.'[6] It takes a world to know creation. It takes a world to know Christ. If our hope is to recognize Christ in this world and stand before him in the next, we will do so together or not at all.

Formation as radical dependence

Certain practices mould us into Christians. Our earthly families bequeath us all the messes that were bequeathed to them, as Philip Larkin famously remarked. So as the Church, we are called together to form a new family. We are family in the sense of being unavoidably related, as we saw above. But the Christian household is also a new unit of formation. In the family of the Church we learn how to be human all over again – new values, new behaviours, new table manners. We learn our humanity from Christ, the one supremely human being, and we learn too from other Christians: from everyone who, like us, is growing daily in Christ through Scripture and sacrament.

Reading the same canonical (that is, authoritative) text is one central part of learning to speak the language of the Christian family. Catholic Christians commit to reading the Scriptures at a given hour and in a given format (through the lectionaries and daily offices) because receiving the wisdom and challenge of the Scriptures is not a private matter. It is part of our mutual formation. Anyone who wants a demonstration of how Christians depend on the Bible should read St Augustine's *Confessions*. An edition that uses italics or footnotes will show best of all how the great theologian weaves the language of Scripture, especially the psalmist, into his own prose. The words of the Church's canonical texts become indistinguishable from Augustine's own thoughts, feelings and reflections. Christians agree that we all depend powerfully on the authors of the biblical texts for our formational accounts of what God has done, and is doing, for his people. It's less easy to agree on how far we should depend on later traditions of biblical interpretation for our understanding of the faith. What we can't do, no matter how conservative our view of Scripture, is avoid other people's interpretations altogether. Every manuscript, every translation of the Bible is a human mediation of God's word to us. That's before we start on sermons, commentaries, theological tracts. Indeed, the Scriptures already contain interpretations of Scripture – some by Jesus himself.[7]

The controversies of the Reformations naturally gave rise to a boom in commentaries on Scripture all over the continent. But if you look at the libraries that scholars amassed, you'll get a surprise. Sectarian allegiances are invisible. Jesuits are reading Lutherans, Lutherans reading Jesuits. Priests and thinkers bought, borrowed and used the biblical commentaries with the best reputations, regardless of the churchmanship of the author. At the peak of the most intense and murderous phases of religious division in European history, the Church can still be found interpreting Scripture together, in humble and mutual dependence. Catholic in the richest sense.

It's important to dwell on the catholicity of the Scriptures precisely because taking the Bible seriously is sometimes imagined as the preserve of reformed traditions. In fact the Scriptures have one purpose only, a purpose shared by all Christians – to point us towards Christ. They are not to be fetishized for their own sake but honoured for their power to sensitize us to the presence of the living Lord wherever he may be in the world around us, and in particular to his presence in the sacraments.

You will hear many definitions of a sacrament, 'an outward and visible sign of an inward and invisible grace' being the most enduring. But how about this? 'Something that can never be done alone.' It doesn't have St Augustine's elegance, to be sure. It may appear too obvious to be worth saying. But it seems it does need saying. Ours is a world in which deepening liberalism and possessive individualism mean that men and women are now seen as authors of themselves. But not us. The life we live as catholic Christians we cannot – thank God – bestow on ourselves. We can't baptize, confirm or ordain ourselves. We can't absolve or anoint ourselves for death, nor can we witness our own marriages (though you'd be astonished how often in the run-up to their own weddings priests are asked if they'll be officiating at it themselves). The Mass, the Holy Communion, the Lord's Supper is the most defining activity of the Church, following the Lord's explicit command to break bread in memory of him. And it can't be said alone. You may love the other people at Mass or you may hate the other people at Mass, but if no one comes to answer the Mass, the Mass isn't offered. We need one another in the most literal and physical way in order to become who we are to be.

Recent scholarship focuses more and more on liturgy as a formational act and not just a devotional one. But its formational power lies in its devotional power. We could come together and sing 'Yellow Submarine' on a Sunday morning, for all the good that would do us. It is our shared orientation towards the One who is that forms us. Towards Christ as our common destiny. In the Spirit who is our shared guide and inspiration. In *The World as Sacrament*, Alexander Schmemann reminds us that each of us brings and offers at God's altar that little part of creation that God has entrusted to our care.[8] Collectively we bring to God's altar the whole of creation and offer it to be restored. What Adam failed to do, we now do. By the will of the Father and the power of the Spirit, we offer the whole world to God. By grace we are empowered to do as Christ does. But only together.

Salvation as radical dependence

We have seen that to live catholicly is to live 'as a whole'. But wholeness is not something we can cultivate in isolation. For Christians, wholeness is a matter not of personal striving but of perfected relationship. And so by definition it is something for which we depend radically on one another. As catholic Christians we ask the saints to pray for us as those whose lives and deaths have brought them close to God. We are accustomed to the idea that we might depend on the saints. More startling is the idea that they might depend on us. The Epistle to the Hebrews details some of the horrors suffered in the Old Testament by the most faithful servants of God. The passage concludes with an extraordinary claim: that whatever the heroism and piety of these saintly figures, God has provided that 'they would not, without us, be made perfect'.[9] We are part of a whole that is destined for redemption as one body. We cannot be spared. Others – even the most glorious of God's chosen – are depending on us for their salvation as we depend on them for ours.

It is easier to believe that heaven will be communal than to experience the communal as heavenly. But this, in the end, is what the catholic life is all about. We are living towards our eschatological wholeness, practising in this world for the perfection of relationship that will be fully revealed when Christ is all in all. As for what that reality will look like, we have the earthly life of Jesus to give us a preview. Jesus, who never met a sick person he didn't heal or a dead one he didn't bring back to life. Jesus, whose healings restored the community to the individual and the individual to the community. Whatever the category of person we fantasize we can manage without, we are wrong. After Christ there is no more inside and outside. After him there is the only the whole. To live according to that whole, to live catholicly, is a foretaste of the life of heaven. The time to begin is now.

Notes

1 J. Turner, 2024, 'Why aren't British Mothers having Babies any More?', *The Times*, 28 March.

2 Revelation 21.2; cf. e.g. Matthew 9.15; Mark 2.19–20; John 3.29.

3 J. Macquarrie, 1999, *On Being a Theologian*, London: SCM Press.

4 S. Tugwell, 1974, *Prayer. Volume 1: Living with God*, Dublin, Veritas Press, pp. 48–9.

5 See R. Williams, 2000, *Lost Icons*, London: Continuum, pp. 184–9.

6 S. Weil, 2002, *Gravity and Grace*, London: Routledge, p. 41.

7 E.g. Matthew 22.41–45, Luke 4.21, Mark 4.13–20.
8 A. Schmemann, 1974, *The World as Sacrament*, London: Darton, Longman & Todd.
9 Hebrews 11.40 NRSV.

4

Visual Theology of the Eucharist: Altarpieces in London, 1880–2024

MTHR AYLA LEPINE

The use of panel paintings as well as textiles, screens and furnishings, both in front of and behind altars, does not align easily into a single historical trajectory. Bonds between interpretations of altarpieces and the meanings and positions of altars have complex origins both materially and liturgically. In Western Europe the altarpiece tradition evolved from the mid-thirteenth century onwards – particularly in Siena. As the art historian David Ekserdjian explains, the location of the altarpiece and the position of the priest at the Mass were closely linked. When *ad orientem* (presiding at the Eucharist facing East with the people) became the norm, altar frontals (*antependia*) were replaced by (or sometimes simply relocated as) dossals.[1] This exploration of altars and altarpieces in relation to catholicity and sacramental theology in the modern Church of England is by no means a comprehensive survey or an attempt to resolve the matter of the histories of altarpieces. By concentrating on altarpieces within the catholic tradition in London from the late nineteenth century through to the present, both within and beyond classic Anglo-Catholic sites, my focus emphasizes how an altarpiece can offer visual theology of its own. Architectural integration, and the diverse opportunities provided by altarpiece commissions by architects and artists alike, is a key aspect of altarpiece theology. Whether an altarpiece is still an altarpiece without an altar or a sanctuary is not in question, even when the work of art has been deconsecrated (or had never been blessed in the first place).

Altarpieces are microarchitectural and microcosmic glimpses of the meaning of the Mass. In the examples offered below, three themes emerge: presence and absence, tradition and innovation, and justice and liberation. One of the altarpieces was destroyed and dismembered, one is extant in the same setting for which it was produced, one has travelled the world and is now in the heart of the community that produced it, and one was intentionally temporary. They include a small 1890s superfrontal designed by Philip Webb and made by May Morris for a suburban community chapel; G. F. Bodley and Thomas Garner's altarpiece for St Paul's Cathedral in 1883 (damaged in the Second World War and subsequently dismantled and partially sold); the altar by Ninian Comper at St Cyprian's, Clarence Gate in 1903; the Keiskamma Altarpiece in 2005 designed and produced by over 130 Xhosa women, which has travelled globally to a huge range of sacred and secular sites including Southwark Cathedral (and is now in the small village of Hamburg, Eastern Cape in South Africa, where it was made); and *Untitled (Altar Piece)* by the American artist Unyimeabasi Udoh, which was installed in the side chapel of St James's Church, Piccadilly for Passiontide and Easter in 2024. There is a century-long gap intervening between the Comper and the Xhosa altarpieces, though both share something deeply significant in common: both are historicist and medievalist interventions within a highly modern context, taking their initial cue from centuries-old traditions in form, representation and meaning.

The chronology aligns with the late-Victorian rise of Anglo-Catholicism, 50 years after the rousing threshold of John Keble's 'Assize Sermon' from the pulpit of St Mary the Virgin in Oxford. This had vital implications for the rise of Oxford Movement theology and, close on its heels, an art and architectural radicalism that supported and extended the revitalization of Catholic liturgy and aesthetics within the Church of England.[2] Artists were highly attentive to this both within and beyond the Church. For the Pre-Raphaelites above all, altarpieces were an integral part of their work both in ecclesiastical commissions (such as Edward Burne-Jones's altarpiece of the *Annunciation and Adoration* for St Paul's, Brighton) and as works of art for the secular market, at least initially (for example, William Holman Hunt's *The Light of the World*, first produced for the High Anglican collector Thomas Combe and later installed in its own side chapel at Keble College, Oxford).[3] Rossetti received a commission from Llandaff Cathedral for an altarpiece in 1856. He described the prospect to the poet William Allingham as 'a big thing which I shall go into with a howl of delight'.[4]

Sanctuary, liberation, justice: Philip Webb and May Morris's superfrontal

At the turn of the twentieth century, a superfrontal was made for a women's community in London. It is not only a Gothic Revival textile; it is also part of the tradition of the 'speaking object', prominent in medieval works of art, in which objects include the inscription *me fecit* ('made me') and the name of the maker, or sometimes of the donor. Almost half a century after the Pre-Raphaelites formed and this circle of artists had evolved and interlaced with the Arts and Crafts Movement, Philip Webb and May Morris's 'Festival Frontal' was made in 1898–9.[5] Many stitching techniques were used, including English medieval Opus Anglicanum-style stitching and a Bayeux stitch, named after the Bayeux Tapestry.[6] Vines and grape clusters swirl around five golden crosses. Later it was part of a major exhibition of Morris and Company's work at the Louvre in Paris. The exhibition opened in April 1914. In August war broke out. The inscription on the cotton backing reads:

> I came from the brains of Philip Webb the architect of our beautiful chapel; he was the great friend & companion of William Morris, Poet Artist & Craftsman ... Philip Webb delighted to give the design for me to May, he said the only woman in England who could work me. And about my travels & how I came to spend nearly five years in Paris. In April 1914 there was a Great Exhibition at the Louvre of the works of William Morris and his friends. I was out [?] & much admired amongst many other wonderful and beautiful things. The Great War came in August 1914 we were all rushed down to the Great Cellars at the Louvre & walled up. For more than four years those who loved us never thought to see us again but we were kept warm & snug tho' the guns & raids were firing over head. In January 1919 I got home again, & so glad to be in my old corner.[7]

Unlike many Morris and Company ecclesiastical commissions, this was highly personal. The commission, together with the altar and lectern, was for an Anglo-Catholic women's community led by Isabella Gilmore. Gilmore, William Morris's sister, was one of the founders of the Church of England's order of Deaconesses.[8] She first trained as a nurse, and in the 1880s became a prominent voice for women's ordained ministry in the Church of England. Philip Webb and May Morris, her niece, made the Festival Frontal for her order's chapel in the 1890s. The chapel, an extension of the Deaconesses' house in Clapham, was paid for by a family inheritance. Another Anglo-Catholic sacred art connection is woven into this narrative too: Gilmore's memorial at Southwark Cathedral is a Neo-classical marble portrait by Arthur George Walker; Comper designed the frame and inscription. The inscription reads:

> First Head Deacon of the Dioceses of ROCHESTER & SOUTHWARK and an honoured leader in the revival of the Ministry of Deaconesses. A SERVANT OF THE CHURCH, A SUCCOURER OF MANY.

The religious life and the growth of women's communities of deaconesses and nuns was a core aspect of catholic life within Anglicanism.[9] Revivalism of any style, in Britain and beyond, in nineteenth- to twenty-first-century projects within and outside the Church, considers the crucial importance of interlacing past and present. Embracing the new and the old simultaneously across styles and periods was a challenging but necessary thing to grasp, even when confined to a reviving as a single stream of historical antecedents with a quasi-purist mindset. Without resorting to the hackneyed claim that 'there is nothing new under the sun', the significance of altarpieces within this realm of the inevitable echoes of past-in-present is vital. The Mass is both here and now and eternal, an invocation of the unbreakable bond between earth and heaven within which we are perpetually interwoven. What better form than an altarpiece for reflecting that bond? Every altarpiece – like every image of Christ – is also a failure, whether artists and worshippers perceive this or not. Attempts to represent holiness in this most sacred of Christian epicentres will always fall short, in the same way that we fall short when engaging in God-talk and attempting to speak about and in relation to God. We dare greatly and reach into the finitude of human nature when we do so, however vulnerably or valiantly.

The same is true for any artist who attempts to explore the image and dual nature of Christ, whether that attempt is figurative (of any gender, colour or style), symbolic or abstract. The injustice, prejudice and oppression of God's own people are often inscribed within altarpieces. Whiteness and its persistently violent racist legacies interrupt the possibilities of eucharistic promise and visual theology as a whole and must be addressed through the lens of contested heritage. What Christianity, whose Christianity, and how these may have been represented or simply ignored, result inevitably in altarpieces – with their particular purpose – presenting a crucial site for critique and reflection.

This is certainly not an argument for iconoclastic destruction, a denial of the profound value of sacred art or a lament for the inadequacy of the arts both theologically and socially. It is, rather, an insistence upon the calibration of both expectations and responsibilities, a corrective to the notion of 'good' sacred art. While there is a great deal of 'bad' and 'good' sacred art (within a wildly different set of categories and questions not to be considered here), this is a plea to embrace the limitations of human endeavour as, certainly, a positive way to encounter the God-given, grace-infused indwelling and outward expression of creativity in the service of the holy, the Church, the Eucharist and Christ himself.

In Ninian Comper's essay 'Of the Atmosphere of a Church', which was written at the invitation of Chichester Theological College in 1939 and finally published by SPCK in 1947, he is uncompromising and clear about the bond between architecture and theology. It's within this spirit that I offer an account of four very different altarpieces across roughly a century and a half of church history. Comper wrote:

> A church built with hands, as we are reminded at every Consecration and Dedication Feast, is the outward expression here on earth of that spiritual Church built of living stones, the Bride of Christ, Urbs beata Jerusalem, which stretches back to the foundation of the world and onwards to all eternity.[10]

In his time as in ours over a century later, the Church of England's internal conflicts created painful division, which produced critical questions of conscience and anxiety for those within and outside the institution. With uncanny freshness for twenty-first-century readers, Comper claims that entering a church, with its altar at the centre of its life and purpose, with the sacrificial love and nourishment that it promises and implies, should remind us:

> to leave all strife, all disputes of the manner of Church government and doctrine outside – 'Thou shalt keep them secretly in Thy tabernacle from the strife of tongues' – and to enter here on earth into the unity of the Church Triumphant in Heaven. It cannot be otherwise, since He Himself, who is the Temple of it, the Lamb slain from the foundation of the world, is there also. Such a conception of a church, however faintly realised, must put to shame the quarrels of Catholic Christians, who profess the same creeds but set up Church against Church.[11]

Emphasis on the altar – its meanings as well as its physical form and its visual theology – could be a route towards transforming fragmentation into unity. It is a place where bread is broken as the Body of Christ to remind each Christian that 'we are one body' through what we share as well as what we believe and what actions we take. If an altar and altarpiece produced by architects and artists can declare and affirm this in materials and imagery, then it is theology in itself.

Construction, destruction, fragmentation: Bodley, Garner and the St Paul's reredos

Richard William Church became Dean of St Paul's Cathedral in 1871 and this heralded the beginning of a High Anglican turn within what is not only a diocesan but also a national and global centre of Anglicanism. He was friends with John Henry Newman and Henry Parry Liddon (who was alongside him at St Paul's) and defended the Tractarians in Oxford. One of the requests made of him when W. E. Gladstone supported his appointment was that he would invite artists to restore and update the cathedral's interior. Church's Anglo-Catholicism would lead not only to the 1880s high altar commission but also to his own condemnation by the Church Association, who attempted to prosecute him under the Public Worship Regulation Act.[12] In this period, perceptions of the role and importance of Canterbury, St Paul's and Westminster Abbey regarding Britain and its empire were complex.[13] A monument – often ignored but deeply inscribed – at the bottom of the steps to the west of the cathedral indicates this Victorian context. For her Diamond Jubilee in June 1897, Queen Victoria visited St Paul's but was too frail to leave the carriage. Despite this the cathedral has been an essential stopping point for every jubilee since. Niels Moeller Lund's 1904 painting *The Heart of the Empire* locates this 'heart' simultaneously in religious and capitalist life. Lund's perspective is from the roof of the Royal Exchange. Distant but prominent is not the Abbey but the dome of St Paul's. When Edward VII took the throne, money drove imperial power more than ever, in an uneasy dialogue with Christianity.

The architectural firm of G. F. Bodley and Thomas Garner, who had co-founded Watts and Company together with G. G. Scott Jr in 1874 and been at the core of the late-Victorian Gothic Revival, were invited to produce a new design for the high altar of St Paul's in 1883. They had worked with Liddon before and were well known by the Dean. Their design's cost was a huge investment, totalling £37,000. The altar complex – not just an altarpiece but a full sanctuary programme including sculptures of the resurrected Christ, the Madonna and Child, and a prominent crucifixion surrounded by saints and angels – was complete by 1888. The altar was elevated on a six-step platform, and its aesthetic was highly and consciously Italian Baroque.[14] Its arrival sparked a 'puritan demonstration' during the liturgy. Liddon recorded in his diary that a woman told him that during the service he had been 'worshipping an idol'. It also led to a legal controversy.[15] From the outset, the commission was both an opportunity and a problem. Christopher Wren's City buildings had been under sustained attack from architectural transformation (capitalism, again) and honouring and preserving them was among Bodley and Garner's public architectural activist causes in this period.

Garner's design met this challenge by leaning into the High Anglican sensibilities of the clergy. Audaciously, Garner's proposal claimed that his design was a utopian vision of what altarpieces in England would have looked like if the Reformation had never happened, while simultaneously referencing (at least partially) Wren's early ideas, which were recorded by his son in *Parentalia*.[16] Stephen Dykes Bower reinterpreted Wren's vision with a baldacchino in the 1950s, because Bodley and Garner's controversial altar was damaged by bombing in the Second World War and subsequently dismantled.[17] The architectural historian Michael Hall suggests that Wren's design was not carried out because it could have been perceived as too Roman Catholic in late-seventeenth-century England.[18] Garner's design amplified the Eucharist as a sacrifice and included the Latin text of John 3.16, *sic Deus dilexit mundum* ('for God so loved the world'), expecting worshippers not only to welcome a Latin inscription but also to complete the passage through visual and sacramental devotion, responding to the emotive image of the crucifixion below.

Reactions to the altarpiece were critical of the design and its theological implications. Reviewing the Royal Academy's Summer Exhibition in 1890, to which Garner had submitted his St Paul's design, *The Architect* flatly said that the design was 'in a manner that Wren could not approve'.[19] Garner and Bodley were highly informed about what Wren would and would not have approved of but, despite their strong public admiration for Wren and their voices in public debate regarding preservation of his churches, this High Anglican high altar project suggests that, to be frank, they were more interested in offering a strong catholic theology of the Eucharist than in pleasing Wren and even contemporary architectural critics. In 1898, Garner converted to Roman Catholicism, and Bodley and Garner's firm dissolved partly because of this. Garner's major architectural commission towards the end of his life was the choir for Downside Abbey, and he was buried at Downside. When St Paul's was bombed in the war, the high altar did sustain minor damage – but it could have been easily repaired. Instead it was dismantled. The crucifix is still in the cathedral's collection, but nearly all the rest of the altar's monumental elements have been dispersed and sold.[20] Dykes Bower's post-war high altar is High Anglican in its own way, referencing Bernini and St Peter's; it is also far closer to Wren's vision and as a result inevitably less controversial, regardless of its visual claims regarding the Eucharist in the mid-twentieth century and the twenty-first.

Death, Resurrection, Redemption: Ninian Comper and St Cyprian's, Clarence Gate

St Cyprian's, Clarence Gate, is a quintessential turn-of-the-century Anglo-Catholic London church. Its simple brick exterior reveals little of what awaits the visitor. Ninian Comper designed it in 1902 and returned for decades afterwards to add to the interior, extending and deepening the meanings of the iconography, with the altar – monumentally and even excessively large – as the church's sacramental and aesthetic epicentre. The stained glass in the east window and the rood screen painting were completed 20 years later and the font's Neo-classical cover arrived in the 1930s. Chairs – not pews – were available at the back and worshippers collected one on the way in, leaving the wooden floor clear as a normative practice. Comper's biographer Anthony Symondson identified the church as a blend of Attleborough parish church in Norfolk (and Norfolk Gothic churches more widely) together with the fifth-century S. Sabina in Rome.[21] Comper claimed that its historicism 'neither seeks nor avoids originality'.[22]

The altar is huge by any standards, and the relatively small size of the church emphasizes its grandeur. Rather than seasonal frontals, the painted leather frontal is intended to be used year-round. The Hebrew Bible, the New Testament and eucharistic theology interlace in unexpected ways, and the overall programme is more fully legible when viewed together with the east window's stained glass. Consistent with Comper's work overall, the figures are white, idealized and inspired by a blend of medieval and Renaissance ideals. Comper's entanglements with whiteness and queerness within Anglo-Catholicism are a persistent and vital aspect of his work, including this early and monumental design for St Cyprian's.[23]

The painted leather altar frontal features Adam and Eve in the centre. Their hands are both touching the tree's fruit. The inscription on the frontal refers to the consequences: *Semen mulieris conteret caput serpentis* ('the seed of the woman shall vanquish the head of the serpent'). This text centres Eve in the story of redemption at the heart of this altarpiece and presents Mary as a Second Eve alongside Christ as Second Adam. Comper emphasizes gender complexity by using a traditional serpent trope: it has a feminine head. Unusually, the roots of Comper's tree conjoin the frontal and dossal. The tree appears dead at the bottom while rooted in the brown earth. The outer figures on the frontal are Moses and David, representing both law and kingship even as they represent the unlikeliness of Moses' leadership (being found in the reeds, rising up to proclaim liberation for God's oppressed people) and David's own flaws and frailty.

The iconography of the frontal and dossal can be read both vertically and horizontally, mapping a cruciform pattern across the altar as a whole. The tree of the knowledge of good and evil is also the tree of crucifixion, with its details implying the New Covenant through the conflation of the cross of death with the promise of resurrection. The crucifixion is framed by scenes including the Annunciation on the left and the Eastern tradition of the Resurrected Christ appearing to the Virgin Mary on the right.[24] This draws not only on the tradition of the Crucifixion and Annunciation taking place on the same day but also links redemption with the Incarnation, Crucifixion and Resurrection. The saints are Matthew, Peter, Mary and John to the left, and Paul, Luke and Mark to the right. These characters represent not only the early apostolic leadership of the Church and the Evangelists but the three figures of Mary are a strong indication of the importance of Marian theology within Anglo-Catholicism.

For the consecration in 1903 Comper wrote an article explaining the architecture and its liturgical meanings. He repeatedly emphasized the altar's importance. Comper describes the church 'as a lantern and the altar is the flame within it', explaining that the geometry of the rood screen in relation to the chancel steps allows for a unique blend of mediated decoration and delineation of the sacred layers of space while also ensuring an uninterrupted view of the altar for the congregation. For Comper, the colour, symbolism and framing of the altar are all visual theology. Including angel-topped riddel posts was a revival of 'English Use', and part of the blend Comper sought between different pre-Reformation architectural, ecclesiastical and liturgical histories.[25] There is nothing purist about the design, which is a deliberate composite of a wide variety of High Anglican perspectives. Rather than asserting what was 'correct', Comper offered a bespoke understanding of what a new, contemporary Anglo-Catholicism could be. In his 1903 article, he asserted that:

> By the richness of its coverings, no less than by its size and austere isolation, [the altar] expresses its supreme and august importance ... To repeat what most needs repeating to-day: it is the emphasis of the table of the altar which is of real consequence; and the reredos and curtains round it and the canopy over it are solely for the purpose of giving dignity to this.[26]

One of Comper's most vocal champions was the poet and architectural writer John Betjeman, who advocated for Victorian church architecture as widely and as publicly as he could. In 1938, J. M. Richards, editor of the *Architectural Review*, who was a keen Modernist and sceptical of sacred architecture that looked back to distant eras for its inspiration, visited St Cyprian's with Hubert de Cronin Hastings. Hastings wrote to Betjeman that they had gone to the church Betjeman loved 'to make sure that you were mad'. Surprised by their positive reaction to it, Hastings told Betjeman that it was 'not everyone's cup of vodka' but that it had 'a remarkable feeling of space and clarity of planning ... I confess that I was very much astonished and so too, strangely enough, was Marx [Richards] who was immediately converted. You have scored again brother.'[27]

This altarpiece was also temporarily relocated during a period of war. During the Second World War the altarpiece was moved into the crypt for safekeeping, where photographs reveal that it became the backdrop for a long communal table where women and men in uniforms and helmets gathered for tea from generous metal teapots in the relative safety of the crypt. This not only demonstrates the value of the altarpiece in the minds of the congregation but also unwittingly the communal nature of every eucharistic celebration. This portability, as with the altarpiece removed during the First World War mentioned above, is a reminder that altarpieces are at once both portable and pertain to permanence, the permanent remembrance of what Christ has done for all time. This interplay of portability and permanence reminds us that all altars focus ultimately on eschatology, the end of all things.

For the congregation, the monumental and visible nature of the gold-backed altarpiece means that when the Mass is celebrated here it is impossible to look away. The poet Nicky Finney describes the responsibility of an artist to 'not look away'.[28] The Eucharist is a broken-hearted insistence upon the open-hearted joy Christ brings out of the violent chaos of the world. It is a liberating, mystical force. For the celebrant, as Mass is always said facing East towards the dossal, it is impossible not to be confronted by the gaze of the crucified Christ, between the images of the Mother of God at the Annunciation and the Resurrection, even as the priest is aware that their feet are planted at the level of Adam and Eve, earthed in the ground of human pain. Every Christian is merely and wonderfully human, longing for the better world that the Eucharist ultimately promises. Every priest at the altar – this and every altar – serves as a mediator for the congregation between the fall and the events of redemption, among images and as a person made in the image of God. The altar's imagery during and outside the liturgy of the Eucharist proclaims a cruciform visual theology with an unbreakable bond between redemption and salvation and between time and eternity. The priest and the congregation step into this visual theology at every liturgy, responding to it and enlivening it.

Trauma, pilgrimage, departures: the Xhosa Women's *Keiskamma Altarpiece* and Unyimeabasi Udoh's *Untitled (Altar Piece)*

The final two altar pieces are contemporary creations which demonstrate the role that an altarpiece can play not only devotionally but as inspiration for activism. These both highlight the solidarity (not just longed for, but actual) achieved through eucharist and the act of making. They demonstrate the role that altarpieces can play in making the solidarity achieved through eucharist real in the experiences of those at the altar, as a reminder of Christ's Body and Blood active in the community now.

The *Keiskamma Altarpiece* is one of a series of artworks produced by Xhosa women who have participated in local arts and community activism initiatives for over 20 years.[29] These South African projects blend together lived experience of the trauma of AIDS and the hope of communities and the Body of Christ with specific references to European art history. They are subversive, not derivative, claiming this tradition as an act of liberation.[30] Using mixed media, they incorporate portraiture alongside pattern and colour, merging the particular and the personal with the insistence upon every person's dignity and yearning for justice and love as a beloved human made in the image of God. The *Keiskamma Altarpiece* was inspired by Matthias Grünewald's *Isenheim Altarpiece*, completed in 1516 for St Anthony's Monastery near Colmar, where patients in physical and spiritual anguish were dying from the plague.[31] Famously, the image of Christ stretched out and mangled on the cross in the central panel is covered in sores that would have been instantly recognizable as signs of death and suffering for plague victims.

The *Keiskamma Altarpiece*'s activism and contemporary insistence upon not looking away from the pain and urgency of those whose voices are often unheard and whose suffering is often unseen is dramatically centred, transposing as well as uniting the sorrow and horror across centuries and continents. The resonances of suffering and salvation go far beyond art-historical scholarship, insisting upon the power of Black liberation theology and womanist theology at the heart of collaborative feminist iconography. Within this framework, Kelly Brown Douglas asserts that 'The cross represents the power that denigrates human bodies, destroys life, and preys on the most vulnerable in society. As the cross is defeated, so too is that power.'[32] The *Keiskamma Altarpiece* embarks on sacred pilgrimages because confrontation with horror and hope creates justice-seeking commitment within the Eucharist. The *Keiskamma Altarpiece* simultaneously has one home and multiple homes, taking a stand and aligning liberation theology with the Eucharist. In 2005 the altarpiece was briefly installed at Southwark Cathedral, temporarily incorporated into the cathedral's liturgical life.[33]

Unyimeabasi Udoh's *Untitled (Altar Piece)* was installed at St James's Piccadilly in Passiontide 2024 and in place throughout Holy Week and Easter.[34] It is a garland behind the altar with individually cut-out letters spelling out the word 'DEPARTURES' in double embossed Japanese paper. For Udoh, 'The word "Departures" evokes something kind of light, ephemeral, and transitory. Here, and then gone.' Udoh's work explores the borderlands of text and image, investigating the uncanny in visual culture. They were also the designer for the Royal Academy's Entangled Pasts exhibition in 2024 and the Starr Fellow at the RA Schools. The parish connection amplified a local long-established bond, with St James's known as the Artists' Church. Udoh's altarpiece deploys text as image, each letter's shadow dancing lightly against the wall. In conversation, the artist reflected on the significance of language for them, as a designer and an artist, about how word and image fuse in the imagination. Their garland also responds to and extends the centuries of sacred art at St James's Piccadilly. It echoes Grinling Gibbons' seventeenth-century carved garland reredos above the high altar. The centre of the reredos, between the altar and (since the 1950s) below a monumental image of the Crucifixion, is a mother pelican feeding her chicks. This is a powerful and enduring medieval image of the sacrifice of the Eucharist.[35] In this context, *Untitled (Altar Piece)* signals both Christ's Passion and the eschatological promise of God, asserting in ephemeral, fragile paper that death and eternal life are simultaneously entangled in the Mass.

Udoh's work expresses the wider relationship between altarpieces and liturgy, as well as memory and anticipation in the cycles of the Mass and of the Church year as a whole. During Holy Week, *Untitled (Altar Piece)* remained in place. The solemn stripping of the altar and the removal of signs of ritual from the church unfolded around the word 'DEPARTURES', left on the wall as if floating in the between-time of the Triduum, next to the open aumbry door. It remained in place, conscientiously among the liturgical traditions of the church, because despite its portability the word it offers promises an imminent leave-taking of its own material. The word remained, accompanying prayers in the side chapel through the hours of the night on Holy Saturday and onwards as a witness to the Dawn Eucharist and the Easter celebrations throughout the days that followed.

The Mass at the heart of catholic life gains its name from the very end of the liturgy in which the deacon proclaims the dismissal, *Ite, missa est.* 'DEPARTURES' contains within itself its own *Ite, missa est* echo, a reminder that participating in the Eucharist finds its completion in the departure of each of us, having been nourished by the Body of Christ and being sent out as members of that Body into the world. 'DEPARTURES' – the word, the liturgy and the work of art – signals that we may 'go in peace'. It reminds us that the Mass itself is small, brief, ephemeral within all life and the beatific vision that awaits us beyond the horizon, when sacraments will cease. The Eucharist is patterned on arrivals and departures. It is an offering to God in gratitude for what God's self has offered us. The mutual, continuous pattern of grace, in the spirit of self-offering, is the setting for every altar and every altarpiece.

Notes

1 D. Ekserdjian, 2021, *The Italian Renaissance Altarpiece*, London: Yale University Press, pp. 12–13.

2 For an overview of the relationship between the Oxford Movement and the Gothic Revival in Anglican visual culture, see W. Whyte, 2020, 'Ecclesiastical Gothic Revivalism', in J. Parker and C. Wagner (eds), *The Oxford Handbook of Victorian Medievalism*, Oxford: Oxford University Press, pp. 433–46.

3 For an overview of Pre-Raphaelite High Anglican works of art, see T.

Barringer, J. Rosenfeld and A. Smith, 2012, *Pre-Raphaelites: Victorian Avant-Garde*, London: Tate Publishing, pp. 114–55.

4 O. Doughty and J. R. Wahl (eds), *The Letters of Dante Gabriel Rossetti, Vol. 2: 1861–1870*, Oxford: Oxford University Press, p. 101 (No. 56.9).

5 L. Parry (ed.), 1996, *William Morris*, London: V&A, p. 251.

6 L. Monnas, 2016, 'The Making of Medieval Embroidery', in C. Browne et al., *English Medieval Embroidery: Opus Anglicanum*, London: Yale University Press, pp. 7–24.

7 Quoted in 'The Festival Frontal', https://collections.vam.ac.uk/item/O89474/the-festival-frontal-superfrontal-webb-philip-speakman/ (accessed 5.08.2024).

8 For an early account of Gilmore's life, see 1924, *Deaconess Gilmore: Memories Collected by Deaconess Elizabeth Robinson*, London: SPCK. See also H. Blackmore (ed.), 2007, *The Beginning of Women's Ministry: The Revival of the Deaconess in the 19th-Century Church of England*, Church of England Record Society, Volume 14, Woodbridge, Suffolk and Rochester NY: Boydell Press.

9 For an extensive bibliography on nineteenth-century Anglican monasticism and women's communities, see: https://historyofwomenreligious.org/women-religious-bibliography/modern-2/.

10 Comper, quoted in A. Symondson and S. Bucknall, 2006, *Sir Ninian Comper: An Introduction to his Life and Works, with Complete Gazetteer*, Spire Books and the Ecclesiological Society, p. 234.

11 Symondson and Bucknall, *Comper*, p. 234.

12 M. Hall, 2014, *George Frederick Bodley and the Later Gothic Revival in Britain and America*, New Haven, CT: Yale University Press, p. 342.

13 For a discussion of Westminster Abbey and imperialism, see G. Alex Bremner, 'Imperial Monumental Halls and Tower: Westminster Abbey and the Commemoration of Empire, 1854–1904', *Architectural History* 47 (2004), pp. 251–82. Regarding St Paul's Cathedral and imperialism, see M. Coughlan et al., 'Round Table: Sculpture and Faith at St Paul's Cathedral, c.1796–1913', *Journal of Victorian Culture* 28, 1 (January 2023).

14 T. Garner, 1890, 'The New Altar Screen in St. Paul's Cathedral', *Transactions of the St. Paul's Ecclesiological Society*, Vol. 2, London: Alabaster, Passmore & Sons, pp. 167–8.

15 'St. Paul's Reredos', *The Press, Canterbury* 46, 7326 (3 June 1889), p. 5.

16 For a full list of Wren's St Paul's designs and the *Parentalia*, see: https://library.asc.ox.ac.uk/wren/concordance.php (accessed 29.07.2024).

17 Anthony Symondson, 2011, *Stephen Dykes Bower*, London: RIBA, pp. 25–9.

18 Hall, *George Frederick Bodley*, p. 341.

19 1890, 'Architecture at the Royal Academy', *The Architect: A Weekly Illustrated Journal of Art, Civil Engineering and Building*, London: Gilbert Wood & Co.

20 See for example, Bonham's London, 21 November 2012: https://www.bonhams.com/auction/20027/lot/216/a-set-of-three-19th-century-relief-carved-marble-panels-from-the-bodley-reredos-after-the-design-by-george-frederick-bodley-ra-by-farmer-and-brindley-london/ (accessed 5.08.2024).

21 Symondson and Bucknall, *Sir Ninian Comper*, p. 87.

22 Quoted in Symondson and Bucknall, *Sir Ninian Comper*, p. 89.

23 For a discussion of Comper, gender and sexuality, see A. Lepine, 2021,

'Ninian Comper's Alabaster Altarpieces in Britain and America: Queer Desires, Holy Spaces', *Theology and Sexuality* 27, 2–3, pp. 95–113.

24 M. Jean Frisk, 2021, 'Easter and Mary', All About Mary, University of Dayton, https://udayton.edu/imri/mary/e/easter-and-mary.php (accessed 6.08.2024).

25 On Comper, Betjeman and the 'English Altar', see E. Wilson, 'Betjeman's Riddel Posts: An Echo of Ninian Comper', *The Review of English Studies* 42, 168 (November 1991), pp. 541–50.

26 Quoted in Symondson and Bucknall, *Sir Ninian Comper*, p. 88.

27 Hastings quoted in Symondson and Bucknall, *Sir Ninian Comper*, p. 95.

28 Nikky Finney, 'Hotbed 66', https://poets.org/poem/hotbed-66 (accessed 6.08.2024)

29 'The Keiskamma Altarpiece: Transcending AIDS in South Africa', The Fowler Museum at UCLA, https://fowler.ucla.edu/exhibitions/the-keiskamma-altarpiece-transcending-aids-in-south-africa/ (accessed 5.08.2024).

30 Brenda Schmahmann, 'A Framework for Recuperation: HIV/AIDS and the Keiskamma Altarpiece', *African Arts* 43, 3 (Autumn 2010), pp. 34–51. See also: www.keiskamma.org (accessed 5.08.2024).

31 Ruth Mellinkoff, 1988, *The Devil at Isenheim: Reflections of Popular Belief in Grünewald's Altarpiece*, Los Angeles: University of California Press.

32 Kelly Brown Douglas, 2015, *Stand Your Ground: Black Bodies and the Justice of God*, Orbis Books.

33 Despite its powerful presence, it received little coverage in the UK. 'Work of Hope', *Church Times*, 9 October 2008.

34 'Unyimeabasi Udoh talks about their New Artwork for St James's', https://www.sjp.org.uk/unyimeabasi-udoh-talks-about-their-new-artwork-for-st-jamess/ (accessed 5.08.2024).

35 C. Walker Bynum, 'Fast, Feast, and Flesh: The Religious Significance of Food to Medieval Women', *Representations* 11 (Summer 1985), p. 15.

Sermon

'How Are You?'

Preached at Evensong and Benediction at
St Peter de Beauvoir Town on 4 May 2024

Fr Peter Allan

Deuteronomy 24.5–end; 1 Peter 3.13–end

> [B]aptism ... now saves you ... through the resurrection of Jesus Christ, who has gone into heaven and is at the right hand of God, with angels, archangels, and powers made subject to him. (1 Peter 3.21–22 NRSV)

How are you? What might we say: Oh, overworked and underpaid ... Getting along ... Still here! Never time to do everything ... And here *we* are: taking time out to pray, to listen, to rest. Perhaps we are hoping for encouragement and inspiration from the Scriptures, but when we look at our two readings today we find ourselves plunged into the depths of the human condition that we know only too well. We recognize this kind of world where practices, rules and regulations are necessary to moderate the effects of human beings who, like ourselves, are not always able to see aright or to make good judgements. But it is also a disappointing kind of world. Hearing Deuteronomy, we experience the all too familiar, and we feel let down. Is this really the way to talk of resurrection life? 'Guard against an outbreak of a leprous skin disease by being very careful'; 'Parents shall not be put to death for their children ... only for their own crimes may persons be put to death'; 'When you beat your olive trees, do not strip what is left; it shall be for the alien, the orphan, and the widow.' We might hope for a radical change in the New Testament, but our reading from the first letter of Peter is also concerned with managing the realities of life in this world: 'Keep your conscience clear, so that, when you are maligned, those who abuse you for your good conduct in Christ may be put to shame.'

Let's try again: 'How are you?' 'In the city and under the protection!' That was, we are told, the response Charles Williams gave to a friend who saw him walking down the High in Oxford and called out, 'Hello Williams, how are you?' 'In the City and under the protection.' Yes, in Oxford, safeguarded by the laws and customs, police and magistrates, but simultaneously a child of God, a citizen of heaven protected and guided by angels, archangels and the communion of saints. Here is a dazzling insight that is at the heart of our Christian faith and that the catholic tradition cherishes particularly. Simply, Christian life is life in 'many dimensions' (to recall Williams again). Martin Rees, the cosmologist and astrophysicist, discussing the advances in contemporary physics, has said that we now know that it is entirely possible for there to be another dimension less than millimetres away and yet invisible to us. What the evolving language of physics is enabling us to say of the world in which we live is also central to our spiritual experience. Catholic Christians are utterly realistic and practical about life in the world, but equally persuaded of the immediacy of the kingdom, 'seek[ing] the things that are above, where Christ is, seated at the right hand of God' (Col. 3.1 NRSV). This is not like a dual-sim smartphone, for then you always have to choose to use either sim 1 or sim 2. This is simultaneous living in the here and now and in the eternal present, the now of God. This is sharing the experience of the incarnate Word, who was fully immersed in our human experience and told his followers, 'I am not of this world' (John 8.23 NRSV).

It is one thing to say something is the case, quite another to understand how it contributes to our life and purpose. How is awareness of such simultaneity nurtured and developed? By all our Christian practices, certainly, but above all through our liturgical prayer. Remember again those two disciples on the road to Emmaus. Walk with them; see the human condition and feel the effect of raw grief and shock leading to self-absorbed gloom – but see how that depression, that despair is gradually transfigured by the presence of the risen Christ. For those two disciples it was a gradual, seemingly impossible restoration of the companionship with Jesus they had known before, but in a new dimension. For us, this is the meaning of our text from the first letter of Peter: 'baptism ... saves you ... through the resurrection of Jesus Christ.' Our Christian life began with the gift of grace in Baptism and is then nurtured by the gifts of word and sacrament. This is a patterned, disciplined way of living – chosen because of the gifts God pours on us through it – and yet it seems the Church is always in danger of forgetting the foundational nature of Baptism and the fruitfulness of daily submission to the word – not choosing the parts of Scripture that seem to fit our mood but responding with curiosity and wonder to what is offered to us day by day. This is the experience of Christian life and worship.

How are you? We talk endlessly about the pressures of modern living, of the chaotic rhythms that clamour for our attention, but the prayer of the hours (the daily office, morning and evening prayer) brings us back to the rhythm of creation. Being opened to a deeper rhythm is not just good for ourselves but for our relationships with others. Unusually for a monastic community, for historical reasons we have had a long tradition at the monastic Community of the Resurrection, Mirfield, of meeting in Chapter for the whole of July. There have been many times when, after heated, tense discussion, the bell has summoned us to church. More often than not we find that singing the psalms and canticles of the Office and waiting on the Word of God in silence is enough to remind us of that other dimension – that other City and those other protections – and we are much less inclined to snarl at one another as we emerge.

Seven times a day do I praise you, says the psalmist – and the liturgical prayer of the Church has always known the importance of this marking the passing of the days and inviting the rhythm of creation itself to permeate the everyday. But even here human fallibility and sinfulness are not far away. All too easily we excuse ourselves from such a discipline: it's vain repetition, we say, or mere formalism. I remember a monk who, at a meeting in another monastery, poured himself another cup of tea as the bell went for Vespers. 'Aren't you coming?' someone asked. 'No,' he replied, 'I said the Offices for the week before I came away!' Indeed, what is first stifled is our expectation that this will be an encounter with the Risen Lord. All too often we participate in worship with low expectations – and, all too often, even those low expectations are exceeded. In part this is because we begin with the mindset that says this is what I have to do for God. Fundamentally, however, it is about God addressing us, being present to and with us and sending us as labourers into the harvest. Our openness to what God may give is squeezed out by the imposition of our own sense of duty, or the sense that, in the midst of our busy lives, this may be a priority, but not the top priority. Addressing this kind of difficulty is not straightforward. One of the most striking elements of the Emmaus story is the way in which the Risen Lord pierced through the self-absorption of the disciples, but our resistance is all too often greater. They had every reason for despair. They had seen the death of Jesus. We, on the other hand, are believers in the resurrection – and can still be so doubtful of the life and presence of God that we come to church dutifully but leave untouched. Yes, we must acknowledge our own resistance to the transfiguring presence of Christ, but don't for a moment doubt God's continuing power and grace.

Singing is vital in all this. What would be the effect if we changed the words of that great hymn from 'How shall I *sing* that majesty ...' to read 'How shall I *say* that majesty ...'? Immediately it feels flat and diminished. We know too that it is much harder to say words together intelligibly than it is to sing them together. But there's more. When we speak we're pretty much in control. We calculate the effect of our speaking and shape the pitch of the voice, the speed, the articulation accordingly. When we sing we are much more vulnerable. It takes considerable professional training to reach a comparable level of control. To sing together both forms us and liberates us. Having shown us our vulnerability, we turn our attention instead to the words we sing – above all the words of Scripture – and discover that, as we sing, Christ is making us, his Body, a reality that we experience and that gives us joy.

Those two disciples, who on the road made the journey from desolation to joy, reveal to us God's grace offered in the liturgy of word and sacrament. That initial journey along the road is a peripatetic liturgy of the word. They begin sunk in human misery. The risen Lord gently and gradually breaks through with his exposition of the words that told of himself – and their hearts begin to change. This is the promise inherent in every serious, attentive gathering around the word, in the gathering of the Eucharist or in the liturgy of the hours. As we, following the model of the Emmaus road, hear the Scriptures and allow the Lord to be present to us through them, so the Risen Christ stands in our midst. The prayer of the Eucharist happens at the supper table in the house and seems almost anti-climactic. Only the briefest of actions is required. The Lord took bread, blessed and broke it and gave it to them – and as they take him into themselves their eyes are opened. It is clear to us that word and sacrament belong together, they interpret and support each other and both enable the miracle of real presence. This is the distinctive mark of our daily Christian life: a life lived consciously in the presence of the risen Christ. It is also the distinctive characteristic of St Benedict's rule for monks. The picture we receive from Benedict is of a group of Christians sharing life together and singing the word that has been given them. Their desire is for God. God has already promised God's presence – 'I am with you always, to the end of the age' (Matt. 28.20 NRSV) – and living and singing together day by day, Christians discover the reality and immediacy of this presence. True, it is a presence that is not discernible by physical sight, but a presence as real as that which convinced the first disciples in the aftershock of the death and resurrection of Jesus.

How are you?
Just great, thank you!

In the city and under the protection, because, as our text has it: 'baptism ... now saves us ... through the resurrection of Jesus Christ, who has gone into heaven and is at the right hand of God, with angels, archangels, and powers made subject to him.' Amen.

5

Discernment

FR BEN KERRIDGE

In the weeks before lockdown began, I contracted Covid and had to isolate. Lacking energy, there was very little I could do. I might have read, I suppose, or listened to grand pieces of music, but in our day and age the only real option in such circumstances is to mindlessly binge-watch a box set. There were two that particularly captured my attention: the first *True Blood* – the soapy, gothic and camp adventures of Sookie Stackhouse among the supernatural inhabitants of the deep south town of Bon Temps in Louisiana; the second, *The Walking Dead* – the story of a small group of survivors after a zombie apocalypse in search of safety and community. I don't suppose either would be recommended as the Archbishop of Canterbury's Lent series – for that indeed was the season – but I noticed that although *True Blood* was compelling (addictive, even), there was something dissatisfying about it, the kind of feeling you get when you have eaten too many Pringles or gobbled a whole packet of Haribo. By contrast, there was something about *The Walking Dead* that made me utterly believe in its premise, as if I were really watching a small group of people struggling to respond to the complete collapse of the world around them – perhaps because in those early days of the pandemic it rather felt as if it was collapsing. The experience of watching *The Walking Dead*, and the sympathy it evoked for these unlikely people, enlarged my soul a little. Albeit a complete fantasy, there was a truth to the story and performances that put me in touch with something about what it is to be human.

Now I am not saying that one series was intrinsically good and the other bad, nor am I suggesting that the effect they had on me would be replicated in anybody else (no doubt for some the watching of *True Blood* is an exercise in deep grace), but what I *am* suggesting is that for me, watching one brought me into a state of what St Ignatius of Loyola might call consolation – an increase in faith, hope and love.[1] Meanwhile, the other, for all the compulsive enjoyment it gave me in the short term – brought me into a state of what Ignatius would call desolation, a sense of turning away from life and ultimately from God.[2] And for Ignatius, it is noticing these movements of consolation and desolation that forms the basis of discernment.

The most common use of discernment in the modern Church of England is as a description of the process that leads to ordination, but it is my contention that discernment is as much a question of which television series we watch. For Ignatius, God is in all things, and therefore all things merit discernment. Of course, discernment *is* about the big questions of choice of life – marriage, ordination, taking the vows of religious life, and about the great questions around the future direction of a church or community – but it is about these questions because even big decisions are only important insomuch as they affect the day-to-day, minute-by-minute relationship we have with God and one another. If you are called to be a priest, it is because that calling will bring you closer to God – and even other people, on a good day – and if it doesn't, there is no real point in it. In fact, Ignatius teaches an indifference to a desire for one way of life over another: 'our one desire and choice should be what is more conducive to a closer relationship with God.'[3] Indifference may seem like a cold word, but for Ignatius it comes from a deeply felt sense that being in relationship with God is the most important thing that a human being could possibly strive for, that it is indeed our purpose, and that all other things follow on from this primal, passionate, love.

He himself came to this recognition of consolation and desolation on his sickbed. After being hit by a cannonball in both a brave and foolhardy defence of Pamplona from the dastardly French, his leg had to be rebroken to be reset and heal straight, not just once but twice. The second time included sawing off a protruding stump of bone, which Ignatius, in his vanity, could not countenance.[4] Nice legs were important to the young Ignatius. He spent months convalescing in the family tower house at Loyola. Goodness knows how the history of spirituality might have changed if he'd had access to Netflix, or indeed a library, but the only two books available were *The Life of Jesus Christ* by Ludolf of Saxony and *The Golden Legend: Lives of the Saints* by Jacobus de Voragine. His choice was between these books and a well-practised tendency to retreat into imaginative courtly and knightly romances, influenced by his favourite novel, *Amadis de Gaula*. In his autobiography he makes mysterious reference to a certain lady, and he spent hours fantasising over the deeds he would perform in her service.[5] We do not know who she was, but the level of discretion leads many commentators to assume she was at least royalty – the Kate Middleton or Meghan Markle of her day.[6]

Over time he noticed that his reading about the lives of Christ and the saints brought him a sense of inner peace, while his romantic fantasies brought him to a sense of dryness and dissatisfaction. Little by little he turned more towards one than to the other and so was converted. After a vision of the Blessed Virgin Mary, he set out from his sickbed not to continue his service to the powerful but to be a pilgrim and find God.

When we talk about consolation and desolation it is important to remember that we are talking about spiritual states, about how we might feel closer or further away from God. Consoling experiences are not necessarily positive in a worldly sense – grief might lead us towards God, loneliness might increase our sense of faith, hope and love, failure might inflame our hearts towards the love of God. Desolation might occur when doing something we enjoy but also might occur because of something we think of as pious or holy. Practising a devotion, being a churchwarden or a rural dean, volunteering for a charity, all might lead us into a state of desolation. It is also worth saying that someone in a state of desolation is not, by any means, further away from God, or less good, than a person in a state of consolation; everybody will move through consolation and desolation in their journey towards God, and desolation has as much to teach us as consolation. In fact, Ignatius counsels spiritual directors to be particularly attentive to directees who don't seem to experience the movements between consolation and desolation.[7] But what is key to discernment is the noticing, the daily act of bringing your life before God and seeing where different choices, events and tasks lead in terms of your relationship with God. At the heart of this is what is known as the *examen*.

The *examen*

The *examen* can be unfairly characterized as saying thank you and saying sorry at the end of each day.[8] Now there is nothing wrong in doing this, and if it brings you closer to God then, of course, go ahead and do it, but the difference between this and the *examen* is that by fitting a series of events into two categories, we are already interpreting them before we have even begun to hold them before God. We risk telling God what to think about them, rather than letting God tell us, or noticing together. The point of the *examen* is to get to the raw data of the day before we begin to interpret that data, to allow God to show us the day, rather than showing God our prepackaged lists of gratitude and regret. Perhaps there is grace in those things we regret or, like the Pharisee praying in the Temple, complacency in those things we are grateful for. On the evening of Easter Sunday, in my exhaustion, I was telling God that the effort and time I had put into the *Triduum* was all an exercise in vanity. God was able to show me something quite different – that through this celebration of the *Triduum*, my vanity notwithstanding, I had experienced moments of real closeness to God. We must allow the *examen* to surprise us.

For Ignatius, the *examen* was the key commitment for each Jesuit: the daily praying-through of the day would keep a Jesuit on track in their relationship with God and able to discern what else God was calling them to do. And as Herbert Alphonso reminds us, it is not an examination of morality but of discernment.[9] And it is through the *examen* that we can discover where consolation truly is, the things we do that bring us life, and slowly move towards them. And what is true for individuals is also true for churches and organizations – what are the things we do that bring us closer to God?

For Ignatius, discernment is not simply about noticing the states of consolation and desolation but also about listening for the impulses and voices that lead to one or the other. He characterizes the voice that leads us closer to God as the good spirit and the one that leads us further away as the evil spirit.[10] We might want to think of the good spirit as the action of the Holy Spirit within us and the evil spirit as the temptations of the devil – the effect upon us of the external supernatural forces of good and evil – or we might want to think of the good spirit as that part of us which desires God and the evil spirit that part of us which resists God (and some prefer to talk about the true and the false voice). I'm not sure that the ontological status we give the spirits is of any great relevance. What is most important is to notice how they act upon us, so that we can recognize which voice we are listening to in any given impulse.

And recognizing the voices is key to discernment, recognizing that in any situation there will be an impulse that leads us towards God and an impulse that leads us away from God. This is true for every person, from the holiest to the most sinful. And the most helpful way of recognizing the good and the evil spirit is not so much by the content of what they are saying – the evil spirit is pretty good at appearing rational, sane, a pious Anglo-Catholic and objectively true – but by the tone in which they say it.

Ignatius makes a distinction between people on a trajectory moving them away from God and people moving towards God. This is not an eternal distinction – I think we can all recognize times in our life when one is more true than the other. For people moving away from God, the voice of the evil spirit can be heard physically in the satisfaction of urges and desires – 'Watch that second episode', 'Have another drink' – whereas the voice of the good spirit is heard in the voice of reason, what Ignatius calls the sting of conscience. But for people moving towards God, the location of the voices reverse: we experience the voice of the evil spirit in our head through fear, anxiety and fallacious reasoning – that way in which we talk ourselves out of doing something that at our deepest level we know we want to.[11] It is worth lingering for a moment on those words – fear and anxiety we probably recognize as the reason we don't do a whole host of things that we wish we had. Fallacious reasoning is the way we justify this to ourselves and perhaps to others. If we've fallen out with somebody, often the real reason we don't call them to make up is fear of rejection or anxiety about what will happen if we do – but we make up all sorts of reasons in our head about why we shouldn't make contact: 'I don't want to disturb him', 'I know he's very busy on a Monday', 'Given what he said, he should really call me', 'The ball is definitely in his court', 'It's not fair', 'Calling him will only encourage him.' If you recognize any of this, then that is fallacious reasoning, and that is the voice of the evil spirit.

The good spirit is felt more in the emotions and the body, through courage, strength, tears, inspiration and most of all a deep sense of peace.[12] That is why a spiritual director will often ask you to talk about how something feels physically, because it is often in our bodies that the voice of the good spirit can be heard. Ignatius gives a wonderful simile of the voice of the good spirit landing like water on a sponge – with quiet absorption – whereas the evil spirit lands like water on a stone, with a disturbing smack.[13] As noted above, the key to distinguishing between the voices is not the content of what they are saying – the evil spirit loves to encourage us to feel self-righteous through pious deeds and judging others – but the tone in which it is said. 'I don't want to disturb her' could come from a place of compassion, from a place of fear or indeed a place of contempt. And that tone is something that will be different for each person and can only be recognized with practice. Ultimately, in the midst of the confusion of these voices, we will recognize the spirits by their fruits: Is this leading me closer to God or further away?

As with consolation and desolation, all of us will experience the voices of the good and the evil spirit, and they will be active in both conditions. The primary way of learning to recognize the different voices is again through the *examen*, paying close attention to the motivations and impulses that led us towards certain actions and states. And Ignatius gives us three pieces of advice for dealing with the voice of the evil spirit. First, the evil spirit is like a bully; a show of strength will scare it away, whereas if you give into it, it will come to dominate you.[14] Second, the bad spirit is like a false lover who wants to keep everything secret; a key way to counteract it is by talking to somebody else about the ways it works upon you.[15] Finally, it is like an enemy general who will survey a castle for its weakest point and attack there; if we ourselves are aware of our weak points, we can more easily defend ourselves.[16]

Spiritual direction

This brings us to another key place for discernment in the Ignatian tradition, which is spiritual direction, the act of talking these things through with somebody else, somebody who is attuned to the movements of the spirits and consolation and desolation. In some ways spiritual direction is a misleading term, as a spiritual director is far more concerned with listening – and encouraging the directee to listen – to the movements of the spirit, than with directing or advising the directee. Many people use the term accompaniment. Ignatius is clear that it is for the directee to discover for themselves how God is calling them, and that this will produce far greater spiritual relish than being told something by the director.[17] It is the job of the director to get out of the way and allow the creator to deal directly with the creature.[18]

From his own experiences of conversion and discerning where God was leading him, and from his experiences of accompanying others upon that journey, Ignatius devised the Spiritual Exercises, a 30-day retreat leading to an election, or choice of a way of life. Normally this was done in one block, away from home, but it can also be done in daily life – the so-called 19th Annotation – where one day of the 30 days roughly corresponds to one week at home, although it almost always takes longer than that. Having done the exercises both in daily life and on a 30-day retreat, I would say each is utterly transformative, and the discernment is between, on the one hand, the opportunity to live in an environment where the only thing you have to do each day is pray, and the possibility, on the other hand, of integrating this prayer and discernment into your daily life. The dynamic of Ignatius' Spiritual Exercises is to some extent directive, but that is essentially because Ignatius recognizes that certain graces need to be received before discernment can occur. In this next section I will look at how the Spiritual Exercises lead to a place where discernment becomes possible, through praying for these graces.

The first grace is a recognition of our primary purpose to be in relationship with God, and therefore a stance of indifference towards the external factors of how that relationship plays out.[19] When we marry, we promise to love in sickness and in health, in riches or in poverty, for better or for worse, until death us do part. We make a vow to be faithful to a relationship without knowing what will happen next. The same is true for our relationship with God – if we are too attached to wealth, for example, we are blinded by our fear of poverty and unable to make a proper discernment. Now true indifference is difficult, and I'm not sure anybody achieves it in this life, but we can always become more indifferent. Conversely, we need to be careful of assuming that what God wants for us is a miserable, short life led in sickness and deep poverty. The freedom of indifference is a freedom to live whatever life God calls us to. Ignatius felt called to be a pilgrim to Jerusalem and this is what set him out on his journey. But although he eventually arrived there, he was soon kicked out by the pesky Franciscans, and while going to Jerusalem was the impetus to leave his sickbed, his vocation was actually something entirely different. He had to learn to be indifferent to Jerusalem. Any true discernment requires the grace of indifference and an awareness of our primary purpose to praise, reverence and serve God.

Any contemplation of our purpose in life as human beings naturally leads on to an awareness of how we fall short of that dynamic, both in terms of how the world works as a whole and in our own individual lives. When Ignatius set out from Loyola he went to spend some time as an ascetic in Manresa. Despite having confessed his sins already he kept wanting to confess them again. He let his hair and nails grow. He began to think there was no hope for him and contemplated suicide. In an act of extreme penance he fasted for a week. His confessor told him to stop, and after a good meal he came to realize that despite his very real sinfulness, God loved him, that he was a loved sinner. This was crucial for Ignatius – he cut his hair and his fingernails, had a wash, and after a beautiful vision on the banks of the river Cardoner, he eventually set on his way, no longer trapped in the need to achieve his own salvation, an interesting parallel with Martin Luther, his contemporary. This second grace is crucial for discernment, for if we do not recognize our own sinfulness and need of grace, or more importantly, if we do not realize that God loves us even though we are sinners, then we are deaf to his call. We can be so caught up in our own sense of worth, or unworthiness, that we cannot hear the gentle voice of love.

The third key grace that is necessary for discernment is to begin to understand and get to know the person who calls us – Jesus Christ. The election, the choice of a way of life, takes place in the context of contemplating the life of Christ, because the more we know Jesus the more we can recognize his voice. Ignatius asks retreatants on the second week of the 30-day retreat to ask for 'an intimate knowledge of the Lord, who became man for me, that I may love him more and follow him more closely'.[20] And my experience of the Ignatian practice of imaginative contemplation, of walking into a gospel scene in your mind to see what happens, is that Jesus is there waiting to meet us. And that felt sense of the individuality of the Jesus I met will stay with me for the rest of my life.

Now our topic is discernment, which can mean the everyday task of orientating your life towards God, and also the big moments of discernment, when we pray in order to discern a particular life choice or big decisions that need to be made. Day-to-day discernment and big decisions are intimately connected – we cannot discern if we are not aware of the movements of consolation and desolation as they manifest in our daily life, and the act of this daily listening and noticing will lead to radical and unexpected choices.

Before launching into what Ignatius has to say about life choices, I will explore what are known as the limits of Ignatian discernment, encapsulated in the helpful mnemonic 'for me, for now, for good', which is to say I can only discern for myself, not for anybody else; I can only discern the next step, not the whole question; and I can only discern between two good things, for there is no discernment between good and evil.

Choices

One of Ignatius' friends and followers, Francis Borgia, was asked to consider becoming a cardinal. He wrote to Ignatius for his advice on what to do and Ignatius wrote back an extraordinary letter outlining his own discernment process in how to respond.[21] Ignatius noticed in himself an impulse to oppose Borgia's nomination in any way he could. But instead of simply giving in to this impulse or rejecting it as irrational, he decided to seek the will of God and asked all the priests in the community to say Mass for three days with the intention that Ignatius might be guided for God's greater glory. Ignatius, over these three days, experienced a certain fear or lack of freedom, asking himself: 'How do I know what God our Lord wants to do?' At other times he felt these fears recede, until on the third day he came to a sense of peace about opposing the election. However, for Ignatius this was not the end of the matter, and he imparts a key truth about his discernment: that he was discerning for himself, not for the Pope or for Francis Borgia or for the Emperor. In the letter to Francis he says:

> There would be no contradiction in its being God's will for me to take this course, while others take a different one and the dignity be conferred upon you. The same divine Spirit could move me to this course for one set of reasons and move others to the opposite for different ones.[22]

To give another example of this key point about discernment, I'll tell a story told by Alfred Agius, a former teacher on the Ignatian Spirituality Course.[23] There was an election for a superior of a religious community. One of the candidates was a clever, charismatic and socially skilled young man, who very clearly had all the necessary qualities. The other candidate was an older member of the community who found it very difficult to look anybody in the eye. One of the members of the community decided to pray about who to vote for, and in his discernment felt the impulse of the Holy Spirit to vote for the older man. 'Really, God?' he asked. As he prayed, this feeling of consolation from voting for the older guy remained, so he did. The votes came in. There was one vote for the older guy, and the rest of the votes went to the younger guy. But the election changed things: because the older guy knew that one of his brethren believed in him, he began to be more engaged in community life and feel more of a part of things; because the younger guy knew that one person hadn't voted for him, he realized he had to be humbler and more inclusive and collaborative to get things done. This story is a wonderful illustration of the fact that God can call people to make opposite discernments, and also that what we discern is only what is in our sphere of discernment – the community member discerned how to vote, not who should be superior of the community. The truth is we cannot see from God's perspective, we never know the whole story, we can only discern for ourselves as best we can, and trust that God knows what God is doing.

This leads on to the next limit, which is that we can only discern the next step. Ignatius is only discerning what he should do in response to a letter from his friend, not the whole story of whether his friend should be made cardinal. This is extremely helpful in any discernment. If we try to discern the whole thing – 'Should I change jobs?' for example – we can get lost in the enormity of the decision. If we discern the next step – 'Should I investigate this other possible job?' – the discernment can become much clearer.

And the final limit is that we can only discern between two good things. There is a useful sifting process here that can really help a discernment. Are the two options before me good? If they are not, then there is no discernment to be made. For Ignatius, in terms of a life choice, this relates specifically to the vows we have made. A married person cannot discern a vowed celibate religious life, for example, or vice versa.[24] There is perhaps more that we might want to say about the issue, but however we frame it, the limit that we can only discern between two goods is ultimately a helpful one.

Having surveyed the limits of discernment, Ignatius talks about three times for making a choice, which I will briefly sketch. The first time is when God makes something obvious – like Paul on the road to Damascus or St Matthew being called by Jesus in the tax booth, there is only one thing to be done.[25] We tend to think of all vocation as being like this but the liberating thing is that for Ignatius, this is just one of the ways God calls us.

The second time for choice is when there are great movements of consolation and desolation and the voices of the good and the evil spirit are very much at work.[26] Discernment here is all about noticing these movements, recognizing these voices and over time coming to a sense about where the deeper consolation lies. One piece of advice he gives for this kind of discernment is to live for a week as if one decision were made, and notice the consolation and desolation, and then live for a week as if the other decision were made, always noticing what's going on inside, as indeed he did over the cardinal's hat.[27] Noticing in which potential decision the greater consolation lay would help the person to realize where God was calling them.

The third time of discernment happens in what Ignatius describes as a state of tranquillity, and here he encourages the person to either make a list of the pros and cons of either choice or to intuitively imagine which choice they would have preferred to make on their deathbed or on judgement day.[28]

My experience of the three times is that there is often flow between them. In what might seem at first like a decision made in tranquillity, deeper movements between consolation and desolation may be uncovered, and following the consolations and desolations of the second time may lead to the spiritual freedom of the tranquillity of the third time, or even, when the deepest consolation is recognized, to the clarity of the first time.

The trouble is, of course, that even when we have discerned something, we have the capacity to get it wrong, and this is especially true because that is what the evil spirit wants – to lead us away from the consolation of following our vocation or listening to the Holy Spirit. Quoting St Paul, Ignatius reminds us that the devil can appear as an angel of light.[29] He gives us some advice about how to notice when the bad spirit may be at work in our discernment.

The first piece of advice is inherently practical: to notice the beginning, middle and end of a course of action.[30] You may, in prayer or on retreat, have resolved to go to Mass each day. A pious thought about which nothing bad can be said. But perhaps, when you arrive at your parish church, you realize that not everybody in the church has made the same commitment as you, and you start to feel a little angry with them for not being there. You also begin to notice that if you stop off for Mass on your way home from work you spend a bit less time with your daughter after school, which begins to affect your relationship with her, and your husband is taking more of the strain of childcare. You begin to grow more and more resentful of the people who don't go to daily Mass and take upon yourself the responsibility of going, because if you don't go the whole thing will finish. But the vicar goes on too long and you start to get angry with her, and it all ends with you stopping going to church at all, even on a Sunday, because nobody will support it. This is deliberately exaggerated, but you get the general idea. If something is leading you into desolation, it may be time to re-evaluate.

Second, Ignatius notices that while there are certain experiences of consolation that are so profound and beautiful that they can only come from God, the evil spirit can often be at work in the afterglow.[31] Let's say I have a beautiful experience of God. After it has finished, I think: I know what I'll do, I'll become a priest. While the experience of God was genuine, the evil spirit can be at work in our mind in the aftermath of the experience. So it's important to notice whether a resolution came as part of the experience itself or whether it came afterwards. Inherent in all of this is that while we may have an experience of something that might feel like peace or joy to begin with, following the voice of the evil spirit will lead to a state of desolation, and that is how we notice what the voice sounds like.

There is more to say about Ignatian discernment. Listening for where God might be leading us in the comings and goings of life is the work of a lifetime, and mastering the theory is not the same as living it day in day out. To do so depends upon the daily contemplation of Christ and the daily listening for God's call. But I wonder whether I might finish by offering a few brief reflections on what Ignatian discernment might have to offer catholic life in the Church of England.

Discernment in catholic Anglicanism

Within what we might broadly call the catholic movement, there are very different ideas and beliefs about the issues of the day. At the heart of these divisions lies a very Ignatian question about who has the authority to discern these questions – the Church of England, the Church catholic, the bishops, General Synod? Within these wider discernments we all have our own smaller discernments to make: How do we vote? Who do we accept communion from? What societies should I join? Should I stay or should I go? The Ignatian principle that we can only discern for ourselves alone, and accept that the Holy Spirit may lead two people to make different discernments on the same question, feels an important principle to hold on to – that in making our own discernments as best we can we are not judging other people's discernments but holding our own discernments within the wider context of the action of God, which is mysterious.

Second, the day-to-day quality of discernment requires a daily interaction with God, and this is a great gift of catholic life in the Church of England: the daily Mass and the offices. Of course, whether a parish has the energy or the resources to offer daily Mass is in itself a matter for discernment, but there is a tendency in the modern Church to judge an act of worship by how many people attend it, rather than by the intrinsic value of being with God and the effect that might have on the life of the Church, even if the Mass were to be said alone. When Ignatius had big decisions to make he would ask for Mass to be offered to shed light on that decision. I think we can learn from him.

Third, we have something to learn from the fact that discernment cannot be second-guessed, it is surprising. If there seems to be a depressing inevitability about cuts in clergy numbers, declining attendance and finances, this is, it seems to me, because we have not adequately discerned the questions. We need to learn how to discern things together as a Church, but that discernment begins with the kind of day-to-day noticing that Ignatius inspired, to discover where the true life, joy and peace are – and they may well be located as much in a tiny congregation worshipping God, loving one another and serving its community, as anywhere else.

Finally, and perhaps most importantly, discernment is far more about discovering who we truly are than it is about what we do. Once we discover our true identity in God, that becomes the criterion for discernment in everyday life and also in the bigger discernments, which become not so much about a binary choice as about the best way of living out your God-given identity, which is as much about how you spend an evening as it is about any of the so-called bigger questions. For Ignatius, God is in all things and all things are to be given back.

Take Lord and receive all my liberty, my memory, my understanding, and my entire will, all that I have and possess. You have given it all to me. To you O Lord I return it. All is yours, dispose of it wholly according to your will. Only give me your love and your grace, that is enough for me.[32]

Notes

1 For a description of consolation, see Ignatius of Loyola, *Spiritual Exercises* (316); Louis J. Puhl, 1951, *The Spiritual Exercises of St. Ignatius: A New Translation Based on Studies in the Language of the Autograph*, Chicago, IL: Loyola Press, p. 142. Further citations of the text of *Spiritual Exercises* are referred to in brackets below and page numbers given for particular editions.

2 For a description of desolation see (317), Puhl, *Spiritual Exercises*, p. 142.

3 See the First Principle and Foundation (23), Puhl, *Spiritual Exercises*, p. 12.

4 Joseph A. Munitiz and Philip Endean (trans.), 2004, *St Ignatius of Loyola: Personal Writings*, London: Penguin, p. 14.

5 Munitiz and Endean, *Personal Writings*, p. 15.

6 See Philip Caraman, 1990, *Ignatius of Loyola*, London: Collins, p. 29.

7 (5) Puhl, *Spiritual Exercises*, p. 3.

8 George Aschenbrenner, in his classic article on the examen, makes the distinction between an examination of conscience and an examination of consciousness, the former an exercise in narrow morality, the latter an exercise in discernment. George Aschenbrenner, 'Consciousness Examen', *Review for Religious* 31, 1 (January 1972), pp. 14–21; see also Herbert Alphonso, 2001, *Discovering Your Personal Vocation: The Search for Meaning through the Spiritual Exercises*, Mahwah, NJ: Paulist Press, pp. 56–65.

9 Alphonso, *Discovering*, p. 57.

10 For Ignatius on the good and evil spirit, see (314–315) Puhl, *Spiritual Exercises*, pp. 141–2.

11 (315) Puhl, *Spiritual Exercises*, p. 141.

12 (315) Puhl, *Spiritual Exercises*, p. 141.

13 (335) Puhl, *Spiritual Exercises*, p. 149.

14 (325) Puhl, *Spiritual Exercises*, p. 145.

15 (326) Puhl, *Spiritual Exercises*, p. 145.
16 (327) Puhl, *Spiritual Exercises*, p. 146.
17 (2) Puhl, *Spiritual Exercises*, p. 2.
18 (15) Puhl, *Spiritual Exercises*, p. 6.
19 (23) Puhl, *Spiritual Exercises*, p. 12.
20 (104) Puhl, *Spiritual Exercises*, p. 49.
21 Martin E. Palmer (trans.), John W. Padberg and John L. McCarthy (eds), 2006, *Ignatius of Loyola: Letters and Instructions*, St Louis, MO: The Institute of Jesuit Sources, pp. 376–7.
22 Palmer, Padberg and McCarthy, *Letters*, p. 377.
23 This story was told to me by Fr Andrew Walker, director of the Ignatian Spirituality Course. It may have changed slightly through retellings.
24 (172) Puhl, *Spiritual Exercises*, p. 72.
25 (175) Puhl, *Spiritual Exercises*, p. 74.
26 (176) Puhl, *Spiritual Exercises*, p. 74.
27 Michael Ivens, 1998, *Understanding the Spiritual Exercises*, Leominster: Gracewing and New Malden: Inigo Enterprises, p. 137.
28 (177–180) Puhl, *Spiritual Exercises*, pp. 74–5.
29 (332) Puhl, *Spiritual Exercises*, p. 148.
30 (333) Puhl, *Spiritual Exercises*, p. 148.
31 (336) Puhl, *Spiritual Exercises*, p. 149.
32 (234) Puhl, *Spiritual Exercises*, p. 102.

Bibliography

Alphonso, Herbert, S.J., 2001, *Discovering Your Personal Vocation: The Search for Meaning through the Spiritual Exercises*, Mahwah, NJ: Paulist Press.
Aschenbrenner, George, 'Consciousness examen', *Review for Religious* 31, 1 (January 1972), pp. 14–21.
Caraman, Philip, 1990, *Ignatius of Loyola*, London: Collins.
Ivens, Michael S.J., 1998, *Understanding the Spiritual Exercises*, Leominster: Gracewing and New Malden: Inigo Enterprises.
Munitiz, Joseph A. and Endean, Philip (trans.), 2004, *St Ignatius of Loyola: Personal Writings*, London: Penguin.
Puhl, Louis J., S.J., 1951, *The Spiritual Exercises of St. Ignatius: A New Translation Based on Studies in the Language of the Autograph*, Chicago, IL: Loyola Press.
Palmer, Martin E. (trans.), S.J., Padberg, John W., S.J., McCarthy, John L., S.J. (eds), 2006, *Ignatius of Loyola: Letters and Instructions*, St Louis, MO: The Institute of Jesuit Sources.

6

Scripture

FR STEFFAN MATHIAS

'The Bible ... what's that? The thing that quotes from the Missal?' So went the well-worn joke when from time to time at theological college someone would mention the Bible. Humour value aside, like all jokes it reveals some deeper realities and unease, which will be explored in this chapter: both about the vitality of the place of Scripture in the catholic life of the Church of England (that the missal or prayer book is predominantly passages of Scripture), and also the hesitations and lack of *ownership* many in the catholic tradition feel about the Bible (perhaps even feeling safer accessing it through the lectionary). On the one hand there is a widespread sense – misguided, I will argue – that the Bible has been claimed by other parts of the Church, that while we excel at the liturgical, the aesthetic and the poetically theological, we lack confidence in Scripture. And on the other, that it is so deeply embedded in our catholic life that we cannot begin to pray without it.

The place of Scripture goes to the heart of our identity. To explore the place of Scripture in the catholic life of the Church of England, we cannot bypass what it means to be Anglican. In fact the place the use of Scripture has in our liturgical and devotional life is at once distinctly *Anglican*, shot throughout our tradition from the Book of Common Prayer to *Common Worship*, and yet is one of the very things that is so demonstrably *catholic* in our tradition, connecting us to the practices of the universal Church (such as the daily recitation of the Magnificat at evensong, which both connects our practice to the wider Church while, in ways we often miss, placing the person of Mary at the forefront of our practices). And yet while contemporary usage of Scripture such as the lectionary readings is so similar in both the Church of England and Roman Catholic Church, the place of Scripture – both theologically and liturgically – is one of the defining ruptures of the Reformation period. The reformation insistence on Scripture in the vernacular – spoken and understood by all – is one of the fruits of the reformation that even the most Anglo-Papalist would be unlikely to want to undo. And, curiously, it now unites us with our Roman Catholic brothers and sisters, whose official teaching today both encourages Scripture to be read and interpreted in a language that is understood, and sees the common translations and reading of Scripture as one of the sources of deepening ecumenical bonds.[1]

Accessibility of Scripture, increased literacy, scholarly study of Scripture are all things that we might imagine have increased a sense of confidence in the place of Scripture in our life, both as Anglicans and as Catholic Anglicans. However, as we shall see, the working out of the enlightenment and reformation attitudes towards Scripture have – if anything – caused a crisis, which impacts the place of Scripture in the catholic tradition of the Church of England today.

A lack of confidence

There is, I will argue, a general lack of confidence in relation to the biblical text felt by both preachers and congregations. Our catholic tradition of preaching tends to focus on the Gospel passages – they are, after all, the life and teaching of Christ; however, they are generally accompanied by passages from the Old and New Testament, particularly from the book of Isaiah, and the letters of St Paul. What makes our preaching practice distinct from our evangelical siblings is that we rarely approach these texts in a systematic or expository style. While there are stylistic and liturgical reasons for this, I would argue that it significantly stems from a lack of confidence deriving from two separate causes: a decline in biblical literacy and the rise of modern biblical studies.

Biblical literacy refers to the general awareness and knowledge of biblical texts both in the Church and in wider society. This has been sharply declining over the last decades: the Bible Society's 2014 report into biblical literacy showed a disconnect between a recognition of the importance of biblical texts (43% of parents felt it is important for their children to read or see Bible stories) and the reality of biblical literacy.[2] For example, for primary school children there were significant gaps in the knowledge of Old Testament texts. Well-known passages are often not known to be from the Bible. The story of Jonah and the whale was only recognized by 41%. Many other texts are simply not known widely at all. Daniel and the lion's den was known by 28%, the story of Solomon by 15%, the Tower of Babel by 11% and the story of Job by 7%.[3] But even when we take a key text such as the nativity, 25% of

8–15-year-olds say they have never read, seen or heard it, rising to 35% when just 15-year-olds are surveyed. As people get older, their biblical literacy appears to decrease. The research among adults suggests significant confusion over whether texts such as David and Goliath are from the Bible (27% of adults failing to recognize that this is so), while at the same time plot-lines from Harry Potter were understood by 34% of respondents as being from the Bible.[4] Interestingly, the report found some elements of biblical literacy were much higher in Wales, suggesting differences in church tradition and culture may shape knowledge of the Bible even within the United Kingdom.[5]

Despite all this, biblical texts seem to continue to inform popular culture, which is in a constant state of 'retelling, reinterpreting and re-appropriating biblical stories, characters and figures', with biblical texts and images remaining ubiquitous, suggesting biblical literacy is a 'contested concept'.[6] That plot-lines from Harry Potter are mistaken for narratives from Scripture is perhaps testament to the pervasive nature of biblical themes and ideas. Those tasked with preaching and teaching may be saturated in biblical images and concepts, while also coming to the point of training with less confidence in the texts, particularly detail and chronology, than would have been the case in past generations.

Biblical scepticism

If there is a general decline in biblical literacy, surely academic biblical studies would provide the remedy? And yet it often ends up compounding the problem, as we can see in theological education. Most candidates will have something like the following biblical studies modules, with each module amounting to perhaps 20 hours of teaching: an introduction to the Old Testament, an introduction to the New Testament, perhaps a short course on biblical Greek, and a further 'advanced texts' class. Teaching generally follows a university model, which focuses on the critical skills needed to approach the text and cannot (and was never designed to) offer in-depth knowledge of the whole of the content of Scripture – knowledge that can only come (frustratingly for those who would like a shortcut) through reading the text. These modules generally focus on the historical–critical approach, the bread and butter of modern biblical studies.

As a classic example of this approach, we can think of the 'Documentary Hypothesis': that the five books of Genesis to Deuteronomy, rather than being written (as was the majority classical view) by Moses, are in fact a carefully woven patchwork of four (or three, or five, depending on the scholar) previous sources, edited over time.[7] Sometimes these approaches, which can feel radical (and disorientating) when encountered for the first time, are simply trying to dig beneath the centuries of Christian interpretation, exploring what is (and isn't) in the text. Take, for example, an academic consensus that the texts of the 'Suffering Servant' in Isaiah, so familiar to us particularly in Holy Week, rather than directly prophesying the coming of Christ (as we often understand), were not written particularly as a messianic prophecy, and were not understood as relating to the passion and crucifixion, even by early Christian interpreters.[8]

Biblical studies, as a discipline, can often make those taking it feel that they are unsure of their own learnt modes of interpretation. In addition, students will learn a range of other approaches to the text: literary, psycho-analytical, feminist, postcolonial, queer and perspectives from social sciences.[9] The radical nature of this change in the status of the text cannot be overstated, as Yvonne Sherwood and David Moore note:

> At issue is the radical disjunction and discontinuity between certain unprecedented eighteenth-century responses to the Bible on the one hand, and all the modes of Christian biblical interpretation that preceded them on the other hand. It is not too hard to imagine that Origen and Augustine, Abelard and Aquinas, Luther and Calvin, for all their significant differences, could nevertheless have conducted a fairly profitable seminar on the biblical text and its proper interpretation.[10]

They also explain how these approaches are foregrounded in the changing nature of the Bible in society:

> Responding to a loss of theological authority, the Bible was rehabilitated on human and cultural grounds in the eighteenth century. The Bible was re-universalized, so to speak, and its relevance newly perpetuated in such unlikely domains as philology, ancient history, archaeology, ancient Near Eastern languages, and the quest for the ever-elusive authorial hand.[11]

And yet it is the discipline, biblical studies itself, that undermines what confidence there is, not because critical approaches themselves undermine the text – I am confident that it is possible to teach using the approaches of secular biblical studies in a way that gives the text life

– but because of the nature of the discipline itself. Moore and Sherwood argue that biblical scholarship 'internalized Enlightenment modes of relating to the Bible – modes anxiously marked by and distinct from the devotional and the confessional, the pietistic and the homiletical, through a fetishistic display of methodological expertise as the primary badge of professional identity'.[12] The mode of theological education does not teach that anyone can approach the text of their faith, but that without a bewildering array of expertise and skills, one cannot even begin. Attempts have been made within the academy to 'restore the Bible as a theological text, such as canonical criticism, which seeks to read the Bible in its final form; however, the name canonical criticism reveals its own limitations', defined in opposition to a historical–critical approach 'simply known as "biblical studies"'.[13]

Lost confidence

If it is sometimes felt that as catholics the Bible isn't our forte, it's important to note that this wasn't always so: the Tractarians and those involved in the earliest days of the Oxford Movement were noted for their deep commitment to Scripture. Timothy Larsen suggests two reasons why this has been neglected in our understanding of the movement: first, we have tended to note what distinguished the Tractarians from the surrounding Protestantism (with objection to catholic practice with reference to the Bible); and second, the later generations quickly adopted more liberal modes of biblical interpretation.[14]

The early figures of the Oxford Movement made clear the primary place of Scripture. Pusey, in his tract on *Scriptural Views of Holy Baptism*, noted that 'in examining whether any doctrine be a portion of revealed truth, the one subject of inquiry must be, whether it be contained in Holy Scripture.'[15] John Henry Newman's Tract 21, *Mortification of the Flesh a Scripture Duty*, is an attempt to demonstrate how 'the Bible was on the side of this method of spiritual formation'.[16] Indeed, Larsen demonstrates that primacy of Scripture was the distinguishing Anglo-Catholic view in comparison to Roman Catholicism, 'on the grounds that the former derived all doctrine from Scripture while the latter believed that tradition alone can sometimes suffice'.[17] This commitment to biblical exegesis can be seen in Pusey, who was even reticent about 'an organized, announced prayer meeting on the grounds that Matthew 6.6 charged believers to pray secretly ... This is fascinating precisely because it is so quirky: it is stereotypically ultra-Protestants who generate hitherto unrecognized and unpractised prohibitions on the basis of biblical texts.'[18]

Exposition of Scripture became a cornerstone of Tractarian writing, both among the leading academic figures and also among lay members of the Oxford Movement such as the novelist Charlotte Yonge, whose five-volume *Scripture Readings for Schools and Families with Comments* 'was essentially a single-author commentary on the entire Bible'.[19] Patristic interpretation was seen as key, but always *secondary* to the biblical text.[20] While Tractarians at times were more 'literalist' than their protestant siblings, they could also display more deference to the behaviour of biblical characters than some evangelical contemporaries. Larsen contrasts this deference with the work of one such, Josephine Butler, who was only too happy to register her disgust at the behaviour of Ishmael and Isaac in Genesis.[21] This moral conservatism was matched with 'a complete and resolute rejection of attempts by modern biblical critics to call into question traditional views regarding the veracity, authorship, date, and composition of the canonical writings'.[22] For example, Pusey's *Daniel the Prophet* sought to defend an early dating of a biblical book that is now almost universally regarded as late post-exilic.[23] Yet within a generation, Anglo-Catholic leaders were characterized by a sharp turn to embrace biblical criticism. Figures such as Charles Gore, who declared that to claim that Moses wrote the Pentateuch, David the Psalms or Solomon Proverbs was 'uncritical'.[24] Through this turn to acceptance of 'secular' biblical studies, the Catholic movement was able to open itself to a sense of critical engagement and intellectual integrity, with the consequence that historical and authorial questions about the text were increasingly entertained.

The Bible in the life of the Church

If the premise so far is that the Catholic movement in the Church of England has lost confidence in the Bible, then contemporary liturgical practice tells a very different story. Our practice is rooted in Scripture itself. Matthew Levering, writing on the Scriptures in Catholic theology, begins with an exploration of how Scripture talks about the interpretation of Scripture, and in it he finds something very catholic: that Scripture interprets Scripture in terms of liturgy and sanctification. After receiving the commandments, Moses reads them to the congregation, builds an altar and performs sacrifices, followed by an intimate 'communion with God' (Exod. 24), followed by extensive discussion of the building of the tabernacle, vestments and liturgical objects (Exodus 32). Levering finds a similar dynamic at work in Josiah's discovery of the lost book of the law in the temple in 2 Kings 23, which emphasizes the people's 'liturgical forgetfulness' in, for example, not keeping the Passover. He also notes Jesus' own practice of merging Scripture and liturgy (Luke 4.21; Luke 24.27–45).[25] He states: 'Scripture is never inert; it is read from within liturgical desire for union with the divine realities that it depicts.'[26] There are three areas where we experience this deep union in our life: liturgy, proclamation and spirituality.

Liturgy

The liturgy is the context in which as catholics we experience the full range of Scripture most solidly, especially in the Daily Office, which is almost entirely scriptural. For example, the whole of Psalm 95 is usually read at the start of each Morning Prayer and the Magnificat of Luke 1.46–55 at each Evening Prayer. With perhaps the exception of the collects, antiphons and hymns, the daily prayer of the office is simply long, extended portions of Scripture, read in a prayerful (rather than academic) fashion. Our eucharistic liturgy is also mostly drawn from Scripture, but in an arguably more piecemeal fashion, even as the liturgy of the Word forms the opening of each and every Mass.

Frank Senn outlines the following places in which Scripture is drawn upon during the Mass:

- the preliminary rites, e.g. antiphons and the entrance hymn (often based on a psalm)
- the salutation 'The Lord be with you' (Ruth 2.4 and Luke 1.28)
- the Kyrie (echoing Luke 18.38)
- the Gloria (beginning with a citation of Luke 2.14)
- the lectionary readings which form the liturgy of the Word
- the Sermon (explicating the texts)
- the Creed (as a summary of the faith proclaimed in the Scriptures)
- Intercessions (influenced by the readings)
- the Peace (citing John 20.19, 21, 26; and Rom. 16.16)
- the Sanctus (Isa. 6.3; and Matt. 21.9, itself a citation of Ps. 118.26)
- Eucharistic Prayers (referencing biblical salvation history)
- Words of Institution (Matt. 26.26–28; Mark 14.22–24; Luke 22.15–20; 1 Cor. 11.23–26)
- Lord's Prayer (Matt. 6.9–13 version)

- Invitation to Communion (Luke 7.6–7)
- Agnus Dei (John 1.29)
- Blessing (commonly Num. 6.24–26 or Phil. 4.7)
- Dismissal (Luke 7.50).[27]

The Invitation to Communion is an interesting test case for this engagement with Scripture. Spoken at the moment when the host is held up and shown to the congregation, it draws on three texts:

> The next day he saw Jesus coming towards him and declared, 'Here is the Lamb of God who takes away the sin of the world!' (John 1.29 NRSV)[28]

> 'Lord do not trouble yourself, for I am not worthy to have you come under my roof; therefore I did not presume to come to you. But only speak the word, and let my servant be healed.' (Luke 7.6–7 NRSV)

> And the angel said to me, 'Write this: Blessed are those who are invited to the marriage supper of the Lamb.' And he said to me, 'These are true words of God.' (Rev. 19.9 NRSV)

Common Worship renders the invitation:

> Jesus is the Lamb of God who takes away the sin of the world.
> Blessed are those who are called to his supper.
> **Lord, I am not worthy to receive you,**
> **but only say the word, and I shall be healed.**

Whereas the Roman Missal renders it:

> Behold the Lamb of God, behold him who takes away the sins of the world.
> Blessed are those called to the supper of the Lamb.
> **Lord, I am not worthy that you should enter under my roof, but only say the word and my soul shall be healed.**

Neither of these texts, of course, stems from any scriptural discussion of the Eucharist, but they do both speak of the person of Christ. Placed at the moment of communion, they both state something about the faith of the congregation and also, pertinent for our discussion, about the status of what (or who) is being raised and presented in the eucharistic bread. *Common Worship*, in order to maintain a broad Church (or ambiguous?) eucharistic theology, obscures the words of the biblical text, rendering it 'Jesus is the Lamb of God', taking away the explicit sense found in the Roman Missal's 'Behold': that what is beheld in the host is Christ himself in the form of the Blessed Sacrament. The arrangement of Scripture in liturgy, and the smallest change in translation, can betray our theological perspectives.

As I have argued elsewhere in relation to the baptism liturgy, *Common Worship* takes a pastiche approach to biblical imagery – a literary technique that draws on multiple texts and symbols – not allowing one image to become dominant.[29] In the case of baptism, this consists of not letting the image of washing clean dominate over other biblical images, such as the waters of creation, freedom of slavery through the Red Sea, living waters flowing from the temple, dying and rising with Christ. This feature of *Common Worship* is echoed in catholic liturgy more broadly. Our liturgical life is a movement of opening up scriptural associations and images, of bringing the story of salvation recounted through Scripture into the life and sacraments of the Church today, while also allowing the freedom for different scriptural associations to dialogue.

Senn goes further, to explore how catholic liturgical symbols, practices and images, draw on Scripture, contrary to the perception we sometimes encounter that they are 'unbiblical':[30]

- 40-day seasons (such as Lent)[31]
- water of baptism[32]
- anointing with oil[33]
- bread and wine[34]
- candles[35]
- incense[36]

Proclamation

The proclamation of Scripture in the liturgy of the Eucharist has been a central, and universal, feature since the second century.[37] In fact this is a somewhat misleading direction of travel: rather than a part of the liturgy, Thomas O'Loughlin demonstrates how the very act of being read in liturgical, eucharistic, contexts helped formulate the canon of Scripture, with the repetitive choice of texts from within the early Christian movement that were deemed, through their repetitive reading, to hold the same or similar status to the 'law and the prophets'. He notes that by the fourth century this use in the eucharistic liturgy effectively gave New Testament writings the status of Scripture on the same level as Old Testament text, to the point where these texts were no longer merely often read but were mandated to be read. However, O'Loughlin also notes that this canonization of New Testament texts through use in the liturgy also led to a corresponding falling away in terms of the place of the Old Testament in the liturgy.[38]

The ritual around the reading of the Gospel (candles, incense, procession, sign of the cross, singing) mirrors the reverence shown to the Eucharist. The Liturgy of the Word and The Liturgy of the Sacrament are the two high points of the two halves of the liturgy, and the two places where we encounter the person of Christ in our liturgical life as the Church. While one encounters different schools of thought as to the purpose and place of preaching, particularly at weekday Masses, it is notable that the proclamation of Scripture is universal, with particular reverence shown to the Gospel even at a simple midweek Mass. The role of Scripture here is sacramental: it is read simply to be heard, in and of itself. We can compare this to the way in some Reformed worship only that which was to be preached on was to be read, leading to a reduction in Scripture being read, with at many services only a single Bible verse being proclaimed and then expounded.[39] Catholic tradition meanwhile holds to what Paul Bradshaw calls 'kerygmatic or anamnetic ministry of the word', which we see most clearly in, for example, the reading of the whole Passion through Holy Week, or particular psalms read at particular times, such as Psalm 95 at the beginning of the day.[40]

Spirituality

Scripture plays an obvious role in the spiritual practices of the Church outside of formal liturgical worship. Devotional daily Bible reading is more common in the catholic life than may often be realized. Resources such as *NewDaylight*, *Word Alive*, *Magnificat*, *UCB Word for Today* – not to mention the explosion of Bible-reading apps – are part of the spiritual practices of many of our congregations. In addition to this, two distinctly catholic prayer practices using Scripture – *Lectio Divina* and Ignatian imaginative prayer – have been popularized beyond just the catholic wing of the Church of England. Both *Lectio Divina* and Ignatian imaginative prayer free the reader (or, properly, the one praying with the text) from questions of historicity. They evade the problems of literalism and they allow the reader a genuine, contemplative and often transformative encounter with God through a medium (Scripture) in which we can have confidence (because we recognize it as the word of God). In addition, practices such as the Rosary and Stations of the Cross use texts drawn from Scripture, encouraging meditation on (largely) scriptural episodes.

Dei Verbum

At the start of the twentieth century the Roman Catholic Church's official approach to the burgeoning discipline of biblical studies, as seen in the encyclical *Lamentabili Sane*, can be described as at best suspicious. The document – mostly a syllabus of what it perceived as the errors of the then modernist approach to Scripture – rejects not just the scepticism that biblical studies had for some texts (e.g. that the Gospel of John may have been written quite some time after the time of Christ), proposing an almost reactionary literalism, but it is also defensive in denying almost anyone outside the magisterium of the Church any authority to interpret Scripture.[41]

The shift by the end of the 1960s, as best expressed in *Dei Verbum*, the major contribution of the Second Vatican Council on the place of Scripture in the Church, is nothing short of extraordinary. *Dei Verbum* offers both a serious attempt to accept the fruits of biblical scholarship and a hermeneutic that accepts the historical 'limitations' of some parts of Scripture, while also offering a life-giving vision of the place of Scripture in the Church. *Dei Verbum* begins its framing of Scripture not with a discussion of Scripture but of revelation, which is the eternal life of the Father that we gain in fellowship with Christ the Son (1 John 1.2–3). It sets forth its aim as to demonstrate how divine revelation is passed on 'so that by hearing the message of salvation the whole world may believe, by believing it may hope, and by hoping it may love'.[42] It then draws on individual moments in Scripture to paint a broad sweep of the story of salvation, creatively drawing on both Old and New Testament texts together to describe creation, the patriarchs and prophets.[43] In so doing, it offers a kind of 'hermeneutic of salvation', suggesting that what we are to take note of in reading Scripture are those parts of Scripture that are about God calling us into relationship with Godself, and that through the person and saving work of Christ, God has achieved salvation and as such 'we now await no further new public revelation'.[44] Notably, it also affirms that God 'can be known with certainty from created reality by the light of human reason (see Rom. 1:20)', but that through revelation we can know religious truths 'with ease, with solid certitude, and with no trace of error'.[45] All this offers a helpful framing for what I often encounter as one of the stumbling blocks in engaging with Christian Scripture: expecting it to be something it is not.

My sense is that one of the elements of Christian theology that causes difficulties in our understanding of Scripture is the distinctive nature of revelation; that is, in essence, that God reveals Godself to us through the person of Christ, and Scripture bears witness to that revelation. The confusion lies in where we place Scripture in this: to compare it to another faith tradition, our understanding of the Bible is different from an Islamic understanding of the Quran. In Islamic understanding, the actual words of the Quran were revealed by the angel Gabriel over a number of years, and so the words themselves and their recitation take on an almost 'sacramental' character. In a classical Christian understanding – leaving aside modern scholarship – different texts of the Bible were written down by different people, in different contexts, for different purposes, at different times. As such they are understood to be inspired by God, yet in are in no way the fullness of God's revelation of Godself, even as they bear witness to it. For Christians, God's revelation is in a person (Jesus) not a text (the Bible). *Dei Verbum* reflects this truth that the fullest revelation of God is through Christ: 'Christ the Lord in whom the full revelation of the supreme God is brought to completion.'[46]

The renewed engagement with scriptural interpretation enabled by *Dei Verbum* was further developed in the 1993 document *The Interpretation of the Bible in the Church*, published by the Pontifical Commission. Here the authors note:

> Catholic exegesis does not claim any particular scientific method as its own. It recognizes that one of the aspects of biblical texts is that they are the work of human authors, who employed both their own capacities for expression and the means which their age and social context put at their disposal. Consequently Catholic exegesis freely makes use of the scientific methods and approaches which allow a better grasp of the meaning of texts in their linguistic, literary, socio-cultural, religious and historical contexts, while explaining them as well through studying their sources and attending to the personality of each author ... What characterizes Catholic exegesis is that it deliberately places itself within the living tradition of the Church, whose first concern is fidelity to the revelation attested by the Bible. Modern hermeneutics has made clear, as we have noted, the impossibility of

interpreting a text without starting from a 'pre-understanding' of one type or another.[47]

All this leaves us in somewhat of a pickle as catholic-minded Anglicans, particularly as the current issues and debates of the Church rage on. *Dei Verbum*, in its wonderfully ambiguous way, offers us a freedom to acknowledge what is beautiful *and* what is troubling in Scripture. If it seems shocking or scandalous to suggest that some part of Scripture is troubling, one only has to read Joshua and Judges. In addition, *Dei Verbum* carries a weight that can free us from a reductive focus on 'authorial intent', an extreme Hirschianism that sees the task of reading Scripture as, for example, trying to decode what St Paul meant in one particular word of one particular verse, and open us to both the task of serious, critical reading of biblical texts, alongside a real sensitivity to how the Spirit is at work in the Church at the present moment.[48] And yet the elephant in the room – for Catholic Anglicans – is what exactly is meant by the 'teaching office of the Church': the magisterium? An ecumenical council? The General Synod? The extent to which we accept the Church of England as the locus of this work of Scripture/Church/Spirit is often a dividing line on the issues of gender and sexuality that have split the Church of England in general and the Catholic movement of the Church of England in particular.

Jacob wrestling with God

So how do we engage with Scripture as catholic Christians? As explored above, Scripture is integral to our Christian life, worship, spirituality and practice. It is read and prayed devotionally; it tells us the story of our faith; it is read in our worship; it has a particular place in devotional practices; it is testament to the revelation of God in Christ; and it is the measure by which our ethics, ecclesiology, theology and life together is measured. As Catholics, our sacramental life makes no sense without it; our liturgy is derived from it, our catholic order is ordained in it. I once heard a Free Church colleague say: 'Scripture is where the power is.' As catholics we can agree.

And yet reading Scripture is hard. My experience teaching across a range of traditions is that those who publicly pretend it isn't hard also tend to be more honest in private conversations about the difficulty that is reading Scripture. The problems outlined: portions of Scripture we find morally ambiguous (or repugnant); lack of biblical literacy; the difficulty of interpretation; a sense of Scripture – understood through the historical–critical approach – of being fragmentary; the question of historicity; not to mention sensitivities to questions of gender, ethnicity, sexuality, and how to read Scripture sensitively alongside our Jewish friends.

I would like to offer in conclusion one approach to this tension. It is a partial, slightly idiosyncratic approach but one that has been productive in teaching across various contexts: the hermeneutic of Jacob wrestling with God (Gen. 32.22–32). In this text, Jacob wrestles, at times unsure with whom he is wrestling; he seems to acknowledge before him both human and divine. And through his long wrestling through the night, he does not acquiesce; he does not turn off his own wrestling or strength or vulnerability (or mind); he continues struggling, and wrestling, and taking seriously what is before him. And ultimately he does so demanding to be blessed, insisting on blessing, on engaging with the fight in order to be blessed; and at the end of the struggle he can say he has seen God face to face.

This encounter between the human and the divine, this slow partial revelation of God who is present and absent, who takes seriously the wrestling of Jacob and blesses him because of it, leaves Jacob changed. And not entirely positively – he leaves with a limp – but with his name changed: 'And he said: not Jacob shall be called anymore your name, but Israel (ישראל), for you have struggled with God and with man and have prevailed.'[49] The very name Israel is given a gloss here, the text proclaiming its etymology from two roots, the Hebrew words for God and struggle: the name Israel is said to mean 'you have wrestled with God' (and man, suggesting a symmetry with what we find in Scripture, divine and human words).[50] This becomes the identity of the people: Israel, 'We Have Wrestled with God'. What follows through the Old Testament is accounts of real wrestling, through almost every page deep inquiry into the nature of humanity and God and their fraught and beautiful relationship; the people who wrestle with God recording their wrestle with God, in all its frank reality. As catholics, when we view Scripture like this, as an account of the honest human wrestle with God, and when we approach it as Jacob, insisting on a deep, honest, sometimes painful engagement with God, then, like Jacob, we can insist on blessing – and blessing we will find.

Notes

1 Pope Paul VI, *Dei Verbum*, 22, https://www.vatican.va/archive/hist_councils/ii_vatican_council/documents/vat-ii_const_19651118_dei-verbum_en.html, accessed 14.02.2024.

2 The Bible Society, *Pass It On* (2014), available at: https://www.biblesociety.org.uk/uploads/content/projects/Bible-Society-Report_030214_final_.pdf, accessed 24.04.2024.

3 Bible Society, *Pass It On*, pp. 32–3.

4 Bible Society, *Pass It On*, pp. 11–13.

5 Bible Society, *Pass It On*, p. 15.

6 Katie B. Edwards, 2015, 'Introduction', in K. B. Edwards (ed.), *Rethinking Biblical Literacy*, London: Bloomsbury T&T Clark, pp. ix–x.

7 This approach culminated in the work of Julius Wellhausen at the end of the nineteenth century, after which it gained widespread acceptance. Baden gives an overview of the premodern questions – at times scepticism – of the authorship of Moses, demonstrating that the ruptures in the texts of the Pentateuch have been noticed since the earliest times. See the introduction and first chapter of Joel S. Baden, 2012, *The Composition of the Pentateuch: Renewing the Documentary Hypothesis*, New Haven, CT: Yale University Press.

8 Mark Z. Brettler and Amy-Jill Levine, 'Isaiah's Suffering Servant: Before and After Christianity', *Interpretation* 73.2 (2019), pp. 158–73.

9 It is worth noting here the near total acceptance of modern biblical studies in contemporary Roman Catholicism, despite previous opposition. The Pontifical Biblical Commission's seminal 1993 text *The Interpretation of the Bible in the Church* (available at: https://catholic-resources.org/ChurchDocs/PBC_Interp-FullText.htm, accessed 8.03.2024) even accepts (though with some reservations) feminist criticism of the Bible as a valuable and worthwhile approach in and of itself, putting it ahead of certain sections of biblical studies to this day.

10 Stephen D. Moore and Yvonne Sherwood, 2001, *The Invention of the Biblical Scholar: A Critical Manifesto*, Minneapolis, MN: Fortress Press, p. 47.

11 Moore and Sherwood, *Invention of the Biblical Scholar*, p. x.

12 Moore and Sherwood, *Invention of the Biblical Scholar*, p. xi.

13 Moore and Sherwood, *Invention of the Biblical Scholar*, p. 47.

14 Timothy Larsen, 2017, 'Scripture and Biblical Interpretation', in S. Brown, P. Nockles and J. Pereiro (eds), *The Oxford Handbook of the Oxford Movement*, Oxford: Oxford University Press, p. 231.

15 Edward B. Pusey, 1835, *Tracts for the Times 67: Scriptural Views of Holy Baptism*, London: Rivington.

16 John H. Newman, 1840, *Tracts for the Times 21: Mortification of the Flesh a Scripture Duty*, London: Rivington.

17 Larsen, 'Scripture and Biblical Interpretation', p. 232.

18 Larsen, 'Scripture and Biblical Interpretation', p. 232.

19 Larsen, 'Scripture and Biblical Interpretation', pp. 232–6; Charlotte Yonge, 1876, *Scripture Readings for Schools and Families with Comments: Genesis to Deuteronomy*, London: Macmillan.

20 Larsen, 'Scripture and Biblical Interpretation', p. 237.

21 Larsen, 'Scripture and Biblical Interpretation', p. 238; Josephine E. G. Butler, 1894, *The Lady of Shunem*, London: Horace Marshall, p. 73.

22 Larsen, 'Scripture and Biblical Interpretation', p. 239.
23 Edward Pusey, 1864, *Daniel the Prophet: Nine Lectures, Delivered in the Divinity School of the University of Oxford. With Copious Notes*, London: John Henry and James Parker.
24 Larsen, 'Scripture and Biblical Interpretation', p. 240; Charles Gore, 1890, *Lux Mundi: A Series of Studies in the Religion of the Incarnation*, London: John Murray.
25 Matthew Levering, 2019, 'The Scriptures and their Interpretation', in L. Ayres and M. A. Volpe (eds), *The Oxford Handbook of Catholic Theology*, Oxford: Oxford University Press, pp. 41–54, pp. 43–5.
26 Levering, 'The Scriptures and their Interpretation', p. 45.
27 Frank Senn, 'The Bible and the Liturgy', *Liturgy* 19.3 (2004), pp. 5–12, pp. 5–8.
28 'Here' is translated 'Behold' in the Authorized Version.
29 Steffan Mathias, 'Freeing the Text: Common Worship Baptism Liturgy as Pastiche', *Anaphora: The Journal of the Society for Liturgical Study* 14.1 (2020).
30 Senn, 'The Bible and the Liturgy', pp. 10–12.
31 Josh. 5.6; Matt. 4.1; Luke 2; Acts 1.3.
32 Gen. 6—8; Exod. 14; Matt. 3.13–16; Rev. 22.1.
33 Psalm 23; Exod. 28.41; Lev. 8.12; Num. 3.3; Isa. 61; 1 Sam. 10.1; Lev. 14.14–17.
34 Gen. 14.18–20; Lev. 23.5–8; 1 Cor. 11.23–24.
35 Ps. 104.2; Rev. 21.23.
36 Ps. 141.2; Isa. 60.6; Song of Sol. 3.6; Matt. 2; Rev. 5.8, 8.4 as well as the sacrificial use in Leviticus.
37 Thomas O'Loughlin, 2022, 'The Bible in the Context of the Eucharist', in G. Jeanes, B. Nichols and P. Bradshaw (eds), *Lively Oracles of God: Perspectives on the Bible and Liturgy*, Collegeville, MN: Liturgical Press, pp. 40–1.
38 O'Loughlin, 'In the Context of the Eucharist', pp. 42–6.
39 Paul F. Bradshaw, 'The Use of the Bible in Liturgy: Some Historical Perspectives', *Studia Liturgica* 22.1 (1992), pp. 35–52.
40 Bradshaw, 'Use of the Bible', p. 40.
41 Pope Pius X, *Lamentabili Sane Exitu: Syllabus Condemning the Errors of the Modernists* (3 July 1907), https://www.papalencyclicals.net/pius10/p10lamen.htm, accessed 1.05.2024.
42 Paul VI, *Dei Verbum*, 1.
43 *Dei Verbum*, 2–4.
44 *Dei Verbum*, 4.
45 *Dei Verbum*, 6.
46 *Dei Verbum*, 7.
47 Pontifical Biblical Commission, *Interpretation of the Bible*, III.
48 Hirsch's work was extremely influential and yet rapidly fell out of fashion; it states that the writer essentially encodes their meaning into a text and the reader's role is in a fundamental way to decode that same meaning; see Eric D. Hirsch, 1967, *Validity in Interpretation*, New Haven, CT: Yale University Press.
49 My translation, emphasizing the Hebrew word order.
50 Wonderfully, for a metaphor about biblical interpretation, many scholars dispute the etymology given in the verse, but this just adds a glorious irony: another place of wrestling with the text.

Bibliography

Baden, Joel S., 2012, *The Composition of the Pentateuch: Renewing the Documentary Hypothesis*, New Haven, CT: Yale University Press.

Bradshaw, Paul F., 'The Use of the Bible in Liturgy: Some Historical Perspectives', *Studia Liturgica* 22.1 (1992), pp. 35–52.

Brettler, Mark. Z. and Amy-Jill Levine, 'Isaiah's Suffering Servant: Before and After Christianity', *Interpretation* 73 2 (2019), pp. 158–73.

Butler, Josephine, 1898, *The Lady of Shunem*, London: Horace Marshall.

Edwards, Katie. B., 2015, *Rethinking Biblical Literacy*, London: Bloomsbury T&T Clark.

Gore, Charles, 1890, *Lux Mundi: A Series of Studies in the Religion of the Incarnation*, London: John Murray.

Hirsch, Eric D., 1967, *Validity in Interpretation*, New Haven, CT: Yale University Press.

Larsen, Timothy, 2017, 'Scripture and Biblical Interpretation', in S. Brown, P. Nockles and J. Pereiro (eds), *The Oxford Handbook of the Oxford Movement*, Oxford: Oxford University Press.

Levering, Matthew, 2019, 'The Scriptures and their Interpretation', in L. Ayres and M. A. Volpe (eds), *The Oxford Handbook of Catholic Theology*, Oxford: Oxford University Press, pp. 41–54.

Mathias, Steffan, 'Freeing the Text: Common Worship Baptism Liturgy as Pastiche', *Anaphora: The Journal of the Society for Liturgical Study* 14.1 (2020).

Moore, Stephen D. and Yvonne Sherwood, 2011, *The Invention of the Biblical Scholar: A Critical Manifesto*, Minneapolis, MN: Fortress Press.

Newman, John Henry, 1840, *Tracts for the Times 21: Mortification of the Flesh a Scripture Duty*, London: Rivington.

O'Loughlin, Thomas, 2017, 'The Bible in the Context of the Eucharist', in G. Jeanes, B. Nichols and P. Bradshaw (eds), *Lively Oracles of God: Perspectives on the Bible and Liturgy*, Collegeville, MN: Liturgical Press.

Pusey, Edward Bouverie, 1835, *Tracts for the Times 67: Scriptural Views of Holy Baptism*, London: Rivington.

Pusey, Edward Bouverie, 1864, *Daniel the Prophet: Nine Lectures, Delivered in the Divinity School of the University of Oxford. With Copious Notes*, London: John Henry and James Parker.

Senn, Frank, 'The Bible and the Liturgy', *Liturgy* 19.3 (2004), pp. 5–12.

Yonge, Charlotte M., 1876, *Scripture Readings for Schools and Families with Comments: Genesis to Deuteronomy*, London: Macmillan.

Sermon

'Hannah's Prayer: Testimony, Thanksgiving and Action'

Preached at Mass at St Peter de Beauvoir Town on 18 May 2024

Bishop Joanne Woolway Grenfell

1 Samuel 2.1–10; John 3.11–16

This Easter, I confirmed several children and teenagers. They made a commitment to take on for themselves the faith that they had been baptized into. One of the girls I confirmed, ten-year-old Jevae Soraya Furlong-Russell, afterwards wrote a testimony for her church of what she had felt. This is what she said:

> Since I have been confirmed, I feel amazing! I was so proud that a lot of my family and friends were able to witness me make a covenant to God and confirm my promise. I felt powerful when Bishop Joanne put her hands on my head and blessed me, she made me feel like God was present and that was amazing. Now, when I eat the Body of Christ, I feel special, and I feel closer to God and am now able to say a little prayer to say thank you to God. My confirmation means that I am now a follower of Christ in my Christian community, and it enables me to be strong and confident out in the community or when I am at school.[1]

If I ever doubt that I have the best job in the world, then testimony like that brings me right back to God in gratitude: that as Christians we get to share in each other's faith, be encouraged by each other and share in thanksgiving for God's goodness to us.

Testimony is an important part of being a disciple of Christ. It's about saying how we've seen God at work in our lives. It's about connecting our own experience with the bigger story of God in action through time and across the world. It's about seeing the story of salvation lived in our communities. God is here, working in and through us. I think it also tells us something important about how we pray – and how we act.

Hannah's prayer of thanksgiving is found in 1 Samuel chapter 2. This is a passage that is very special to me. It's because of this passage that my eldest child, our eldest child, is called Samuel. Though she has been married a long time to Elkanah, Hannah hasn't been able to conceive a child. And this makes her very sad. It also makes her feel shame, because in the Israel of her time, children were considered a sign of God's blessing, and infertility brought shame. She is mocked and excluded. So for many years, Hannah pours out her heart to God in prayer, asking him for a child and promising that if she were to have one, she would give him back to God in thanksgiving.

When her prayer is answered, she gives birth to a boy whom she names Samuel, and she brings him to the tabernacle to be trained as a priest to serve God. And then she gives her testimony, these extraordinary words filled with praise and thanksgiving, both for what God has done in giving her a child and in a more universal sense for all God's acts and interventions throughout creation.

I know that Hannah's prayer of thanksgiving has been a help to many individuals, for many different reasons – not only to those who have found their prayers to be answered but also to those who haven't, those who hear that they, like others who feel weak, shamed, excluded or forgotten, are raised up. They are reminded by Hannah's words that God will intervene, perhaps in ways that we don't fully understand in this world, so that they too can walk in their full stature as the children of God.

It's a prayer that I found helpful after several miscarriages when I wasn't sure that I would ever be a mother. So I did use its words of thanksgiving when our Samuel was finally born. But I also used it before then to remind me of God's faithfulness and God's raising up of the broken-hearted. I knew from Hannah's witness that, although we don't get to decide how, God does intervene through history on the part of those who suffer, are downtrodden or who endure shame or persecution. And I was able to share in Hannah's gladness.

Do you notice that it's God in whom Hannah rejoices – not her son Samuel? She is grateful to God for the gift of life and for more than that, for the restoration of her strength and dignity. And so she sings out God's greatness, faithfulness, and holiness. God alone can save and restore.

Hannah moves beyond what's personal into a more public thanksgiving. And it's this that allows other people to find a place within her testimony and her thanksgiving. She is able to warn herself and others that there's no place for boasting of their own strength. She is able to remind her community that God is judge as well as the one who brings the gift of life: he judges those who wage war and those who are gluttonous or greedy or boastful rather than living in peaceful thanksgiving. God's actions aren't random but work systematically to bring down those who are wicked, to bring redress to those who are hurt and to raise up the poor from the ash heap.

Hannah's prayer is often recited as part of Jewish rituals of worship. It's used as a *haftara*, a leave-taking or a parting prayer. And its use probably comes from a time of persecution when it was forbidden to read the Torah. So her testimony is used to remind God's people that even though they have to leave safety and even though they may be persecuted, God is still at work in and through them. Remembering the past faithfulness of God keeps present hope alive.

I also find it helpful to know that, in Hebrew, the word for prayer is a reflexive form of the verb to judge. So not just to judge but to *judge ourselves*. The purpose of prayer isn't to change God or to change God's mind. Instead, prayer judges us, it helps us to see ourselves in the light of God's love and to use that knowledge to transform who we are. Prayer brings us a new relationship with God and each other. Prayer is the work of our hearts, individually and together. We need to be transformed and renewed. And God makes that possible through prayer.

I wonder what being transformed looks like. When you pray, what difference do you see – in your own lives and in the world around you? Take a moment to think. Sometimes it's obvious and we know what to give thanks for. But sometimes it isn't at all obvious and we can continue to feel lost and uncertain. Faith doesn't give us everything we want or an easy life. And if you feel that your heart is still breaking, despite pouring out all your longing to God, then know that Hannah is still praying with you, still there, reminding you of God's solidarity with all who weep.

Most of all, I think that transformation through prayer looks like a changed attitude. And that's partly why it's so important to hear each other's prayers of thanksgiving and testimony, so that we can keep being reminded of the goodness of God and cultivate our own posture of generosity. In other words, I think prayer leads to solidarity. When we're more at one with God and more tuned into the injustice that Hannah cries out about, then perhaps we become a little more human, a little more aware of the needs of the world and more inclined to do something about them. Testimony gives voice to our prayers, connects them with the needs of others and shapes our action. It leads us to feed the hungry at the food bank – and to campaign for a living wage. It compels us to reduce our burning of fossil fuels once we realize that our usage means rising sea levels and flooded communities on faraway shores. It leads us to challenging and changing healthcare inequalities so that a mother giving birth to a child, to her Samuel, has the same access to medical and surgical interventions as a woman on the other side of the world. Prayer leads to solidarity, which leads to action.

When we join a Christian community in baptism, confirmation or some other act of commitment, we join our voices and our actions together in community. As well as praying privately we show solidarity by praying together and learning from each other. We voice together the justice we long to see – knowing that God does and will intervene but also knowing that we need to be committed to working for the kingdom that we believe can be present all around us.

So I am grateful to Jevae for giving voice to her gratitude to God and for showing how this was going to make a difference to how she is in her community and school. Remember what she said: 'My confirmation means that I am now a follower of Christ in my Christian community, and it enables me to be strong and confident out in the community or when I am at school.'

I learned something from her testimony. And that something was simply this: that prayerful thanksgiving changes me and enables me to act as a follower of Christ in the world. Prayer gives action wings to fly. And when I speak and especially when I act for good, for God, others will also see God and will believe. They will see God at work in the world, intervening for the downtrodden, and they will see people of faith, acting out of love.

So there's a challenge for each of us: to bring our thanksgiving to God in prayer and to take our thanksgiving out into the world. And there's also a challenge for the whole Church: to voice our thanksgiving for all that God has already done for us, and to ask God to help us work out where we need now to give and to act, so that others too will be caught up in his kingdom.

> Hannah said:
> My heart exults in the LORD;
> > my strength is exalted in my God.

May it be so with us.
Amen.

Notes

1 Quoted with permission.

7

Prayer

FR NICOLAS STEBBING CR

Lord, teach us to pray

Sr Wendy Beckett, in her book *On Prayer*, tells an amusing story:

> A learned Jesuit was asked to give some talks on prayer in New York cathedral. At the end of the first talk an old priest came up to him, full of admiration and said, 'Father, how did you do it. That was amazing. After all prayer is so easy.'[1]

Prayer is not complicated and we must make sure we keep it simple. So we start with Jesus, as the disciples did: 'Lord, teach us to pray, as John taught his disciples to pray.'

If we want to learn about prayer we must ask Jesus to teach us. For a Christian, all prayer goes through Jesus to our Father in heaven. Throughout the Gospels we see Jesus praying to his father in heaven. Jesus is the best teacher we have when it comes to prayer.

Jesus' most famous teaching on prayer was, of course, the Lord's Prayer. What does this prayer teach us?

First, it is very simple. We don't need to indulge in high-sounding rhetoric; we simply say what we want.

Second, it is directed to our father in heaven. Simply that we have a father in heaven is amazing. We should think of that more often. Our father in heaven loves us. We can speak to him with the confidence of a child speaking to its father. Of course, he is not any old father; he is a special father. 'May your name be holy' is one way of saying 'May everyone recognize how wonderful you are.' When we pray our first concern must be God, not us.

Third, we pray for the world, that it may come to God and allow God to rule its ways. The prayer sets its sights high: 'on earth as it is in heaven'. God intends earth to be like heaven. One day earth will be gathered up into heaven. We need to be working for that day even now.

Fourth, in the very heart of the prayer comes the petition for ourselves: 'Give us this day our daily bread.' Food, yes. We need it. But this short petition covers all our needs. We could stop there and think of our needs: for health, friends, a decent job. There is nothing wrong with asking for these things. Jesus himself said: 'Ask and you will receive' (Matthew 7.7). Yet we do have to remember that our father knows our needs better than we do. We have to trust him. He is not a machine that responds to the pressing of buttons. He is not a genie that gives us what we want. He gives us what he knows we need. And this sentence goes on to ask for what we need most: forgiveness of our sins.

Do we mean that when we pray it? Do we admit we have sins? This should not be something we just say, something we rattle off. I suspect we all rush through this bit about trespasses. We don't want to think about them. Sometimes we should stop here in saying the Lord's Prayer and remember just what sins we do have that need forgiving. This won't put God off. God knows perfectly well what our sins are. If this prayer makes us feel a bit rotten, a bit sorry, that is no bad thing: 'a broken and a contrite heart, O God, you will not despise' (Psalm 51.17 NRSV). Prayer to God is based on humility. We know he is infinitely great. We know we are small and weak and do many things wrong. The wonder is that God loves us and lets us speak to him at all. And again we have to remember that forgiveness comes at a cost. God is always ready to forgive. God does forgive, but we cannot receive that forgiveness unless we forgive others. Once again we need to stop. Are we holding on to resentments and hurts? Are we refusing to forgive anyone?

By now we know we are weak and easily led astray so we end our prayer with another act of humility. We don't just blithely tell God we won't sin again. We admit we are weak and ask him to keep temptation away from us, and keep us out of evil. We need God's help every step of the way if we are going to live the way he wants us to live. Again we do need to ask ourselves: Do we really mean this prayer? There are temptations that really are temptations because we like what they offer. That may even be true of the evils. When we think of particular temptations and particular evils that are part of our life, do we really want God to keep them away from us? It's easy to rattle off the Lord's Prayer several times a day. When we stop to think about it we can be quite shocked at what we are saying!

Why do we pray?

That little scamper through the Lord's Prayer tells us quite a lot about the different kinds of prayer: adoration, petition and confession. But behind all that is the question: Why do we pray? We may say that prayer starts with petition, asking God for things we need, but that begs the question: Why do we ask God in the first place? Why do we think there is a God who will answer prayer? Why do we think he is interested in us and our little ways? It is because prayer starts with God. God calls us to himself. He calls us to prayer.

When I was 18, I paid my first visit to a monastic community. They ran a mission station in the Eastern Highlands of Zimbabwe. It was a beautiful place: mountains all around, ten fathers of my present Community of the Resurrection in white cassocks and grey scapulars, a beautiful church full of the sense of prayer, two communities of sisters and a host of school children. I was completely blown off my feet by this; but most of all, there was this sense of God. God was everywhere, but particularly in church. I spent hours before the Blessed Sacrament, feeling his presence and knowing he was calling me. It was not an imperious call. It was a call of love. 'If you want a full, exciting life, come, follow me. Come and learn to pray.' It is where my call to monastic life began. God calls us because he loves us and he has things he wants us to do. Indeed, it is because he loves us that he wants to share his work with us. He doesn't just want us as passive admirers.

Throughout the Bible we hear God calling.

In Genesis 3, when Adam and Eve go into hiding, God seeks them out and calls: 'Where are you?' In Genesis 12 he calls to Abraham to leave his country and go to another. In Exodus 3 he calls out to Moses from a burning bush and tells him to go and rescue his people. In Isaiah 6 God asks: 'Whom shall I send?' And Isaiah offers himself. In Jeremiah, God tells the young prophet that he had called him before he was even born. In the Gospels it is always Jesus who calls disciples: 'Come, follow me.' The practice for a rabbi was to wait until disciples asked to study with him. Jesus doesn't give them that choice. He simply calls them. And in Acts, Saul is on his way to persecute Christians when God stops him and calls him, turning his life around.

These are famous examples but I think it is true for us too. God calls us to himself because he loves us. He wants to see us. He wants to walk with us. He wants to talk to us. He wants the pleasure of our company. It might help us to pray with more delight if we remember, each time we go to prayer, that we are responding to God's call. We don't have to hammer on the door to gain entrance to his court. We don't have to shout and scream to get his attention. It may sometimes seem like that but that is not God's fault; it is ours. Our sins and our wrong expectations get in the way. God is always listening. God is closer to us than the marrow of our bones (Hebrews 4.12). Our problem is how to respond to this. How should we pray?

Let's go back to the teaching of Jesus:

'Two men went up to the temple to pray, the one a Pharisee, the other a tax collector ...' We all know what happened. The Pharisee thanked God for making him such a jolly good chap. The tax collector could only say, 'Lord, have mercy on me, a sinner.' It was the tax collector God listened to.

We probably all know the Jesus Prayer: 'Lord Jesus Christ, Son of God, have mercy on me, a sinner.' It is a very good place to begin our prayer. I personally use it as my default prayer. It calls on Jesus whom we know as the Man in Galilee, acknowledges him as Lord, sees him as the Son of God, through whom we can speak to God, and it asks for mercy, one thing we know God will always give. Perhaps most importantly, it admits we are sinners. That is the foundation of our relationship with God because that is the truth. If we try to pretend we are not sinners we are trying to build a relationship on a lie. Even to say we are not very big sinners is dodging the truth. Sin is sin, whether it is big or small. It will always get in the way of our relationship with God, till we confess it. Then, extraordinarily, it becomes a gateway into the wonder of God's love. All of us who go to confession know how amazing it is that the very things we are most ashamed of become an occasion for the love of God. The more sin we can find in our lives the more blessed we shall be. That doesn't mean we should put sin there! There is plenty to find if we look properly. The more honest we can be, the more we can search out, the more we shall find God's forgiving love poured out on us. Prayer needs to start with humility – the humility of telling the truth. It moves very quickly from there to the glory of knowing we are beloved daughters and sons of God.

The Pharisee was not entirely wrong with his prayer. He began with thanks. That is a very good place to start praying. The trouble was that he thanked God for making him so good. He should have thanked God for being so good. The psalms are full of that kind of thanks and praise. 'Praise the LORD, O my soul, and all that is within me, praise his holy name' (Psalm 103.1). 'The heavens declare the glory of God; And the firmament shows His handiwork' (Psalm 19.1 NKJV). Almost every page of the psalter says something of the goodness, the wonder and the glory of God. We can use those psalms for our own prayers. We can thank God for being so good. We can thank him for giving us such a wonderful world to live in. We can thank him for the family and friends who fill our lives with joy. We can thank him for the many gifts he has given us, Christian life and its joys. We can even thank him when we realize that, through his grace, we have actually left certain sins and weaknesses behind. That is really good news. But we have to tell the truth. There is always more work to be done. There is a lot in each of us that has not yet turned wholly to God. We confess that, not so that we can wallow in our sinfulness but so that we can move on into the love of God.

Love

We speak quite often of the love of God. What is this love? Love is not a thing; it is a person. Or it is something a person does. God loves us. There are moments when we feel that love overwhelming us; times when we know we are forgiven; times when something really good happens to us; moments in prayer or at Mass when God's love really touches us. These are important moments we need to treasure. However, there are long periods when we feel nothing. Prayer time is full of distractions. It is even boring. We try to feel loving towards God but our feeling doesn't leave the head. We are tempted to give up and go and find something more useful to do. Would it not be better to read a book or study the Bible? Perhaps I could go and see a sick friend? Those are good things to do but they mustn't replace the times of boredom when prayer is hard and nothing seems to happen. These times of boredom are really important.

Real prayer does not take place in the head but in the heart. Prayer is not all a matter of having great feelings or thinking wonderful ideas. The real place of prayer is deeper than that. When we get to that place we won't usually feel anything very much. At most there may be a quiet sense of being in the right place. I don't know what's going on, I just know that God is here. God wants me here and that's enough. Sometimes a picture helps, like the one conjured up in Psalm 131.2: 'I hold myself in quiet and silence, like a little child in its mother's arms' (NJB). We don't talk all the time with those we love. We spend long times in silence, content to be in each other's company. That is a good picture of prayer.

The boredom of prayer is also a time of testing. Am I praying just to get good experiences or am I giving myself to God? John Dalrymple writes:

'We do not pray in order to gain something for ourselves. We pray in order to give something to God. It is a sacrifice. That is the language of love.'[2] If we stay with the boredom, without complaint, without trying to find something interesting to replace it, we are showing we trust God is there. We trust God to get on with doing useful things with us at a level we don't feel. Most of us don't feel what is going on in our bodies. Hearts beat, lungs take in oxygen, food is digested, impulses go back and forth and we only feel it when something goes wrong! Staying with boredom or dryness of prayer is a sure way of showing we trust God. After a while we find we get used to it; we become sure that something really is going on and we don't want anything else. We have grown up. We don't need the toys and excitement of childhood. Maturity is something else. It also tells us something really important: prayer is not something we do; it is what God does. It takes time to realize this.

When I was about 22, I thought I was really good at praying. I could kneel in front of the Blessed Sacrament and feel wonderfully happy to be with God. I had lovely thoughts. I expected to get better and better at praying. In fact I seem to have got steadily worse. Most of the feelings have gone. I mostly don't know what I'm doing. I pray for people and causes. Sometimes they get better – but I wonder: Was that because of me or would it have happened anyway? Often they don't get better. Has God ignored me or has he used my prayer for something else? Wars go on for years and my prayers seem to make no difference. Am I ever going to get better at prayer?

The trouble is that we tend to think of prayer as an activity like learning a language. If I work at German I get better and better, understand it more and come to speak it fluently. Prayer tends to go in the other direction. We get worse and worse and know less and less. Actually we are being forced to give up control. It is not I who pray but God who prays in me. Like Alice in the Looking Glass, in order to go forwards I have to walk backwards. It is not easy to give up control, especially in a world like ours, today, when we are trained from childhood to be in charge, to take decisions, to decide what we want to do in life and do it. We have to let God take control of our prayer. How do we do that?

I think the key point is that we have to get away from the idea of prayer as an activity: saying prayers. What we want is to become prayer.

When I was ordained priest in what was then Rhodesia, I was sent out to a rural mission. It was a wonderful time for me. The countryside was beautiful, the people were delightful. I had a children's home full of affectionate kids, and two nuns who looked after me. I rode around on a motorbike, spoke Shona and simply loved it all. The only trouble was that there was a civil war going on. Things got more and more violent; atrocities were committed on both sides. Negotiations came to nothing and the people who suffered most were the village people who had no defences and were hit by both sides. It became clear that I could not stay much longer. Eventually one of the sisters told me: 'It's time to go, Father.' I knew it was time to take up the vocation God had given me ten years before. It was time to pray. It was time to leave the country I loved, the people I loved and the work I loved, to go and live in a monastery in gloomy Yorkshire. Only in this way could I make a serious contribution to stopping this horrible war.

That sounds pretty arrogant. I was never going to stop the war on my own. Yet we all say prayer is important. We all say prayer is more powerful than anything else yet we tend to use prayer as a last resort, when nothing else has worked. In fact prayer comes first because God comes first. Those of us who enter monastic life don't simply want to be in a place where we spend lots of time praying. We want to be in a place where prayer and work, life and God are so integrated that we become the prayer. Our vows commit us, at least in principle, wholly to God. It takes the whole of our life for the principle to become anything like reality. Sin always messes it up. We are continually reminded of our weakness and failure. That should stop us getting proud, and keep us in that humility that Benedict sees as fundamental to monastic life. Yet how does this work? We need a quick reminder of Catholic spirituality to understand that.

The first thing we need to remember is that we are baptized into Christ. We live in Christ. All our prayer is through Christ. Whether we pray to Father, Son or Holy Spirit, we are praying in Christ. We are in the Body of Christ. Christ is the head, we are the members. We never pray entirely on our own. Not only do we have Christ with us but we have all those millions of Christians with us as well. And that includes the dead who remain part of the Body when they have died. This concept of the Church can be a bit scary! It's also very encouraging. All those Christians support us and we support them. We are on a journey together, all going in the same direction. That is the prayer of the Church. The Church's prayer goes on all the time. It is a bit like a train. We get on and off when we take part in the prayer. Some of the prayer is the official worship of the Church, the services of Mass, Morning and Evening Prayer. Thousands of priests and people join together every day in praying this formal prayer of the Church. It is, you might say, the bread and butter of the Church's prayer, going on all the time, in countless forms, countless languages all over the world. It is the foundation of our life. It provides a huge energy of love, commitment and praise for God to use. It is a really important part of the bloodstream pumping its way around the Body. We need to do all we can to keep that prayer going and bring others into it.

The more we remember that we pray in Jesus, the more alive our prayer will be. We don't have to shout the Jesus Prayer up into the sky in the hope that Jesus will hear. He is as close to us as it is possible to be. If we whisper, he will hear it and be part of it. This is true also of our reading of Scripture. The Gospels are, of course, alive with Jesus. Here are his words. Here we see his actions. Paul's epistles too are full of Jesus. He is continually bursting out of them. Paul has an intense awareness of Jesus inside him and that presence of Jesus keeps breaking out in his words. And the Psalms ... these were the words that Jesus himself used. When we pray with the psalms we are using the same prayers Jesus used. That should make them even more alive to us.

Then there is what we monks call the *Opus Dei*, the Work of God. That mostly refers to the times we go to chapel to pray the Office, four, five or six times a day. Sometimes we enjoy it, sometimes we are tired. It is hard work, not recreation. Ideally the whole of the day becomes joined to that Work. Everything we do in the monastery is part of that prayer. Prayer is not a hobby; it's not a form of recreation. It is work and it is a way of life. I think that is true for all of us, not just for monks and nuns. I have said already that prayer is there to serve God, to honour and praise him and to change us to become like him. Prayer also serves the world. We pray for friends and people we know are sick but we also pray for peace in Ukraine, an end to the violence in Gaza and an end to the suffering in the Sudan. That prayer is hard work. We sometimes weep over it. It is hard to sustain this work because often nothing seems to change. We hope our little prayers are somehow alleviating the suffering, maybe bringing a bit of hope into someone's life. We will never have the satisfaction of saying: 'I stopped that war!' Yet every part of our prayer, the praise we offer to God, the confession of our sins, the actual attention we give to the problem all play a part in doing God's work. Don't be surprised if you feel tired after a time of intercession. You have been working hard. It is a great privilege to be able to share this work of God. It is not easy.

As we come towards the end of this chapter I would like to share two sayings that have been of immense importance to my own understanding of prayer. You have probably heard them before but they bear continual repeating.

The first is from Abbot John Chapman: 'Pray as you can; don't try and pray as you can't.'³

It is a great temptation to look around us and see others praying and want to imitate them. Or we read books on prayer and find all sorts of different ways of praying. Should we try them all? Or we read the great spiritual classics and feel inadequate because we are nowhere near being like John of the Cross or Teresa of Avila in our prayer. Well, we are not St John or St Teresa. We are who we are. It is good to talk to others about our prayer. It is good to read books and sometimes it is good to try out new ways of praying. Yet we must always remember that we are each on our own journey with God. He has a particular way for each of us because he knows us. He is leading us and we must trust him. Most of us will use the same basic forms of prayer for years on end. That is fine. People often worry: Am I growing in prayer? Am I growing in Christian life? Real growth is slow, almost imperceptible. Weeds and flowers grow quickly and die. Trees grow very slowly. They may seem not to grow at all for ages but they are putting down strong roots, getting firmer inside. Then we suddenly notice they are bigger. We need to grow slowly and steadily, and trust God to get it right.

My second quotation comes from Alan Ecclestone in *Yes to God*, though I am sure others have said it: 'Prayer does not change God; it changes us.'⁴

There is a lot one could say about this. It doesn't simply mean that God is always right, though he is. It is more that prayer helps us to understand what God is about. We grow in understanding of the situation God is dealing with. When the war in Ukraine started, I expect we all prayed fervently for peace. We still pray for peace but we know now how difficult it is going to be to get peace established there. So much has happened over centuries to poison relations between Russians and Ukrainians. There needs to be reconciliation, not just a cessation of fighting. Stopping the fighting will be difficult without massive involvement from the West, and who knows? That may make it worse. We are caught up in the tragedy that is Ukraine and Russia. Fundamentally it is about sin, on both sides. Violence, power, revenge, jealousy and stupidity are all involved. So are courage, compassion, generosity and Christian love. That is the mixture that war always contains. Our prayer for Ukraine is not simply a prayer for peace, though it is that; it has become a prayer for the whole human condition, including ourselves. We have been changed through our prayer for Ukraine.

In the end, prayer is a journey that takes us to God. Whatever kind of prayer it is, the destination is the same and we shall be changed. We need to remember just how high the stakes are and what a glorious adventure we are engaged in. We are not simply little human beings praying from our little churches or tiny bedrooms. We are children of God who:

> have come to Mount Zion and to the city of the living God, the heavenly Jerusalem, and to innumerable angels in festal gathering, and to the assembly of the first-born who are enrolled in heaven, and to a judge who is God of all, and to the spirits of just men made perfect, and to Jesus, the mediator of a new covenant, and to the sprinkled blood that speaks more graciously than the blood of Abel. (Hebrews 12.22–24 RSV)

That is always true when we pray. That is the company we keep and the place we are called to. It changes us to become what God wants us to be and what we ourselves want to be. For 'our God is a consuming fire' (Hebrews 12.29 NRSV).

Notes

1 Wendy Beckett, 2007, *On Prayer*, London: Bloomsbury.
2 John Dalrymple, 2010, *Simple Prayer*, London: Darton, Longman & Todd, p. 42.
3 John Chapman, 2003 (1935), *Spiritual Letters*, London: Continuum, p. 109.
4 Alan Ecclestone, 1975, *Yes to God*, London: Darton, Longman & Todd.

8

Community

MTHR MITZI JAMES

Nurturing catholic life in the Church of England

> We are essentially social beings, and I am only one part of the reflection of the great mystery of God. We are each of us simply one fingerprint or footprint of God. We are essentially connected with one another. The pattern of the universe is that we are one. (Richard Rohr)[1]

As we navigate the complexities of the changing climate, political, secular and of course Anglican, many of us feel that our catholic voice is getting quieter and quieter; it feels increasingly more important to preserve, cherish and celebrate the rich traditions and spiritual practices that have shaped us and have shaped our shared faith for centuries.

This chapter is a reflection on my experience as a curate and parish priest in North London, in the hope that this set of experience might help all those seeking to live out the catholic life in their local communities, in order to become aware of and foster a sense of community participation and engagement.

Like a lot of people, especially clergy, I know the feeling of imposter syndrome all too well. Even on my best days I can relate to the person who said that they feel they have the theological understanding of a bright 8-year-old. Jesus does say that we need to approach life like children, and the inclusive Anglo-Catholic home where I feel most alive and most at home is a place where I know there is room in our Anglican Communion and Community for all – young, old, gay, trans, cis, straight, black, white, neurodiverse. We might not get on or agree with each other but our community means that we at least see each other.

First, I'd like to explore what it means to embrace catholic life within the Church of England. For me, it is not about division or exclusivity but rather about embracing the fullness of our Anglican heritage. It is about honouring our roots, acknowledging our shared history with the

Catholic Church and recognizing the beauty in our liturgical traditions, sacraments and spiritual disciplines.

When we Catholic Anglicans talk about building a world where all people can achieve justice and fulfil our potential as human beings, we really do mean all people. We share a vision with Dr Martin Luther King for 'beloved community'.

To be a Christian is to recognize that we can't be fully whole unless we also recognize that we are part of wider whole, the Body of Christ, that enables us to realize who we are called to be in community. We each have different gifts that are our contribution to the whole and enable us to flourish as part of the beloved community of humanity and of the Church. The catholic life is in part a journey of discovery of the particular gift we've been given, the particular part of the whole that we are called to be.

Building beloved community is not about loving the people who are easy to love. It is about loving even those who are difficult to love. It is about loving them over there, the others: the people who voted for the opposite party to us in the political elections on Thursday, the people who destroy community as much as those who build it, the people we find it difficult to love. All in the knowledge that such a community of love begins to transform the hearts of those who would tear down and destroy rather than join us as we build up community in love.

A feature of many catholic Anglican churches and communities is acceptance. We are accepted quietly to be as we are in a pew at the back of church in Mass or in the silent prayer of adoration during Benediction. By being accepted and then sustained by catholic faith, we know we are all part of God's beloved community. Or at least we should, even if it is difficult to know in our heart what we might know at an intellectual level in our minds.

Catholic life in community

How do we develop and encourage this move from knowing intellectually that we are all part of this beloved community of the catholic faith to making it a reality in the hearts of those we serve so that they also have this place in beloved community?

First, we need to really know this in our minds through education to enable understanding. Knowledge is the cornerstone of appreciation. We must educate ourselves and our community about the depth and breadth of Catholic traditions within Anglicanism. From studying the writings of the early Church fathers and mothers, reflecting on the liturgy of the Eucharist and by exploring the richness of our spirituality and the spiritual traditions that make up the catholic life.

By embracing the Sacraments (yes, all seven of them ...), we move our understanding from the head knowledge to knowing in our hearts that we are part of this beloved community. The seven Sacraments of the Church are at the heart of the catholic life. By actively participating in the Eucharist, Baptism, Confirmation, Confession, Marriage, Holy Orders, and Anointing of the Sick, we not only strengthen our own faith but also build a deeper sense of community and communion with God and each other. It's for this reason that these sacraments, including marriage and ordination, need to be open to all those called to share in them.

An example of this on a practical level came to me thanks to the restrictions in place during the Covid-19 pandemic, which meant that for a time we could only worship and celebrate the Mass outside. For months I'd passed a homeless man on a bench outside church. I was almost always in my cassock and so a visible reminder of the presence of the Church in my community. This man came from a Roman Catholic background and so had only ever seen male priests; one day he called me over to settle an argument. He wanted me to confirm to his friend that I was a Roman Catholic priest, even though I am a woman! My new friend of course lost his bet but we struck up a friendship and I told him that they were both welcome to attend Mass at any time.

It was during those outside Masses that the circle of our community was drawn more widely. Suddenly my homeless friend on the bench was more clearly part of our beloved and worshipping community, even as he remained on his bench. It was about six months later, at Easter, when my friend, with tears in his eyes and hands outstretched, walked up the path and back into that community to receive communion – a very visible sign that this person who wanted to remain outside was just as much a part of our beloved community as those of us who have been longing to return inside our church buildings and to the normality of our worship outside the conditions of the pandemic.

Reflecting on our liturgical practice enables us to better communicate our beliefs and values. Embracing a sacramental approach to worship can help nourish the spiritual lives of our congregations. Ritual can speak powerfully to those who might not speak our language or understand the language of sermons and Christian teaching. The use of incense and vestments engages all of the senses to communicate what we believe as catholic Christians.

While how we worship engages those inside our congregations, community engagement enables our catholic life to extend beyond the walls of the church. It encompasses how we live out our faith in our daily lives and interact with the world around us. Encouraging acts of charity, social justice and pastoral care within our community fosters a spirit of compassion and service reflective of catholic values.

One of the ways in which we demonstrate this vision for beloved community is how we are visible reminders of Christian presence. For clergy this means we're seen in our community in our cassocks and our clerical collars. For others it can mean wearing a cross or a crucifix, or being known for having a community presence because of and not despite our catholic faith, as an act of catholic witness. Where I was formed for priesthood at the College of the Resurrection in Mirfield, one of our distinctive approaches to formation for ministry was that we always wore cassocks for worship and meals – two important tables. For some visitors to the college this was tantamount to 'swanning about in our cassocks', but it was in fact a valuable reminder of the importance of visibility in community. When riots broke out in London in 2011, Bishop Rob Wickham has spoken about how, because he lived right in the midst of the riots, he needed to be with his community and so he rushed to put on his cassock precisely because he needed to be a visible presence in the midst of an unfolding situation. This was such an instinct of community presence, and he was in so much of a rush that he forgot that he was still wearing a pair of crocs!

This visibility through our distinctive clothing and insignia enables us to serve our community in this ministry of presence. It can be our badge of Christian presence in community, our uniform. It can sometimes feel like a protective armour in the midst of difficult community situations but it can also make us vulnerable. Visibility is an important act of witness but can leave us vulnerable to the hostility that often accompanies Christian witness.

This confidence in our catholic witness in community enables us to celebrate our catholic heritage even as we also recognize the diversity within our wider Church of England family. Embracing different expressions of faith and theological perspective enriches our spiritual journey and strengthens our bond as a community united in Christ.

Our confidence in catholic witness enables all of us, both lay and ordained, to be leaders in our communities. Through embodying the values of humility, reverence and devotion, catholic Christians in their everyday lives set examples for others to follow. They live out an attractive vision of the catholic life so that that those we encounter just have to find out more. Encouraging congregational involvement in liturgical ministries is a vital part of developing the visibility and confidence of lay leadership in catholic witness. Regular spiritual formation programmes can further cultivate a vibrant catholic identity within our community.

The presence of each and every person called to lead in whatever capacity is an essential part of beloved community. One of the reasons I was attracted to the College of the Resurrection was that the importance of daily prayer was instilled in those training for priesthood. I'd visited another seminary and was told on the open day that if it came to your tutor's knowledge that you had missed morning prayer, you would get an email asking why you weren't there. At Mirfield we were told that if we missed morning prayer it mattered, not because we would be disciplined but because if we weren't there the worshipping assembly would be poorer, because our voice, even a voice as terrible as mine, would be missing. We would be missed. This to me sums up beloved community – each of us has our valued place. Each of us has a voice to be heard.

The College of the Resurrection is a theological college set alongside a monastic community, the Community of the Resurrection. This community is in the Benedictine tradition of catholic spirituality, with its special focus on hospitality. This is often seen in the two tables: the altar of the Eucharist and the table of dining and fellowship. During the pandemic this hospitality was made real on the first day of lockdown when one of the brothers came into the common room with a tray of scones that he'd baked for us, not only nourishment for the body but a very visible witness to the value of hospitality in that community.

Monastic community is one of way of living out the catholic call to beloved community. One of the brothers at Mirfield spoke of his deep love of Christ, his deepest desire to be a faithful Christian. He was also completely honest about the fact that he had tried to live out his love for Christ in the world but found it too hard. For him, his vocation to beloved community took him into a monastic community as the crucible to live out his love for Christ. For others of us, we are called into our local communities to live out the same life. I found his honesty refreshing as he recognized how hard it is to live out this call. It can be just as hard in monastic community as in our local communities.

We shouldn't kid ourselves that living in beloved community is easy. It's so much easier to pray for people we love and like. I also know that living in community is incredibly challenging but also incredibly lifegiving. Here, the Sacrament of Reconciliation can be unbelievably important. Being honest in Confession about those we struggle to like or love, those we really struggle to get along with, can help us in the fostering of beloved community that is our call. One Confessor taught me that resentment, hatred and being unforgiving is like drinking poison and waiting for the other person to die. Being honest about our resentment, even our hatred, and where we struggle to forgive is a path to life. Living in the College of the Resurrection alongside the Community taught me to pray not just for those I wanted to pray for or felt compelled to pray for but, as the CR brethren pray every evening, for all those for whom I ought to pray, all members of our community.

Community engagement

Community engagement plays a fundamental role in shaping and sustaining catholic identity within the Church of England. Catholic parishes have traditionally been very strong on matters of social justice and advocacy. This does not only refer to activities of service or outreach, such as food banks or warm spaces. While these may have an important part to play there's also a significant place for catholic spiritual practice that is open to the presence of those who may be new, or even initially averse, to Christian faith.

Community involvement provides opportunities for individuals to participate in shared worship experiences such as the Eucharist, liturgical celebrations and communal prayer. Through these shared practices, individuals develop a sense of belonging and connection to the broader Catholic tradition of Anglicanism.

Catholic practices such as silence or adoration before the Blessed Sacrament can be gateways into beloved community for those who are new or even hostile to the faith. I've begun to offer a space for silent prayer before the weekly evening Eucharist and it is very well attended by people I have never seen in church before. Offering our community the opportunity to rest, particularly to rest in God in the Sacrament, and with no demand on their time, is I think one of our catholic superpowers.

I am sure you too have noticed or experienced the overwhelming demand on our time from all corners. This, I think, is just part of living in the kind of capitalistic age that we live in, one in which we are endlessly invited to accelerate – accelerate to do more, take on more. But we have very few criteria by which to evaluate what is worthy of our time or how much time to spend, and so everything that presents itself has some level of appeal, whether it's being fit and exercising through to eating a certain way through to the way we spend our time with family and friends and in cultural enrichment. We in the church are competing with all this and with all the opportunities for self-development. In such a world, being known as one of the few places for silence and rest can be a means to community engagement. It's also important for us to notice in ourselves. What if we started our community involvement not by doing more but by stopping, taking time instead to listen to our communities?

Listening is the key building block of community organizing. In the tradition of community organizing exemplified by Saul Alinsky and nurtured in catholic communities in America and other European contexts, one of the golden rules is that institutions have 'no permanent friends' and 'no permanent enemies'. Something community organizing challenges us to do is to ask: Who exactly is our community?

One of the features of catholic Anglican life is our ability to embrace an expansive vision of beloved community. Anglican Catholicism embraces individuals from diverse backgrounds who come together as a unified community around the altar. In beloved community, differences are transcended by embracing a shared catholic identity that encompasses a diversity of backgrounds: from those who have had a difficult experience of other forms of Christianity to those who have been fed by other forms of catholic Christianity outside the Church of England. Our welcome and vision for beloved community in progressive Anglo-Catholicism means that many people are in our communities because they are sure of our welcome to women and members of the LGBTQIA+ community and others who have found in us a place of sacred belonging in our model of beloved community.

Who is your community? If you're called to the prophetic task of living out the catholic life in the Church of England, this question is vital. Not just the beloved community in which you are challenged to play your part, but who is the community that will feed you, support you, and guide you and help you find your own sacred place of belonging?

In conclusion, fostering catholic life within the Church of England is not about finding a new supplier of Rosa Mystica incense or how many inches of lace one wears (however much I like it) or imposing rigid dogma or stifling innovation. It is about embracing the fullness of our Anglican tradition, rooted in the ancient faith and guided by the Holy Spirit. By nurturing a deep sense of reverence, devotion and community, we can ensure that the flame of catholic life continues to burn brightly in our midst, illuminating our path towards God.

O God and Father of us all, you send labourers into your vineyard: set on fire many hearts with a sense of their vocation and with an eager response to your call. To those whom you have gathered at the College of the Resurrection give grace to prepare in all earnestness and zeal, that with entire concentration of heart and life they may labour hereafter in your holy Church, through Jesus Christ our Lord, who lives and reigns with you and the Holy Spirit, one God, now and for ever. (The prayer of the College of the Resurrection, Mirfield)

Notes

1 Richard Rohr, 2022, 'Humanity is a Community: The Embodiment of God', *Center for Action and Contemplation*, 7 July, https://cac.org/daily-meditations/the-embodiment-of-god-2022-07-07/ (accessed 4.07.2024).

Sermon

'The Love of God Lived Out'

Preached at the funeral of Fr Michael Farthing
(29 February 1928–28 December 2019),
St Mary Magdalen, Oxford on 16 January 2020[1]

Fr Peter Groves

Anglicans are apt to enjoy nostalgia, and Anglo-Catholics particularly so. In a city as churchy as Oxford it's all too easy to reach across the generations with tales of the great men and women who have lived and served the Christian faith and whose lives were closely bound up with this city and this county. Here in St Mary Magdalen's, which dates back a thousand years and has lived through most of the upheavals of English Christianity, it's hard to be unaware of the past. But it's also essential to learn from it and not simply to shrug one's shoulders and sigh that the days are gone when there were giants in the land.

Of the many words one might use to describe Michael, giant would not come very high on the list. I remember well a previous requiem Mass in which we both participated – I felt the lovely black vestments were a little too long for me, but poor old Michael was practically at the stage of having to hitch up his skirts for fear of tripping over the sanctuary step. When I was licensed to this parish as priest in charge, I had several assisting colleagues who were well over six feet and towered over me at the high Mass. It was nice, from time to time, to have a deacon who made everything look in proportion, even if those proportions were pretty tiny.

But of course, in another sense Michael was a giant, and a giant of the Lord's own making. More than 60 years of priesthood, and a Christian life dating back to his infancy, saw him grow not just in faith and in years but in the wisdom of the gospel that comes only with practice, with doing, the essential experience of living out the love of Christ in Christian ministry, for which there is no possible substitute. As many of you know, we liked to tease Michael about his date of birth – 29

February 1928. In 2012, he celebrated his 21st birthday having been 84 years upon this earth. But that paradox, most ingenious as W. S. Gilbert calls it, came for me to reflect something essential about the priest who was known and loved in this place as in so many places before: his years, his knowledge and his experience were close to unrivalled, but his kindness, his generosity and his commitment remained always youthful because they were the outworking in his own life and person of the love of God which is eternally new.

Michael came to Christian ministry from an existing life of service, having joined the Royal Navy in the immediate aftermath of the Second World War when global and political uncertainty continued to dominate. He spoke of the importance of his naval chaplains and the discipline of prayer in the formation of his own vocation. He went to Durham to study and then came to Oxford to be trained under one of those aforementioned giants in the land, the great Fr Arthur Couratin of St Stephen's House. Serving his curacy at St Mark's in Marylebone he met a young member of the choir named Jennifer Woods, and the rest was history. Apart from that first parish, the whole of Michael's ministry was spent in this diocese of Oxford – Newport Pagnell, Standlake, Lower Windrush, Wheatley – and then at the Cathedral, and here at Mary Mags, and St Cross and countless other parishes and communities that benefited from his care and generosity. The memories we treasure today, of a loving husband and father and grandfather, of a priest and pastor and teacher, of a friend and colleague and mentor, are a part of our tribute to someone who gave so much to so many. Personally, I will always be tremendously grateful for his gentle wisdom and support, offered 15 years ago to a young and very inexperienced priest in charge: Michael never imposed anything, but his guiding hand, often almost unnoticed, saved me from many of the pitfalls of that inexperience. His and Jenny's friendship to everyone here, and especially to my children to whom they are second grandparents, is a gift that carries on giving in our thoughts and in our hearts.

But there is much more than memory to celebrate. It would be easy to say that they don't make them like they used to. Michael represents a generation in the life of our country, as well as in the life of our Church, to which we all owe an enormous amount. The exemplary model of priesthood he displayed has been an inspiration to younger clergy and ordinands literally for decades, and how fitting it is that the first woman to serve as a bishop in our diocese was guided and nurtured in her vocation by Michael more than 30 years ago. The world he knew and in which he ministered is in some ways distant from us, and we might mourn for a time when the Church's face and presence in the communities of our country was personified by Michael and his ilk. But at the same time, nothing is lost, because the faith Michael lived and taught is a faith for the here and now, a gospel of love and of hope that transcends the rose-tinted visions we are so ready to conjure. No matter how keen we are to look back, the truth remains that there is nothing nostalgic about the love of God, nothing old-fashioned about his grace and presence in our lives.

That grace and that love were not just the reason for Michael's ministry, they were the very content of that ministry. Christianity does not call us away from the world to a remote and distant heaven, it proclaims the good news of heaven on earth, it celebrates the God who is with us in the child of Bethlehem and the preacher and healer from Nazareth. Everything Michael did as a priest – every Mass celebrated, every sermon preached, every baby baptized, every couple married, every sick person anointed, every lonely person visited, every child affirmed and taught, every parishioner supported and upheld, every hospital ward attended, every deathbed sat beside, every soul commended to God, every mourning family comforted – every one of these things is nothing other than the love of God lived out in our world and in our lives, lived out in the ministry of the Church which is the Body of Christ, and through the sacred order of the priesthood to which Michael was called more than 60 years ago.

As we celebrate God's love in the life of our departed brother we are marking the end of a life. But we are also celebrating the end of a life, not in the sense of termination but end in the sense of purpose or goal. Michael's life was directed by, and directed towards, the love of Father, Son and Holy Spirit. The Easter faith Michael proclaimed sustains and assures us that if there is an end of things, it is only the end, the goal, of the love that will not be contained and bursts the realms of emptiness and death. The Hebrew name Michael means: Who is like God? The answer was Michael's whole life.

Notes

1 Fr Michael Farthing was Vicar of Wheatley for 13 years before retiring in 1996. He inspired a generation of women and men to discern their vocation (including more than one author of this volume), both in his time as parish priest and in retirement as a member of the congregation at St Mary Magdalen's in Oxford.

9

Baptism

MTHR CHRISTINA BEARDSLEY SMMS

'It joined us together, the well.'[1]

Catechumenate and catechesis in Catholic life today

The earliest known Christian baptistry, at Dura Europos in eastern Syria, dates from the third century AD. Among its wall paintings is the image of a woman, arms stretched downward, hands gripping a thick black rope hanging into a well.[2] Formerly identified as the Samaritan woman, recent scholarship argues it is an Annunciation scene.[3] Either way, for that early Christian congregation the symbol of a well conveyed the significance of baptismal water for life in the Spirit, making the meeting of Jesus and the Samaritan woman an apt place to begin this chapter on baptism.

In baptism the new Christian encounters the Living Water, Jesus Christ, and through Christ, 'the ocean of light which is the Trinity'.[4] Baptismal waters – poured over candidates or into which they are plunged – are no drop in a bucket. They are more like a fountain – in Latin *fons*, from which the word 'font' derives – an outward sign of a spring, welling up to eternal life: the inward grace of participation in the life of the Blessed Trinity; fullness of life in the Spirit.

Jesus' conversation at a well is also a good starting point because what has emerged in researching this chapter is the importance of the catechumenate, both accompaniment and catechesis, when preparing adults for baptism; the focus of this chapter is mainly adults. Jesus' encounter with the Samaritan woman at the well is a masterclass in catechesis, which is from the Greek word for 'to echo' or 'to resound'; in this instance, learning to echo 'the teaching and life of Jesus'.[5] Initially, Jesus and the Samaritan woman talk at cross-purposes – the echo delayed – but Jesus is alongside and the woman puts questions, which good catechesis encourages. Initially she fixates on the prosaic, like the well's depth. Deeper than any cistern, Jesus' words, which offer Living Water, the life of God, find an echo in her heart.

'A spring of water welling up to eternal life' (John 4.14 RSV)

In the Catholic Church's catechumenate liturgies, the *Rite of Christian Initiation of Adults* (RCIA), the encounter between Jesus and the Samaritan woman, recorded in John 4.5–42, is mandatory as the Gospel at Sunday Mass when the First Scrutiny is celebrated with those elected and enrolled for baptism at Easter.[6] The time of instruction, or catechumenate proper, complete, this liturgy marks a more intense stage of initiation. 'Scrutiny' here assumes openness to God, who searches and knows us (Psalm 139.1). The three scrutinies, for use at Sunday Mass on the Third, Fourth and Fifth Sundays of Lent, 'complete the conversion' of those to be baptized. Their aim is 'purification and enlightenment'.[7] The scrutinies remind Sunday Mass congregations that their baptismal calling includes further accompaniment of the baptism candidates on the next stage of their Christian pilgrimage and, if their own love for God or neighbour has grown cold, that they too should seek conversion by the Holy Spirit.

Since 2006, *Common Worship: Christian Initiation* has provided similar texts, called, 'Rites Supporting Disciples on the Way of Christ', which are also appropriate for those preparing for confirmation or reaffirming their baptismal faith.[8] Yet a decade later, Simon Jones noted that 'very few communities seem to make use of this catechetical material published in *Christian Initiation*.'[9] Presumably this is because the catechumenate model isn't normative in Church of England parishes, even catholic ones, as RCIA is in the Catholic Church. Although Church of England liturgical scholars have admired RCIA, they've tended to avoid traditional terms like 'catechumen' or even exorcism, believing that they could be a barrier.[10] Their preferred image of 'the Way' is biblical and attractive, but not engaging with this richer, archaic language risks losing depth of meaning. Language about baptism, especially its poetry, is discussed below.

RCIA and *Common Worship* are agreed, though, that Christian Initiation must be understood in terms of evangelization or mission. RCIA describes the catechumenate as the revival of an 'ancient practice of the Church' in a form 'suited to contemporary missionary activity'.[11] Belonging to 'a community whose *mission* is to serve God's Spirit in redeeming the world' is step four of the Church of England Liturgical Commission's four-stage theological framework for baptism.[12] This is the Samaritan woman's experience when, carrying Living Water to her neighbourhood, the message re-echoes in response to her catechesis, drawing others into the ocean of God's love.

Modern catholic memory: First Communion 2018

What happened that Thursday night has stayed with me: a First Communion Mass at my local parish church on the Feast of Corpus Christi 2018. The building crowded with 90 children and their immediate and extended families. The girls in party or bridesmaids' dresses, the boys in crisp white shirts. Go-pack tables laden with food, rapidly consumed after Mass, with the parish priest and myself left alone to clear the debris into black plastic bin bags.

Modern Catholic in ethos, the evening felt more Roman than Anglican. Partly due to the social demographic: as if we were in an episode of *Broken*, the fictional television drama about a northern Roman Catholic parish, broadcast at the time. Partly because First Communion is a long-established Roman Catholic tradition, though now widely adopted by catholics and others in the Church of England, previous Anglican practice having been admission to Communion following confirmation administered by a bishop.

It would be mistaken to think that the switch from confirmation to First Communion for children has undermined Christian Initiation of the young in today's Church. The admission of children to Communion, based on their baptism, has gained traction precisely because the theological understanding of baptism has changed. Over the last 30 years or so, a growing consensus has emerged that baptism is the primary sacrament of Christian Initiation.[13] No longer in need of 'completion' by confirmation, which is increasingly understood as akin to a pastoral rite or a commissioning, baptism is now regarded as the sacrament of full membership of the Body of Christ, and hence admission to Holy Communion may follow immediately. Insight into the life-long overflowing fullness of Baptism has given further theological justification for admitting young children to Holy Communion. Already established in Anglican churches – it was introduced in my local, West London parish in 1986 – the practice has become increasingly popular as the understanding of baptism has developed.

That 2018 First Communion, based on close liaison with the parish school, had strong baptismal associations:

- The white garments, favoured by children at First Communion, connect tangibly with 'the clothing' at baptism: a semi-conscious re-donning of the Christening robe, reminiscent of the *albae* or white garments worn for eight days by the newly baptized in the early Church.
- Children making their First Communion receive catechesis or instruction beforehand. In our parish this has lasted for up to a year, with further instruction following the rite of admission: a pattern reminiscent of the early Church's pre-baptismal catechesis and post-baptismal mystagogy – meaning leading into the mystery (of God) – 'from two Greek words (*mystes* and *agogos*) signifying that a guide will become an initiator of the catechumens'.[14]
- Lay people share in preparing children for First Communion, but holding the ceremony on a Thursday evening (albeit Corpus Christi) rather than a Sunday, like leaving the clergy to tidy up afterwards, indicated lack of congregational engagement with Christian nurture of the young. Renewed appreciation that accompaniment belongs to the baptismal calling of all God's People's should help address that.

Plumbing and poetry

According to the leadership theorist James March, 'Leadership involves plumbing as well as poetry.'[15] The same is true of baptism. Plumbing in terms of sourcing water – river, sea, pool or font. Poetry in terms of the rite, the prayers said over the water and over the candidates. In classical theological terms, the 'plumbing', or water, constitutes 'the matter' of the sacrament of baptism, and the 'poetry', or words – specifically, 'I baptize you N, in the name of the Father, and of the Son, and of the Holy Spirit' – 'the form'.

Architectural history illustrates how the poetry of Christian iconography has inspired richly decorated baptisteries and fonts. Whatever its decoration, and however awkward its location might seem liturgically, the church's font will usually be preferable to a portable font, which can become a practical hazard. This is not simply aesthetics. How and where baptism is celebrated has theological resonance. Just as we honour the altar as the locus of Christ's eucharistic presence, so the font should be honoured as the place not simply of our initial incorporation into Christ but of its life-long effects. Fortunately, Catholic liturgy offers the eucharistic community frequent poetic reminders of their baptismal calling: holy water stoups at the door for signing oneself with the sign of the cross, and sprinkling with water at the start of Mass as *Asperges* or *Vidi aquam* are sung. Reordering can also be an opportunity: the Cantharus installed in the Community of the Resurrection's Church, Mirfield, is both a fountain for sprinkling and a total-immersion font.

'Like a mighty flood'

Working in the Portsmouth Diocese when Bishop David Stancliffe was Cathedral Provost (1982–93) helped me to appreciate the significance of baptismal plumbing and poetry. As a member (from 1986), and later Chair (1993–2005) of the Church of England's Liturgical Commission, David shared widely the theological and liturgical principles underlying the completion of Portsmouth Cathedral, especially in relation to baptism. Today the west end of Portsmouth Cathedral is a light, broad space: a giant narthex, symbolically a place of enquiry, approach, preparation and ultimately, if appropriate, decision for Christ. The font, specially designed for the reordered cathedral, stands at the heart of the building, under the central tower, which provides a womb-like sense of enclosure befitting a site of spiritual rebirth. Based on a ninth-century Greek design, and cruciform, the Portsmouth Cathedral font also resembles a coffin, both shapes being powerful reminders that baptism immerses us into Christ's death before raising us to life with him.

The Portsmouth Cathedral font is large enough to stand or sit in, like 'a bath', a term applied to baptism in early Christianity. Bathing or washing facilities were common in private houses and public buildings and easily adapted for baptism, as at Dura Europos. The Portsmouth font, which can hold 'a substantial amount of water' as recommended by *Common Worship*,[16] is a striking and poetic piece of plumbing!

Once dried with towels, the newly baptized emerge from the shelter of the baptistery into the brightness of the quire, to continue their journey, with other members of God's People, to the altar, situated in the Sanctuary beyond, to which they'll return, often, to be sustained on their Christian pilgrimage.

Poetry in motion

Two churches I'm acquainted with have moved their fonts east, to create useful social space at the west end of their buildings. One font is situated south of a nave altar. These relocated fonts afford maximum visibility to a seated congregation but undermine the symbolism of a pilgrim people on the move. Yet this liturgical accompaniment of baptismal candidates should also reflect the role of sponsors who are willing to 'walk' with enquirers, both before and after their initiation. As Larry Chapp writes, many 'people ... come to the faith because they have established an open and honest relationship, even friendship, with a serious person of faith who was willing to engage them in the full depth of their humanity'.[17]

'A forest of symbols'?

The *Common Worship* baptism liturgy deliberately drew on 'the enormous variety' of New Testament imagery 'to illustrate the richness of all that God gives us through the sacrament'.[18] Some of these additional themes include liberation, recognition, new birth and building.[19] Simon Jones considers this range of images 'one of the new rite's great strengths, but also its principal weakness', in that it led to a call for alternative accessible-language texts.[20] These are concerns that Jones thinks came mainly from clergy, as parents surveyed by the Baptism Project seemed not to share them.

An explosion of imagery about baptism is true of tradition, as well as Scripture, like this wonderful patristic passage from *Oratio* 40, 3–4 by St Gregory Nazianzus:

> Baptism is God's most beautiful and magnificent gift ... We call it gift, grace, anointing, enlightenment, garment of immortality, bath of rebirth, seal and most precious gift. It is called *gift* because it is conferred on those who bring nothing of their own; *grace* since it is given even to the guilty; *Baptism* because sin is buried in the water; *anointing* for it is priestly and royal as are those who are anointed; *enlightenment* because it radiates light; *clothing* since it veils our shame; *bath* because it washes; and *seal* as it is our guard and the sign of God's Lordship.[21]

A 'forest of symbols' on this scale is an opportunity, surely, rather than a problem. A treasure trove to be explored in catechesis, and after baptism, but not during the service!

Pusey, Patristics and poetry

It ought to excite Catholic Anglicans that the Oxford Movement leader Edward Bouverie Pusey (1800–82) was a pioneer of the modern reassessment of baptismal theology. Pusey's *Tracts for the Times* on baptism demonstrate extensive knowledge of patristic theology and empathy with its typological approach to biblical texts. For example, Pusey notes how the Fathers understood water and Spirit not only in reference to baptism, but 'regarded them as a sort of key to the rest of Holy Scripture, which any way bore upon the same subjects'.[22]

As Pusey's contemporary J. B. Mozley observed: 'There was wanted a restoration of the doctrine of Baptism. ... the whole current language about it had to be deepened and enriched; a whole sentiment ... awakened. Dr Pusey did this' and was suited to the task as one 'instinctively at home' in the 'deep and powerful' writings of the Fathers, baptism being the subject 'which brings out all that holy poetry which so peculiarly belongs to them'.[23]

Pusey writes of 'the warm undefined language of the Eastern Churches', giving as his examples being 'made a member of Christ, the child of God, and an inheritor of the kingdom of heaven'.[24] This suggests that he preferred it to the Augustinian understanding of Baptism in which we are 'by nature born in sin, and the children of wrath, we are hereby (by the spiritual grace of Baptism) made the children of grace'.[25] He does however acknowledge that context shaped these different emphases. Drawn to the Eastern doctrine of *theosis*, the 'overwhelming mystery' expressed by the early Church as 'our being "Christophori", "Theophori" [Christ-bearers; or God-bearers]',[26] nevertheless Alf Härdelin thinks 'Pusey ... at least laid the foundation of what we could call a paschal spirituality.'[27]

The Paschal Mystery

The 'strong Western tradition' of participation in the Paschal Mystery through baptism and Eucharist has tended to eclipse a 'broader and more complex range of images, including ... new birth by water and the Spirit within the new creation',[28] which Pusey also favoured. Yet it was precisely Pusey's pastorally sensitive handling of Patristic texts that anticipated the *ressourcement* ('return to the sources') theology of the early twentieth century, which informed both the Liturgical Movement and the Second Vatican Council, radically altering catholic thought and practice, especially in relation to Christian Initiation.

Pusey's tracts had set out to demonstrate that Baptismal Regeneration (or rebirth) was the Scriptural, Patristic and Church of England understanding of baptism; regeneration being – in words quoted by Pusey's biographers – 'the act by which God takes us out of our relation to

Adam and makes us actual members of His Son'.[29] A similar focus on God's activity appears in *The Paschal Mystery* by Louis Bouyer, in a sentence that neatly encapsulates the essence of Mystery theology: 'The Christian religion is not simply a doctrine: it is a fact, an action, and an action not of the past, but of the present, where the past is recovered and the future draws near.'[30]

This dynamic Paschal theology, embracing Christ's risen glory as well as his death and passion, is key to the liturgy according to the *Catechism of the Catholic Church*: 'Christ ... acts through the sacraments in what the common Tradition of the East and the West calls "the sacramental economy"; this is the communication (or "dispensation") of the fruits of Christ's Paschal mystery in the celebration of the Church's "sacramental" liturgy.'[31]

Later Catholic Anglicans, like Dom Gregory Dix and A. G. Hebert, were significant players in the Liturgical Movement. Hebert's *Liturgy and Society* (1935) was particularly influential, with its emphasis on Christian worship's power to transform the social order as well as individuals. In this he was influenced by the nineteenth-century Church of England theologian F. D. Maurice, for whom baptism signified that Christ was the Head of every person, and thus that all deserve respect. A supporter of workers' co-operatives, as well as education for the working class and for women, Maurice embodied the sociological implications of his baptismal theology.

Reinvigoration of the Church's communal life, and its agency in the world as the Body of Christ, was an important aspect, among others, of the theological, liturgical, sacramental and ecclesiological transformation of Catholicism in the twentieth century. The outcome of a remarkable confluence, this holistic catholic vision invites a faith response to God at work in the Paschal Mystery. As Aidan Kavanagh explains,[32] RCIA's norm of baptism:

> rests on the economic principle that baptism is inadequately perceptible apart from the eucharist; that the eucharist is not wholly knowable without reference to conversion in faith; that conversion is abortive if it does not issue in sacramental illumination by incorporation into the Church; that the Church is only an inept corporation without steady access to Sunday, Lent, and the Easter Vigil; that evangelization is mere noise and catechesis only a syllabus apart from conversion and initiation into a robust ecclesial environment of faith shared.

Easter Vigil 2024

Preaching at this year's Easer Vigil, I was energized by my preparatory reading for this chapter. Such was the *Constitution on the Sacred Liturgy, Sacrosanctum Concilium*, which pictures baptism as being 'plunged into the paschal mystery of Christ'.[33] Or, more recently, Peter Waddell, for whom baptism involves being 'immersed in joy'.[34] Taking up the theme of the Triduum as an immersive experience, I observed:

> Immersion is a core element of this Vigil because we journey to the font, the place of baptism, which means immersing ... But tonight something, or rather, someone, is missing ... where are the candidates for baptism? In the early centuries of the Church ... the catechumens, who'd been instructed in the faith for up to three years, were baptized at this or the Pentecost Vigil. The whole Church was involved in their preparation, as catechists or as sponsors. Baptism was immersive and renewing, for everyone, not just the candidates.

Next morning, on social media, the Bishop of London shared how, that same evening, at the Easter Vigil at St Paul's Cathedral, she had baptized 22 candidates and confirmed 101 people. No shortage of candidates there; but in many parishes the number of adults preparing for baptism is low, perhaps because baptism's missionary dynamic, and how the catechumenate, catechesis and sponsorship relate to that, is under-appreciated. Yet there it is in the Great Commission, where the Risen Christ instructs his disciples to 'make disciples of all nations, baptizing them in the name of the Father and of the Son and of the Holy Spirit, teaching them to observe all that I have commanded you' (Matthew 28.19–20a RSV). Here, discipleship or learning call for catechesis or teaching, with both integral, along with the ethical and the social ('all that I have commanded you'), to Christ's mission through the Church – mentoring and teaching, like the call to holiness, being open to every Christian via the catechumenate in which sponsors have such a significant role. To quote Larry Chapp: 'Evangelization is a relational act between persons of equal dignity who are engaged in that most human of activities: a conversation.'[35]

A Facebook question about catechesis

Prior to Easter 2024, a young Roman Catholic layman posted on Facebook that he was leading the RCIA programme in his parish and asked about the kind of adult catechesis being offered in Church of England parishes. A Church of England layman, a liturgist, replied, including a link to the 'Commentary by the Liturgical Commission' that concludes *Common Worship: Christian Initiation*.[36] The Commentary emphasizes the importance of the 'catechumenal process', citing the 1995 report *On the Way*, whose principal author, it is now known, was the late Michael Vasey.[37] It appears that Vasey's untimely death in 1998 stalled promotion of the catechumenate within the Church of England.

However, the RCIA catechist on Facebook was interested in the content of Anglican catechesis rather than the rites. What were Church of England enquirers being taught about the Christian faith, and by whom? Simon Jones has expressed the hope 'that the widespread use of the Church of England's adult discipleship course Pilgrim ... will encourage fresh interest in a catechumenal approach to initiation'.[38] The Pilgrim course offers a catechumenal approach to initiation, covering Doctrine, Spirituality, Ethics and Lifestyle, and does stress the importance of connecting catechetical groups with the wider congregation by means of the *Common Worship: Christian Initiation* rites.[39]

Adult catechesis has a higher priority and has been better resourced in the Roman Catholic Church than in the Church of England, including among Catholic Anglicans. When I was a healthcare chaplain, one of my Roman Catholic colleagues, also part-time in a parish, assumed oversight of its RCIA programme in succession to the parish Sister. He immediately received a pay rise and a larger office in recognition of this responsibility in parish life. To be fair, RCIA was promulgated in 1972, so the catechumenate model has had half a century to embed in the Catholic Church, with the *Catechism of the Catholic Church* available since 1994 as a comprehensive teaching resource. There is growing convergence though. Like RCIA and early Christian practice, the *Common Worship* rites envisage a liturgical handing over of the Apostles' Creed and the Lord's Prayer to candidates for prayer, study and reflection. The *Catechism of the Catholic Church* – referenced in Pilgrim – discusses both texts, as does Pilgrim. *Common Worship* also suggests handing over Our Lord's Summary of the Law and the Beatitudes, recommended in *On the Way*.[40]

Yet as Kavanagh warns, catechesis is reduced to a syllabus if disconnected from conversion and initiation into the faith community.

'Faith Shared'

In the mid-1980s I had a colleague whose enthusiasm for the catechumenate emerged when a young single mum requested baptism. Sponsors were arranged to accompany her on the journey, a 'welcome and nurture group' convened where she could grow in faith, and a spirituality group established for post-baptismal formation. Sadly, this vision didn't long survive my colleague's move to another parish because, as a staff team, we were unfamiliar with the catechumenate model and soon fell back into established patterns like confirmation preparation.

Forty years on such regression would be inexcusable. The theology of baptism reinvigorated, and the catechumenate restored to its place in the Church's mission, this catholic vision of Christian Initiation is compelling.

I loved it then for its single-minded commitment to those coming to faith; in the words of Megan Mckenna, that 'the *only* priority, the primary symbol and the place of transformation is their person and the communities that embrace them.'[41]

I love it even more now that evangelization is seen to entail 'a catechesis for justice'; as the USCCB *National Directory for Catechesis* puts it: 'Our faith in the sovereignty of God and the destiny of the human person compels us to work for justice, to serve those in need, to seek peace, and to defend the life, dignity and rights of every person.'[42]

This prompts me to end, as I began, with the woman at the well. Compared with the Church of England's agonizing over identity, sexuality, relationships and marriage, Jesus is matter of fact and unfazed by the Samaritan woman's 'lifestyle' (John 4.17–18), which in no way inhibits her from evangelizing her own community. Michael Vasey articulated something similar in *On the Way*, based no doubt on personal experience: I once heard him say, 'I have Jewish heritage, I'm disabled and I'm gay – I'm stuffed!' This is the passage:

> Great care needs to be taken over the handling of particular moral issues that may arise during initiation ... A catechetical process that fails to respect the conscience of individuals or attempts an over-rigid moral formation risks damaging the individual. It also risks making the Church culturally and socially monochrome: one of the potential strengths of catechumenal approaches lies precisely in its capacity to help the Church respect the diversity and particularity of those coming to faith.[43]

Here is another reason, along with those already outlined, to commend the catechumenate model of Christian Initiation as well suited to catholic life in the Church today.

Notes

1 Pope St John Paul II (Karol Wojtyla), 1980, 'The Samaritan Woman', in Jerzy Peterkiewicz (trans.), *Easter Vigil and Other Poems*, London: Arrow Books, p. 19.

2 Everett Ferguson, 2009, *Baptism in the Early Church: History, Theology, and Liturgy in the First Five Centuries*, Cambridge: Eerdmans, pp. 441–2; André Grabar, 1986, *Christian Iconography: A Study of its Origins*, Princeton, NJ: Princeton University Press, Plate 42.

3 Mike Cummings, 2016, 'Yale Art Gallery Painting might be Oldest Known Image of the Virgin Mary', *YaleNews*, 12 February, available at: https://news.yale.edu/2016/02/12/yale-art-gallery-painting-might-be-oldest-known-image-virgin-mary, accessed 25.03.2024.

4 Pope St John Paul II, 'Letter of the Holy Father Pope John Paul II to Priests for Holy Thursday 1998', 7, available at: https://www.vatican.va/content/john-paul-ii/en/letters/1998/documents/hf_jp-ii_let_31031998_priests.html, accessed 22.07.2024.

5 Jennifer Strawbridge, 2019, 'Making Christians and Lifelong Catechesis', in Steven Croft (ed.), *Rooted and Grounded: Faith Formation and the Christian Tradition*, Norwich: Canterbury Press, p. 52.

6 International Commission on English in the Liturgy: A Joint Commission of Catholic Bishops' Conferences, 1987, *Rite of Christian Initiation of Adults. Approved for use in the Dioceses of England and Wales, Scotland*, London: Geoffrey Chapman, p. 73; 1984, *The Sunday Missal, A New Edition*, London: Collins, pp. 527 and 736.

7 *Rite of Christian Initiation of Adults*, p. 70.

8 Archbishops' Council, 2006, *Common Worship: Christian Initiation*, London: Church House Publishing, pp. 29–56.

9 Simon Jones, 2016, *Celebrating Christian Initiation: Baptism, Confirmation and Rites for the Christian Journey*, London: SPCK, p. xii.

10 Michael Vasey, 1995, *On the Way: Towards an Integrated Approach to Christian Initiation*, London: Church House Publishing, p. 40.

11 *Rite of Christian Initiation*, p. 3; see also Congregation for the Clergy, 1997, 'Catechesis in the Church's Mission of Evangelization', *General Directory for Catechesis*, Part 1, https://www.vatican.va/roman_curia/congregations/cclergy/documents/rc_con_ccatheduc_doc_17041998_directory-for-catechesis_en.html.

12 *Common Worship: Christian Initiation*, pp. 319–21.

13 Jeremy Haselock, 2000, 'Introduction', in Gilly Myers, *Using Common Worship: Initiation Services, a Practical Guide to the New Services*, London: Church House Publishing, pp. 2–4; Simon Jones and Philip Tovey, 2001, 'Initiation Services', in Paul Bradshaw (ed.), *A Companion to Common Worship: Volume One*, London: SPCK, pp. 159–61.

14 Bernard Piault, 1963, *What is a Sacrament?*, London: Burns & Oates, pp. 26–7.

15 Joel M. Podolny and James G. March, 'A Conversation with James G. March on Learning about Leadership', *Academy of Management Learning & Education* 10, 3 (September 2011), pp. 502–6, p. 504.

16 *Common Worship: Christian Initiation*, p. 100.

17 Larry S. Chapp, 2023, *Confession of a Catholic Worker: Our Current Moment of Christian Witness*, San Francisco, CA: Ignatius Press, p. 130.

18 Haselock, 'Introduction', p. 2.

19 *Common Worship: Christian Initiation*, p. 323.

20 Jones, *Celebrating Christian Initiation*, p. xix.

21 Cited in 1994, *Catechism of the Catholic Church*, London: Geoffrey Chapman, p. 277, paragraph 1216; added italics.

22 Edward Bouverie Pusey, 1836, *Scriptural Views of Holy Baptism, as Established by the Consent of the Ancient Church, and Contrasted with the Systems of Modern Schools*, London: Rivington, p. 32.

23 J. B. Mozley, 1892, 'Dr Pusey's Sermon', in *Essays Historical & Theological Vol II*, London: Longmans, Green & Co., pp. 149–63, p. 162.

24 Pusey, *Scriptural Views of Holy Baptism*, p. 48.

25 Pusey, *Scriptural Views of Holy Baptism*, p. 48.

26 Pusey, *Scriptural Views of Holy Baptism*, p. 22.

27 Alf Härdelin, 1986, 'The Sacraments in the Tractarian Spiritual Universe', in Geoffrey Rowell (ed.), *Tradition Renewed: The Oxford Movement Conference Papers*, London: Darton, Longman & Todd, p. 90.

28 *Common Worship: Christian Initiation*, p. 336.

29 Henry Parry Liddon, J. O. Johnston and Robert J. Wilson (eds), 1893, *Life of Edward Bouverie Pusey Vol. 1*, London: Longmans, Green & Co., p. 346.

30 Louis Bouyer and Mary Benoit (trans.), 2022 (1951), *The Paschal Mystery: Meditations on the Last Three Days of Holy Week*, Providence, RI: Cluny Media Edition, p. xv.

31 *Catechism of the Catholic Church*, p. 247, paragraph 1076.

32 Aidan Kavanagh, 1991 (1978), *The Shape of Baptism: The Rite of Christian Initiation*, Collegeville, MN: The Liturgical Press, p. 122.

33 Pope Paul VI, *Sacrosanctum Concilium* (1963), 1.6, available at https://www.vatican.va/archive/hist_councils/ii_vatican_council/documents/vat-ii_const_19631204_sacrosanctum-concilium_en.html, accessed 28.08.2023.

34 Peter Waddell, 2012, *Joy: The Meaning of the Sacraments*, Norwich: Canterbury Press, p. 20.

35 Chapp, *Confession of a Catholic Worker*, p. 130.

36 *Common Worship: Christian Initiation*, pp. 313–55.

37 *Common Worship: Christian Initiation*, p. 355.

38 Jones, *Celebrating Christian Initiation*, pp. xii–xiii.

39 Stephen Cottrell, Steven Croft, Paula Gooder and Robert Atwell, 2013, *Pilgrim: A Course for the Christian Journey. Leader's Guide*, London: Church House Publishing, pp. 56–66.

40 Michael Vasey, 1995, *On the Way: Towards an Integrated Approach to Christian Initiation*, London: Church House Publishing, p. 45.

41 Megan McKenna, 1998, *Rites of Justice: The Sacraments and Liturgy as Ethical Imperative*, Maryknoll, NY: Orbis Books, p. xi; emphasis original.

42 United States Conference of Catholic Bishops, 2005, *National Directory for Catechesis*, Washington DC, p. 170.

43 Vasey, *On the Way*, p. 73.

Bibliography

Archbishops' Council, 2006, *Common Worship: Christian Initiation*, London: Church House Publishing.

Bouyer, Louis (trans. Mary Benoit), 2022, *The Paschal Mystery: Meditations on the Last Three Days of Holy Week*, Providence, RI: Cluny Media Edition [orig. George Allen & Unwin 1951].

Bradshaw, Paul (ed.), 2001, *A Companion to Common Worship Vol. 1*, London: SPCK.

Catechism of the Catholic Church, 1994, London: Geoffrey Chapman.

Chapp, Larry S., 2023, *Confession of a Catholic Worker: Our Current Moment of Christian Witness*, San Francisco, CA: Ignatius Press.

Cottrell, Stephen, Steven Croft, Paula Gooder and Robert Atwell, 2013, *Pilgrim: A Course for the Christian Journey. Leader's Guide*, London: Church House Publishing.

Croft, Steven (ed.), 2019, *Rooted and Grounded: Faith Formation and the Christian Tradition*, Norwich: Canterbury Press.

Ferguson, Everett, 2009, *Baptism in the Early Church: History, Theology, and Liturgy in the First Five Centuries*, Grand Rapids, MI: Eerdmans.

Grabar, André, 1968, *Christian Iconography: A Study of its Origins*, Princeton, NJ: Princeton University Press.

Härdelin, Alf, 1986, 'The Sacraments in the Tractarian Spiritual Universe', in Geoffrey Rowell, (ed.), *Tradition Renewed: The Oxford Movement Conference Papers*, London: Darton, Longman & Todd.

Haselock, Jeremy, 2000, 'Introduction', in Gilly Myers, *Using Common Worship: Initiation Services, A Practical Guide to the New Services*, London: Church House Publishing.

International Commission on English in the Liturgy: A Joint Commission of Catholic Bishops' Conferences, 1987, *Rite of Christian Initiation of Adults. Approved for use in the Dioceses of England and Wales, Scotland*, London: Geoffrey Chapman.

Jones, Simon, 2016, *Celebrating Christian Initiation: Baptism, Confirmation and Rites for the Christian Journey*, London: SPCK.

Kavanagh, Aidan, 1991 (1978), *The Shape of Baptism: The Rite of Christian Initiation*, Collegeville, MN: The Liturgical Press.

Liddon, Henry Parry, J. O. Johnston and Robert J. Wilson (eds), 1893, *Life of Edward Bouverie Pusey Vol. 1*, London: Longmans, Green & Co.

McKenna, Megan, 1998, *Rites of Justice: The Sacraments and Liturgy as Ethical Imperative*, Maryknoll, NY: Orbis Books.

Mozley, J. B., 1892, *Essays Historical & Theological Vol. II*, London: Longmans, Green & Co.
Piault, Bernard, 1963, *What is a Sacrament?*, London: Burns & Oates.
Pusey, Edward Bouverie, 1836, *Scriptural Views of Holy Baptism, as Established by the Consent of the Ancient Church, and Contrasted with the Systems of Modern Schools*, London: Rivington.
Strawbridge, Jennifer, 2019, 'Making Christians and Lifelong Catechesis', in Steven Croft (ed.), *Rooted and Grounded: Faith Formation and the Christian Tradition*, Norwich: Canterbury Press.
The Sunday Missal: A New Edition, 1984, London: Collins.
United States Conference of Catholic Bishops, 2005, *National Directory for Catechesis*, Washington DC.
Vasey, Michael, 1995, *On the Way: Towards an Integrated Approach to Christian Initiation*, London: Church House Publishing.
Waddell, Peter, 2012, *Joy: The Meaning of the Sacraments*, Norwich: Canterbury Press.
Wojtyla, Karol (trans. Jerzy Peterkiewicz), 1980, *Easter Vigil and Other Poems*, London: Arrow Books.

Sermon

'Singing the Lord's Song'

Preached at Evensong and Benediction at
St Peter de Beauvoir Town on 27 April 2024

Mthr Kathryn Fleming SCP

Psalms 84 and 86; Deuteronomy 15.1–18;
Ephesians 6.10–end

It was my A-level year when my father died. My A-level term actually, the day before my first exam.

One of those liminal seasons when you are acutely aware that things are changing for ever – but don't perhaps fully understand the changes.

I believed this meant I was 'grown up'.

Well, that's the first mistake! Forty-five years on, I'm still waiting, but let's pass over that for now. I thought this threshold was about loss – of a beloved parent, of my identity at a school that had been the safest and happiest of communities for a shy only child – but it turned out to be a transition into a new, more intense way of being, which challenged all I had learned of life so far.

You see, as I travelled home to face the new reality, the God whom I'd viewed from a cautious distance met me in a railway carriage somewhere near Pevensey Bay. The John Donne poem ('A Hymne to God the Father') that I was revising feverishly for Monday's exam suddenly became a non-negotiable truth, as that self-same God came so close I could absolutely feel his arms holding me steady.

'I fear no more', Donne said, and his words effected what they described, assuming a sacramental significance outside their immediate context. Everything changed, as grief and anxiety were newly coloured by a love beyond my imaginings.

A few weeks later on the eve of the funeral, the school choir's big summer concert was the Brahms *German Requiem*. My love of music came from my father, so despite the concern of many wise adults that this would be 'far too much', I was determined to sing, and when we reached the fourth movement, a setting of Psalm 84, it turned out to be an experience of utter bliss.

'How lovely are thy dwellings fair', we sang – and everything was light and truth and tentative faith confirmed as I found myself plunged head over heels into the Communion of Saints.

'Blessed are those who dwell in thy house; they will be always praising you.'

I could practically *hear* my father's voice, his distinctive baritone there beside me, so that we sang together as we had done countless times before – and I had a glimpse, for a moment, of how in worship we can lift our voices to join in the eternal music round God's throne.

So with all that in mind, it's probably no surprise to learn that I'm firmly grounded in the catholic tradition, or that singing has remained very much my first language of the soul, my easiest route to encountering God. While I am passionate about seeking and loving God in all things with heart, mind and soul, I find myself standing with the author of *The Cloud of Unknowing* and sharing his experience of searching:

Because he may well be loved, but not thought. By love he can be caught and held, but by thinking never.

When the rational fails to land me safe on Canaan's side, when my intellect founders and the voices in my ears assert as one that 'This is all folly', when I simply cannot *think* myself into the presence of God, then I need those things that awake me to love, life and faith once more: those things that the Church terms the Sacraments. These are parables for the senses, ordinary things of the here and now, wine and water, oil and bread, which lift us, both here and now, to the edges of eternity where we can taste and see for a moment the glory we strain towards.

And again and again I've found that music acts as one of them, for it has power to bypass our defences – of logic, of busyness, of simple inattention – and forces us to be present in and open to the moment. And the moment is, most often, where we find that we can meet with God.

Augustine famously said that *those who sing pray twice*. On a bad day, it may be that we find ourselves substituting singing for any other kind of engagement in prayer, relying on it to provide instant emotion such that we can evade honest encounter. It would be disingenuous to pretend that singing 'Sweet sacrament divine' cannot sometimes become every bit as self-indulgent as some of those choruses from another tradition that could be dismissed as 'Jesus is my boyfriend' music. But those surely are the worst days.

More often, though, come those wonderful days when loving worship is shaped as we sing, when music builds a bridge to God like nothing else and expresses the truth of God in ways that words can simply never aspire to, as it opens a window wide on to heaven.

If music just doesn't do it for you, please don't panic.

The whole of life, the whole of creation, is a sacrament if we but open our hearts to the God who is always longing to welcome, to feed and transform us, so that together we, the Church, may live the life of the Kingdom, even here, even now.

Yes, our worship will always be inadequate. How could it not be, when you consider the greatness of a God beyond all words, beyond all telling? Evelyn Underhill knew this, writing: 'If God were small enough to be understood, He would not be big enough to be worshipped.'

But when we worship, when we turn hearts and souls and senses to God, however much we may struggle with that process, we will find ourselves carried, if we're only willing to allow it. Just that tiniest movement towards God, 'Where heaven is but once begun', sweeps us up in the song of praise that started as the world began and will continue even beyond its end.

And, you know, the notes of praise that we sing together in this place will resound in God's heart for ever, for God delights in every movement of the heart towards him.

Alleluia.

Thanks be to God.

10

The Bridegroom and His Bride: Learning about Celibacy from Early Christian Fathers and Mothers

PROFESSOR MORWENNA LUDLOW

Introduction

In 1841 Marian Rebecca Hughes took vows of poverty, chastity and obedience, the first Anglican woman to do so since the Reformation. She recorded the vows in her diary: 'This day Trinity Sunday 1841, was I enrolled one of Christ's Virgins, espoused to Him and made His handmaid ... Written by me in the 24th year of my life at 12 o'clock at night on my knees.'[1] Marian took her vows in private, witnessed by E. B. Pusey and a family friend; she received communion from John Henry Newman immediately afterwards at a public service. But while Pusey had suggested as early as 1839 establishing a women's religious house in England, Hughes took her vows before the first such community even existed: it was a remarkable commitment of faith and hope. In 1851 she established the Society of the Holy and Undivided Trinity in Oxford, first in her own house and later in a purpose-built convent.

Marian was not, of course, the only woman involved in such a foundation: in 1848 Lydia Sellon founded the Society of the Most Holy Trinity in Plymouth and Devonport. She was 27 and she too was influenced by the Tractarians: Pusey was her spiritual director and life-long advisor.[2] Both women were characterized by unusual determination and a vocation to serve the poor and vulnerable. For both, their vocation as a religious sister was inseparable from this social mission. Other communities followed, often in response to calls from parish priests in the Anglo-Catholic tradition working in areas of great need and social deprivation. There were communities for men too, such as the Community of the Resurrection, which had strong connections to Christian

Socialism. Each community had its own independent character but broadly speaking they adapted post-Reformation Roman Catholic forms of community life and were influenced theologically by scholars like Pusey and Newman who were steeped in a much longer tradition of catholic Christianity and were eager to renew the Church of England by drawing on those sources.[3]

Given that the topic of celibacy has been a repeated theme in recent discussions of sex and marriage in the Church of England – usually from conservative Evangelicals – it is a timely moment to ask what the catholic tradition in Anglicanism can learn not just from pioneers like Hughes and Sellon but from their much earlier forebears. In this chapter I will focus on just three themes: the variety of ascetic expressions in the Early Church; the metaphor of Christ the bridegroom; and the outward-looking, missional character of early ascetic movements.

Before I continue, it will be useful to clarify some terminology. Early Christian language about asceticism reflected the fluidity of its forms. The term 'virgin' (*parthenos* in Greek; *virgo* in Latin) was usually used of those committed to sexual abstinence, both men and women; it applied to those in community, those living in their own household and those in a solitary form of life. It did not necessarily refer to a biological state or to the fact of never having had sex. 'Chastity' in English has come to mean sexual virtue in general terms (often defined as not having sex outside marriage) and 'sexual continence' can be understood in the same way; but when Augustine of Hippo prayed 'Give me chastity and continence, but not yet' (*da mihi castitatem et continentiam, sed noli modo*), it is quite clear that he is praying for the strength to commit himself to a life of permanent vowed celibacy.[4] Here I will be mostly discussing voluntary celibacy – the choice to undertake a single life for religious reasons, accompanied by marks of a disciplined life, like a routine of prayer and a restricted diet and, often, formal vows. We will also encounter examples of those who were either married or living in some kind of partnership, but who committed themselves to sexual abstinence. These relationships are best described in terms of sexual continence rather than celibacy.

The variety of ascetic expressions in the early Church

Anglican debates today are still coloured by the Reformers' condemnation of the corruption of monastic foundations and individuals' failure to maintain clerical celibacy – debates that obscured the variety of early Christian attitudes to sexual continence. As Richard Finn points out:

> Early Christians who shared a concern for the virtues associated with sexual restraint were far from united in their understanding of what this meant for sexual conduct ... How widespread were the different forms of sexual abstention? Were all equally acceptable everywhere? How did permanent sexual renunciation feature within the identity of the individual who embraced it?[5]

Evidence from very early Christianity is elusive, not least because it was unimportant or impossible for many people to keep a written record of their activity. But there are hints about those who took literally Jesus' exhortation to leave family and follow him. For example, the second-century apocryphal text, the *Acts of Paul and Thecla*, tells the story of a young woman's fascination with Paul's preaching – which in this text is portrayed as having a very strong emphasis on celibacy.

Paul said in this text:

> Blessed are the pure in heart, for they shall see God [Matt. 5:8]; blessed are those who have kept the flesh chaste, for they shall become a temple of God; blessed are the continent, for God shall speak with them; blessed are those who have kept aloof from this world, for they shall be pleasing to God; blessed are those who have wives as not having them, for they shall experience God [1 Cor. 7.29; Rom. 8.17]; blessed are those who have fear of God, for they shall become angels of God ... Blessed are the bodies of the virgins, for they shall be well pleasing to God and shall not lose the reward of their chastity. For the word of the Father shall become to them a work of salvation in the day of the Son, and they shall have rest for ever and ever.[6]

Thecla broke off her betrothal, left home and eventually became a travelling preacher. In the narrative, her baptism, her commitment to celibacy and her commitment to evangelism are closely connected. Although Thecla may never have been a historical individual, many scholars think that she and her 'band of young men and maidens' reflect an early Christian tradition of peripatetic celibate preachers. There is some evidence that these missioners travelled in male–female celibate pairs.[7]

Another early ascetic tradition is often labelled *Enkratite*. There were those, especially on and beyond the eastern borders of the empire, who took up the strictest habits, including voluntary poverty and abstinence from meat, wine and sex. These ideals were reflected in Tatian's *Diatessaron* (a harmony of the four Gospels in Syriac that was used as the main Gospel text in Syriac churches until the fifth century), which gives John the Baptist a vegetarian diet (milk and honey) and says that Anna 'remained seven years a virgin with her husband'.[8]

However, the existence of a specific historical group called the *Enkratites* seems to have been an invention of early Christian anti-heretical writings, inspired by 1 Timothy 4.3, which condemns those who 'forbid marriage and abstain from certain foods, which God created to be received with thanksgiving by those who believe and know the truth' (NRSVUE).[9] Those who rejected marriage (like some Gnostics and Marcion) because they thought that all materiality was bad were condemned by the Church.

Nevertheless, there is evidence that celibacy was so valued in early Syriac-speaking Christianity that it was a condition for baptism. Those who were already in marriages renounced them or perhaps simply abstained from sex. A late second-century Syriac rite combines baptism and vows of sexual renunciation.[10] While Christians further afield debated the question, only Syriac (and Marcionite) churches required celibacy for all the baptized. The severity of the demand was mitigated by the fact that the age of baptisands varied; many were baptized as adults and some probably waited until they had had children.[11]

In time the strict requirement of celibacy for all those being baptized developed into a distinctive and selective form of Syriac Christian asceticism: the 'Sons and Daughters of the Covenant'.[12] They took vows of poverty and chastity and played a role in their communities similar to that of a deacon in early Christian tradition, serving the poor under instruction from their bishop. They lived with each other or remained with their own families. Various writers warn against men and women attempting to live together in chaste marriages. The Sons and Daughters of the Covenant were a kind of dispersed celibate community with a public presence in the community, mixing with others but distinguished by their dress and set apart by their vows. Some were consecrated to this form of life from childhood.[13] There is evidence for them from the third century and they still feature prominently in texts from the fifth century: the Persian martyrs, Martha and Thekla and her friends (killed in Iran under Zoroastrian rule) were 'Daughters of the Covenant' and, as in the story of Thecla, their vows of celibacy were one factor contributing to their persecution.[14] Other kinds of Syriac Christian ascetic were more solitary, living apart from society in small groups or as hermits.

Hagiographies describe the extreme rigours undertaken by the stylites, for example, who sat on pillars.

For those living in the Roman empire, Christian asceticism was often deemed to have started with Antony of Egypt, whose life was lived in tension between seeking complete isolation and teaching others. But even Antony was not the first: he joined a group of hermits placed under the instruction of a spiritual father outside his village. The lives of these early holy solitaries were taken as blueprints of the ascetic life, and Athanasius' *Life of Antony* was, after the Bible, the most widely circulated and translated early Christian book. Later forms of asceticism in Egypt became more organized: very large communities of hermits in lower Egypt around Kellia and Scetis (living and praying apart but meeting occasionally for teaching); then the establishment of monasteries for both men and women by Pachomius and his sister Maria, and Shenoute. Christians from around the empire came to visit these communities to learn from them and put their way of life into practice back home. Two such men were Eustathius of Sebaste and Basil of Caesarea, who were very influential in establishing monastic communities in Anatolia, including in the imperial capital Constantinople. Basil's sister, Macrina, was probably influenced by Eustathius as she set up her own monastic community in her household on the family estate in Anatolia. The development of this community from an individual to a household to a more formal monastery seems to have been fairly typical for the fourth century, both for women and men.[15]

Other visitors inspired by the ascetics of Egypt were western founders of religious communities in and near Jerusalem, such as Melania the Elder, a wealthy Roman widow, and her granddaughter Melania the Younger. The latter was married but, after the death of two children as infants, persuaded her husband Pinian that they should both dedicate themselves to a religious life, including giving up sex. Although Melania and Pinian became the most famous exemplars of 'chaste marriage', it may have been a relatively popular option for Christians wanting to mark a new depth of commitment to their faith, especially if they had already produced an heir. High infant and maternal mortality rates made abstinence more attractive.[16]

In the West, ascetic teachers like Jerome and Pelagius attracted followers among elite families in Rome. Ascetic communities followed more slowly. We know, for example, that Jerome joined a household community in Aquileia and Augustine founded one near Milan before returning to North Africa to set up more formal communities. Augustine had lived with a woman for 15 years who bore him a much-loved son: his story reminds us that while baptism did not require celibacy, for young men like Augustine who chose the celibate life it marked the point of their decision.

The marriage metaphor: Christ the bridegroom

A recurrent theme in early Christian asceticism is the idea of Christ as bridegroom. This stems from Jesus' own presentation of himself as bridegroom, from Ephesians 5, which compares the relationship between Christ and the Church to that between husbands and their wives, and from the imagery of the Song of Songs. Unlike much current Christian discourse, early Christianity frequently (even usually) saw Christ's relationship to his Church as displacing human marriage rather than being the model for it. The individual believer's marriage to Christ – represented by baptism – often replaced earthly marriage, especially in Syriac Christianity.[17] In becoming a member of the Church through baptism, the believer was renouncing all others to become wedded to Christ.

When celibacy became a particular calling, not a baptismal requirement, the commitment to asceticism was frequently portrayed as entering Christ's bridal chamber, and liturgy used elements traditionally associated with marriage (e.g. crowns, veiling) to symbolize a believer's union with Christ.[18] In the fourth century, the Syriac Christian Aphrahat wrote an 'exhortation to the Sons and Daughters of the Covenant', urging his addressees to be prepared to meet their spouse:

> Let us keep the appointed meeting with the Glorious Bridegroom so that we may enter with him to his bridal chamber. Let us have oil ready for our lamps so that we may go out to meet him in joy ... Let us listen to the voice of the Bridegroom so that we may enter the Bridal Chamber with him. Let us prepare the gift for the wedding and go out to meet him in joy.[19]

It is clear that Aphrahat is addressing men and women, promising heavenly blessings both to 'those who do not take wives' and those who 'are delivered from the punishment of Eve's daughters'. In this group:

> There is no male or female there, no servant or freeborn, rather, all are children of the Most High, and all the pure virgins who are betrothed to Christ will have their lamps shining brightly there as they enter, with the Bridegroom, to his bridal chamber.[20]

This imagery was not restricted to the Syriac tradition: it is prominent in treatises on virginity by Basil of Ancyra and Gregory of Nyssa, again addressing both men and women.[21] For Gregory, the soul is portrayed as female: this bride seeking her husband must be pure not so much in a physical or sexual sense but in terms of being free from greed, pride, envy and malice. Bridal imagery runs throughout his Homilies on the Song of Songs, in which the 'bride' represents both the Church corporately and the soul of each individual believer.[22] Over time the imagery of the 'bride of Christ' was applied especially to female ascetics: in the West there was a growing requirement for their sexual purity (biological virginity) and their marriage was symbolized with a veil. In the meantime, also in the West, the increasingly strong emphasis on clerical celibacy was justified in terms of keeping the Church pure for its heavenly bridegroom, so that its sacraments might be true:

> And so [Christ] desired that the Church, whose bridegroom he is, should have her visage shining with the splendour of chastity, that in the day of judgment, when he comes again, he might find her without spot or blemish, as he ordained by his apostle. Hence all we priests and Levites are bound by the unbreakable law of those instructions to subdue our hearts and bodies to soberness and modesty from the day of our ordination, that we may be wholly pleasing to our God in the sacrifices which we daily offer.[23]

Early asceticism as outward-looking: social concern and mission

Early Christians took up ascetic practices for a variety of reasons. Some saw strict sexual continence as a universal dominical command, others as an ideal. Not all reasons were endorsed over time by the catholic Church. In particular, the kind of asceticism that denied the goodness of creation (and specifically the goodness of the human body and the materials that nurtured it) was condemned; the universal requirement of celibacy for baptism was relaxed. Nevertheless, one very striking and consistent feature of early Christian asceticism is the connection between strict sexual abstinence and an outward-looking perspective on the world. This missional attitude has two broad forms: teaching/preaching and the alleviation of suffering.

Jesus' call to discipleship was associated with leaving family behind (Matthew 10.35–39; Luke 14.25–27); Paul's recommendation to 'remain unmarried as I am' in 1 Corinthians 7 might have its context not just in the expectation of a time of crisis (v. 26) but in the need for disciples to travel to preach into that situation. Certainly, in Christianity's early years there seems to have been a strong expectation that missionaries would be celibate. In the Acts of Paul and Thecla, Thecla wants to give up marriage and to be baptized so that she can fulfil a call to travel and preach.[24] Montanist prophets connected their gift of visions (and thus their ministry to others) to sexual abstinence.[25] If it is correct that some early apostles travelled in couples, it seems likely that they were sexually abstinent – not least so as to avoid pregnancy, childbirth and childcare enroute. When Christianity was more established and mission less of an imperative, it was common for local parish clergy to be married; nevertheless, celibate ascetics continued to be witnesses to the gospel. Even the hermits of the Syrian desert, for example, became important sources of advice, mediation of disputes and pastoral care.[26] It is possible that the common expectation that senior clergy would be celibate reflected the demands placed on bishops to travel within and outside their dioceses.

In later centuries, sexual abstinence was associated not so much with preaching but with the alleviation of poverty and suffering. Gregory of Nyssa wrote that marriage distracts one with its many joys and sufferings; those who were celibate, on the other hand, could enjoy a (more) uninterrupted focus on the divine. This facilitated not only contemplative prayer but also serving the poor. In the monastic enterprises of Basil, Gregory's brother, this focus on the divine was inseparable from love of neighbour. Basil boasts to a local governor that, in addition to a 'magnificent house of prayer' and accommodation for themselves, the community has built 'hospices for strangers, for those who visit us while on a journey, for those who require some care because of sickness', for whom they also provide 'the necessary comforts, such as nurses, physicians, beasts for travelling and attendants'. The community has workshops for training people in 'occupations ... necessary for gaining a livelihood'.[27] Basil's efforts were not alone. They were part of a general movement in the 350s–370s, especially focused on Asia Minor.[28] This mix of shelter, food and medical care reflects the context in which lack of food, exacerbated by poor harvests, and precarious or bad housing inevitably brought with them ill health. Furthermore, a disease like leprosy made its sufferers homeless and hungry.[29] In time, hospitals were established outside the major cities, supervised by the newly established 'area' or 'country' bishops (*chorepiscopoi*) – assistant bishops (usually celibate) who worked under the direction of their diocesan, especially in localities that would be difficult for the diocesan to cover.[30]

Even in cases where celibacy was not connected to organized schemes of these kinds, it was strongly associated with giving money to the poor. For example, Athanasius' *Life of Antony* tells how he went to church and, in that day's Gospel reading, heard Jesus' instructions to the rich young man (Matthew 19.21). So, Athanasius relates:

> Antony, as though ... the passage had been read on his account, went out immediately from the church, and gave the possessions of his forefathers to the villagers – they were three hundred acres, productive and very fair – that they should be no more a clog upon himself and his sister. And all the rest that was movable he sold, and having got together much money he gave it to the poor, reserving a little however for his sister's sake.[31]

The core features of this famous story were repeated many times in later lives of holy men and women. But the fact that the simultaneous call to baptism, celibacy and giving family wealth to the poor was a common topos need not diminish its historical credibility. There is ample evidence that private wealth passed from rich families to the poor, sometimes directly, sometimes via an individual ascetic or monastic institution who became responsible for its distribution. Although the latter sometimes led to accusations of hoarding, early monastic communities had a strong ethos of using spare resources for the poor.[32] Although people sometimes exaggerated how much disposable income or excess food communities had, the evidence shows 'that ascetic and monastic almsgiving of some kind was not only taken for granted by Christians of the period, it was integral to a theology of virtuous monastic labour'.[33]

This use of resources was only possible for celibate individuals and communities whose members had none of the distractions and responsibilities of family life. But it caused controversy and had to be defended by Christian writers, including Basil, who argues that his buildings for poor relief are a gift to the city as important as traditional donations by wealthy citizens.[34] When Melania and Pinian gave away vast amounts of family wealth they scandalized their aristocratic peers. As their story highlights, Christian promotion of voluntary celibacy meant not only giving up wealth (as one might give up rich food or wine) but also deliberately abstaining from producing children through whom one would pass wealth to the next generation. It thus stepped out of a fundamental structuring principle of Roman society.[35] In that context, voluntary singleness was a profoundly counter-cultural option.

Concluding reflections

For too long in Britain, church history treated monasticism as a corrupt practice rightly expunged by the Reformation. More recently, academic accounts of early asceticism have focused on the strange behaviour of ascetics at the expense of their spiritual (or indeed other) motivations.[36] It should be possible to write about early Christian asceticism without yielding to the temptation of treating it as predominantly either wrong or strange. It should be possible to learn from early ascetic practices without simply using them to validate what we should do today. For this reason I have focused on three themes I hope can inform current debates.

First, early Christian asceticism was characterized by 'an almost bewildering variety of experiments'.[37] Celibacy could be chosen by virgins, by those widowed or by renouncing previous sexual relationships. Some, like Melania the Younger and her husband, chose to remain married in law but vowed themselves to chastity; of such couples, some joined a monastic community while others remained together at home. Some ascetics, like the Sons and Daughters of the Covenant, lived public lives of service fully involved in their communities; others were hermits seeking greater isolation. Some ascetics, usually wealthy individuals (including some women), travelled widely, touring sites before founding their own communities. Even formally organized communities followed various models: groups of hermits under one father, a single monastery for either men or women or a 'double monastery' where men and women lived and worked in separate quarters but worshipped together under one leader.

This variety enjoins on us humility regarding present-day ascetic experiments: the history of asceticism shows that it (like episcopacy) is a church practice much characterized by local adaptation. We should take seriously those who feel that celibacy is the correct response to their own sexuality. Amid all the variety, however, one thing is constant: celibacy as a religious practice is voluntary. When celibacy was a baptismal requirement it applied to adults who chose the time of their baptism; in time it ceased to be a requirement. Early debates about clerical celibacy frequently distinguish between junior, local clergy (who were often permitted to marry) and senior clergy. There was a wise concern for choice and the dangers of imposing too severe a discipline on those who were not fitted to it. Even though clerical celibacy was imposed in the West it remained contentious, as the Reformers' arguments showed. Looking back at the broad span of Christian tradition from a perspective that is catholic and reformed, it seems important to re-emphasize the concept of voluntary celibacy. Insisting that one's own choice of celibacy should apply to all who fall into a similar category (e.g. ordained or lesbian/gay) seems not to be faithful to this.

Second, it is very clear that for early Christians the passage from Ephesians 5 was used not as a pattern for human marriage but to displace or replace it. Either Christ was the spouse of the Church corporately (which imposed a responsibility for purity on its priests) or individuals were espoused to Christ the bridegroom through baptism or vows of celibacy. The powerful paradox that Christ the bridegroom offers an intimate, quasi-exclusive, relationship to all believers echoes Paul's similarly paradoxical adoption metaphor: in baptism the believer's relationship with God is like the exclusive relationship between an adopted heir and his adoptive father. Arguments that the marriage motif runs throughout Scripture as a symbol for salvation need not only to take seriously the rich plurality of soteriological motifs in the Bible but also to grapple with the fact that the marriage motif is complex and subverts the value of human marriage.

Third and finally, although some early Christian asceticism was distorted by excessive self-denial (which often denied the goods of creation and became a source of selfish pride), much was distinguished by service to the poor and needy. Here again there is much to learn. Consistently the early Church warns against celibacy motivated by a self-regarding pride. On the other hand, there is much to value in a voluntary celibacy that opens up time for attention to one's neighbour.

Glancing back, we can see these features in our opening examples. The early steps to formal ascetic communities were characterized by bold experimentation and significant variety. We saw that Marian Hughes expressed her vows in terms of espousal to Christ – a daring, voluntary commitment that allowed her to step outside the usual expectations of a woman of her time. The new Anglican religious communities were notable for their work of mission to and care for the vulnerable. As with all ascetic experiments, there were mistakes. But the best traditions of Christian celibacy see it not as closing something down but as a voluntary opening up of oneself: to Christ, to one's neighbour and to the future kingdom.

Notes

1 Valerie Bonham, 2004, 'Hughes, Marian Rebecca (1817–1912), Anglican Nun', in *Oxford Dictionary of National Biography*, Oxford: Oxford University Press.

2 Peter G. Cobb, 2004, 'Sellon, (Priscilla) Lydia (1821–1876), Founder of the Society of the Most Holy Trinity', in *Oxford Dictionary of National Biography*, Oxford: Oxford University Press.

3 Adam D. McCoy, 2020, 'The Anglican Tradition', in Bernice M. Kaczynski (ed.), *The Oxford Handbook of Christian Monasticism*, Oxford: Oxford University Press, p. 622.

4 Augustine, 2014, *Confessions (The Loeb Classical Library 26 & 27)* (trans. Carolyn J.-B. Hammond), Cambridge, MA: Harvard University Press, VIII.7 (17).

5 Richard Finn, 2009, *Asceticism in the Graeco-Roman World*, Cambridge: Cambridge University Press, pp. 80–1.

6 Anon, 2005, 'Acts of Paul and Thecla', in Patricia Cox Miller (ed.), *Women in Early Christianity: Translations from Greek Texts*, Washington DC: Catholic University of America Press, pp. 155–66, paragraphs 5 and 6.

7 Joan Taylor, 2021, 'Male–female Missionary Pairings among Jesus' Disciples', in Joan E. Taylor and Ilaria L. E. Ramelli (eds), *Patterns of Women's Leadership in Early Christianity*, Oxford: Oxford University Press; Ilaria L. E. Ramelli, 'Colleagues of Apostles, Presbyters, and Bishops: Women Syzygoi in Ancient Christian Communities', in Taylor and Ramelli, *Patterns of Women's Leadership*.

8 Françoise Briquel Chatonnet and Muriel Debié, 2023, *The Syriac World: In Search of a Forgotten Christianity* (trans. Jeffrey Haines), New Haven, CT: Yale University Press, p. 62; Finn, *Asceticism*, p. 82; cf. Luke 2.36.

9 Finn, *Asceticism*, p. 72.

10 Chatonnet and Debié, *Syriac World*, p. 63.

11 Finn, *Asceticism*, pp. 84–94.

12 Sebastian Brock, 1992, *The Luminous Eye: The Spiritual World Vision of Saint Ephrem the Syrian*, Kalamazoo, MI: Cistercian Publications, chapter 8.

13 Chatonnet and Debié, *Syriac World*, pp. 63–4.

14 Sebastian P. Brock and Susan Ashbrook Harvey (eds), 1998, *Holy Women of the Syrian Orient*, Berkeley, CA: University of California Press, chapter 3; see also Introduction.

15 Susanna Elm, 1994, *Virgins of God: The Making of Asceticism in Late Antiquity*, Oxford: Oxford University Press.

16 Kate Cooper, 2013, *Band of Angels: The Forgotten World of Early Christian Women*, London: Atlantic Books, chapter 8.

17 Robert Murray, 1975, *Symbols of Church and Kingdom: A Study in Early Syriac Tradition*, Cambridge: Cambridge University Press, pp. 152, 157.

18 Finn, *Asceticism*, p. 84; Murray, *Symbols*, pp. 132, 142; David G. Hunter, 2007, *Marriage, Celibacy, and Heresy in Ancient Christianity: The Jovinianist Controversy*, Oxford: Oxford University Press, p. 225.

19 Aphrahat, 2011, 'VI. The Demonstration on the Sons of the Covenant', in *Aphrahat Demonstrations* (trans. Kuriakose Valavanolickal), Piscataway, NJ: Gorgias Press, pp. 121–60, pp. 122–3, 128.

20 Aphrahat, 'The Demonstration on the Sons of the Covenant', p. 141.
21 Elizabeth Castelli, 'Virginity and its Meaning for Women's Sexuality in Early Christianity', *Journal of Feminist Studies in Religion* 2, 1 (1986), pp. 61–88; Elm, *Virgins*, pp. 113–21.
22 Gregory of Nyssa, 2012, *Homilies on the Song of Songs* (trans. Richard A. Norris Jr), Atlanta, GA: Society of Biblical Literature, 15:1; 16:1.
23 Siricius, quoted in Hunter, *Marriage, Celibacy, and Heresy*, pp. 215–16.
24 'Acts of Paul and Thecla', paragraphs 40–1; cf. Finn, *Asceticism*, p. 93.
25 Finn, *Asceticism*, p. 87.
26 Theodoret's *Life of Simeon Stylites*; Peter Brown, 'The Rise and Function of the Holy Man in Late Antiquity', *The Journal of Roman Studies* 61 (1971), pp. 80–101.
27 Basil of Caesarea, 1926, *Letters* (trans. Roy J. Deferrari), Cambridge, MA: Harvard University Press, Letter 94.
28 Peregrine Horden, 2012, 'Poverty, Charity, and the Invention of the Hospital', in Scott Fitzgerald Johnson (ed.), *The Oxford Handbook of Late Antiquity*, Oxford: Oxford University Press, pp. 720–23.
29 Horden, 'Poverty, Charity', p. 728.
30 Horden, 'Poverty, Charity', p. 720.
31 Athanasius, *Life of Antony*, paragraph 2 (available at https://ccel.org/ccel/schaff/npnf204/npnf204.xvi.ii.iii.html, accessed 2.05.2024).
32 Richard Finn, 2008, *Almsgiving in the Later Roman Empire: Christian Promotion and Practice (313–450)*, Oxford: Oxford University Press, chapter 3.
33 Finn, *Asceticism*, p. 98.
34 Basil of Caesarea, *Letter 94*.
35 Peter Brown, 1988, *The Body and Society: Men, Women, and Sexual Renunciation in Early Christianity*, New York: Columbia University Press.
36 For example, Brown, *Body and Society*, p. xv.
37 Elm, *Virgins*, p. 125.

Bibliography

Anon., 2005, 'Acts of Paul and Thecla', in Patricia Cox Miller (ed.), *Women in Early Christianity: Translations from Greek Texts*, Washington DC: Catholic University of America Press, pp. 155–66.
Aphrahat, 2011, 'VI. The Demonstration on the Sons of the Covenant', in Kuriakose Valavanolickal (trans.), *Aphrahat Demonstrations*, Piscataway, NJ: Gorgias Press, pp. 121–60.
Athanasius, *Life of Antony* 2: Nicene and Post-Nicene Fathers translation, https://ccel.org/ccel/schaff/npnf204/npnf204.xvi.ii.iii.html, accessed 19.12.2024.
Augustine, 2014, *Confessions*, trans. Carolyn J.-B. Hammond, The Loeb Classical Library 26 & 27, Cambridge, MA: Harvard University Press.
Basil of Caesarea, 1926, *Letters*, trans. Roy J. Deferrari, Cambridge, MA: Harvard University Press.
Bonham, Valerie, 2004, 'Hughes, Marian Rebecca (1817–1912), Anglican Nun', in *Oxford Dictionary of National Biography*, Oxford: Oxford University Press.

Brock, Sebastian P. and Susan Ashbrook Harvey (eds), 1998, *Holy Women of the Syrian Orient*, Berkeley, CA: University of California Press.

Brock, Sebastian, 1992, *The Luminous Eye: The Spiritual World Vision of Saint Ephrem the Syrian*, Kalamazoo, MI: Cistercian Publications.

Brown, Peter, 1988, *The Body and Society: Men, Women, and Sexual Renunciation in Early Christianity*, New York: Columbia University Press.

Brown, Peter, 1971, 'The Rise and Function of the Holy Man in Late Antiquity', *The Journal of Roman Studies* 61, pp. 80–101.

Castelli, Elizabeth, 1986, 'Virginity and its Meaning for Women's Sexuality in Early Christianity', *Journal of Feminist Studies in Religion* 2, 1, pp. 61–88.

Chatonnet, Françoise Briquel and Muriel Debié, 2023, *The Syriac World: In Search of a Forgotten Christianity*, New Haven, CT: Yale University Press.

Cobb, Peter G., 2004, 'Sellon, (Priscilla) Lydia (1821–1876), Founder of the Society of the Most Holy Trinity', in *Oxford Dictionary of National Biography*, Oxford: Oxford University Press.

Cooper, Kate, 2013, *Band of Angels: The Forgotten World of Early Christian Women*, London: Atlantic Books.

Doran, Robert (ed.), 1989, *The Lives of Simeon Stylites*, Edinburgh: Alban Books.

Elm, Susanna, 1994, *Virgins of God: The Making of Asceticism in Late Antiquity*, Oxford: Oxford University Press.

Finn, Richard, 2008, *Almsgiving in the Later Roman Empire: Christian Promotion and Practice (313–450)*, Oxford: Oxford University Press.

Finn, Richard, 2009, *Asceticism in the Graeco-Roman World*, Cambridge: Cambridge University Press.

Gregory of Nyssa, 2012, *Homilies on the Song of Songs*, trans. Richard A. Norris Jr, Atlanta, GA: Society of Biblical Literature.

Horden, Peregrine, 2012, 'Poverty, Charity, and the Invention of the Hospital', in Scott Fitzgerald Johnson (ed.), *The Oxford Handbook of Late Antiquity*, Oxford: Oxford University Press.

Hunter, David G., 2007, *Marriage, Celibacy, and Heresy in Ancient Christianity: The Jovinianist Controversy*, Oxford: Oxford University Press.

McCoy, Adam D., 2020, 'The Anglican Tradition', in Bernice M. Kaczynski (ed.), *The Oxford Handbook of Christian Monasticism*, Oxford: Oxford University Press, pp. 621–33.

Murray, Robert, 1975, *Symbols of Church and Kingdom: A Study in Early Syriac Tradition*, Cambridge: Cambridge University Press.

Ramelli, Ilaria L. E., 2021, 'Colleagues of Apostles, Presbyters, and Bishops: Women Syzygoi in Ancient Christian Communities', in Joan E. Taylor and Ilaria L. E. Ramelli (eds), *Patterns of Women's Leadership in Early Christianity*, Oxford: Oxford University Press.

Taylor, Joan, 2021, 'Male–female Missionary Pairings Among Jesus' Disciples', in Joan E. Taylor and Ilaria L. E. Ramelli (eds), *Patterns of Women's Leadership in Early Christianity*, Oxford: Oxford University Press.

11

Marriage

FR CHARLIE BELL

Over the past few years it seems that the Church of England has had rather a lot to say about marriage. If we were being uncharitable we might even suggest that it has become obsessed with the 'ideal' of marriage to the point of it becoming not only a rather weak identifier of supposed 'orthodoxy', but also in elevating marriage to such a degree in the Christian world view that those who are not married are perceived to have something wrong with them! It's therefore essential that any discussion of marriage places it within a wider framework – that of the Christian life more generally – and seeks to do so without suggesting that those who are not married are somehow deficient in grace. Marriage, then, is a particular instrument of the superabundant grace of God, but in being so it is not the only path of access to that grace.

Yet because so much has been said about marriage, and so much of it apparently lacking in basic reflection on its core features beyond 'one man and one woman' or engagement with its history as institution and as sacrament, there is a need to call catholic Anglicans back to the reasons why the Church adopted it as a Sacrament, and try to situate this complex and changing institution within both its historical and contemporary contexts. In other words, we need to ask ourselves whether marriage deserves such a central role in our self-understanding as Christians – and particularly as catholics in the Church of England.

Our recent ecclesial debates on marriage have regularly come back to a discussion of the Church of England's 'doctrine' of marriage, which has been used as a rather unfortunate – and not entirely accurate – shorthand for what would more properly be labelled as 'description', found in Canon B30 (recognizing of course that Canon B30 itself refers to 'the Church's doctrine of marriage as herein set forth', although this appears to be a somewhat contingent point related to 'our Lord's teaching'). Much is made of the first part of the first part of Canon B30, but for our purposes it is helpful to hear the whole thing:[1]

MARRIAGE

1. The Church of England affirms, according to our Lord's teaching, that marriage is in its nature a union permanent and lifelong, for better for worse, till death them do part, of one man with one woman, to the exclusion of all others on either side, for the procreation and nurture of children, for the hallowing and right direction of the natural instincts and affections, and for the mutual society, help and comfort which the one ought to have of the other, both in prosperity and adversity.
2. The teaching of our Lord affirmed by the Church of England is expressed and maintained in the Form of Solemnization of Matrimony contained in *The Book of Common Prayer* (BCP).
3. It shall be the duty of the minister, when application is made to him for matrimony to be solemnized in the church of which he is the minister, to explain to the two persons who desire to be married the Church's doctrine of marriage as herein set forth, and the need of God's grace in order that they may discharge aright their obligations as married persons.

This Canon is helpful to our purposes here not because it has some kind of eternal doctrinal significance but because it points us towards the understanding of the *nature* and *purpose* of marriage as an institution within the context of the Church of England – at least at the time of the revisions of the canons in the 1950s. At this juncture, it is also important to note that the description found in this particular canon does not take account of the significant liturgical development that has taken place since – we might think here of the *Alternative Service Book* and of course of *Common Worship* – and hence cannot be credibly argued to be unchanging nor unchangeable.

We will return to the 'man and woman' element of 'one man and one woman' towards the end of this chapter, but for now it is worth taking a step back and recognizing the context in which this canon was written, and what the canon is trying to portray. Despite the protestations of some within the modern Church of England, this canon is not written with the purpose of opposing same-sex marriage – not least because when it was written, homosexuality was illegal within the UK and it would simply not have featured in the discussions of the time. Instead, the canon is making a positive statement about the nature of marriage, referring to numbers of participants (that is, two), the exclusive, permanent, lifelong, for-better-for-worse of marriage and the purpose of marriage, here described as procreation and nurture of children, hallowing and right direction of natural instincts and affections, and mutual society, help and comfort.

Part Two of the canon refers to the BCP, and upon closer inspection it is clear that the vast majority of the text mirrors precisely that in the BCP. There is a good reason for that – the canon as it stands now is indeed effectively lifted from the extant marriage liturgy of the time. Hence we find similar themes of *purpose* as those we found in the canon, namely that it is for the procreation of children, for the mutual society, help and comfort, in prosperity and adversity, and in *nature* it is to be exclusive, permanent and lifelong, albeit more by implication than by direct statement. In the BCP, of course, we also meet another purpose of marriage – as a 'remedy against sin, and to avoid fornication; that such persons as have not the gift of continency might marry, and keep themselves undefiled members of Christ's body'.

Yet in the BCP we also hear what appear to be rather audacious claims for the estate of marriage, not least given the history to which we shall soon turn.[2] Marriage is described as having been 'ordained' for the purposes outlined as 'such an excellent mystery, that in it is signified and represented the spiritual marriage and unity betwixt Christ and his Church', having been 'instituted of God in the time of man's innocency'. The relationship between Adam and Eve is therefore described as 'marriage'. There is also a rather tenuous reference made to the wedding at Cana, at which the Lord is supposed to have 'adorned and beautified' the 'holy estate' with 'his presence', and a rather surprising reference to St Paul which suggests that he commends marriage 'to be honourable among all men'.

There is not the space here to fully engage with the significant reliance on complementarian theology in the liturgy, but it is important nonetheless to mention it, not least because it highlights the culture-bound nature (at least to a significant degree) of the differences between the BCP liturgy and the marriage liturgies that have developed in the late twentieth and early twenty-first century. This is important not only because such a change in emphasis changes the nature of the liturgy (most obviously in the vows and exhortations) but also because such a change points to a developing understanding of what it is in marriage that we might be solemnizing and that, as catholics, we might wish to call sacramental.

Of course, Cranmer doesn't call marriage a sacrament, but the language consistently used is that of 'honourable' or 'holy estate'. In addition there is a clear expectation that a blessing is said over the newly married couple, and in the rubrics of the service Cranmer also makes clear that 'it is convenient that the new-married persons should receive the holy Communion at the time of their Marriage, or at the first opportunity after their Marriage.' It is notable that this relationship with the sacramental – with the Eucharist – is missing from *Common Worship* and from standard practice and expectations in the contemporary Church of England.

This relationship with the receiving of Holy Communion, however, is not only a relationship with the overtly sacramental – rather, that relationship with the sacramental contains within it a relationship with the communal or shared Christian life. So Cranmer's vision of marriage, building on Sarum usage, does not relate merely to the couple's becoming one flesh (a phrase he does not in fact explicitly use) but also to the place of marriage in the life of the Church, both for the individuals who are being joined in marriage (specifically in the reference to those without the 'gift of continency' keeping themselves 'undefiled members of Christ's body') and also for the wider Church. The 'holy estate' that is entered into is therefore something solemnized by the Church because it builds up the couple and the Church. Something of this has been lost in the contemporary practice of the Church, but this is perhaps inevitable in an Established Church.

Establishment, as central to the Church of England's self-understanding, inevitably adds complexity to any understanding of marriage that sees it primarily as an ecclesial event or as an institution whose sacramentality is primarily expressed within the context of the *ecclesia*. We meet here the tension between marriage as sacrament and marriage as institution, a tension that continues in debates over widening the doctrine to include same-sex couples and debates on marriage versus Holy Matrimony. Of course, in a country and Church in which the vast majority of inhabitants were communicant members of the Church of England, then the link with holy Communion and church life was easier to both insist upon and envisage, but in the twenty-first-century UK, if the Church of England is to remain Established in the current sense, including the right for parishioners to get married in their parish church (to someone of the opposite sex), then there is inevitably going to be some form of compromise or need to re-engage imaginations on the meaning and context of sacrament.

From a catholic perspective, the fact that the vast majority of those coming to solemnize marriage in church are *not* likely to receive communion 'at the first opportunity' poses a particular challenge because of the belief in its sacramentality, rather than marriage merely being an institution that the Church has adopted. That said, while not described as a Sacrament (with a capital 's') by all within the Church of England, recent debates on same-sex marriage have suggested that a recognition of its sacramentality, at least, is now the majority position – although it does sometimes appear a little unclear as to what marriage is then held to be in the eyes of the Church. The re-emphasis on the idea of Holy Matrimony points, perhaps, to Cranmer's vision of a 'holy estate', although the relationship of this with civil marriages remains somewhat unclear (an issue with which Cranmer, of course, did not have to engage).

Nonetheless, the Church's public pronouncements have – at least until recently – suggested that 'a marriage is a marriage',[3] even if it is not clear what exactly that marriage is. For catholics in the Church of England, who do not have the privilege of freedom that the non-Establishment status of the Roman Catholic Church gives it in thinking through how this relates to sacramentality, there remains work to be done in the changed world of 2025. To put it concisely: How do we hold together the centrality of Establishment to our self-understanding as *ecclesia anglicana* and its contemporary consequences with our belief in the sacramental nature of (all?) marriage? How do we receive that sacramental nature and in what way is it expressed? Do we, indeed, hold to the idea of all marriages being sacramental? Do we hold to the idea of marriage, however performed, as being a Sacrament? And just as importantly, why do we do so?

We will return to the idea of 'holy estate' and sacramentality later – for now, let us briefly address another of Cranmer's rubrics that has also apparently been forgotten in recent debates on marriage, and that is the link between marriage and procreation (by which it appears he means reproductive sex). Much has been made of the necessity of procreation *for* marriage (rather than the other way around, that procreation is *best* undertaken in the 'holy estate' of marriage), yet Cranmer is clear that this is not his understanding. In a brief but unmistakable phrase, he makes it clear that the prayer for 'fruitfulness' in marriage is not to be prayed when 'the woman is past childbearing' age. In Cranmer's vision, therefore – in contradiction to so much that is currently spoken about in Church of England debates on the *necessity* of marriage to be open to reproductive sex – openness to procreation (in his understanding) does not appear to be a prerequisite for marriage, but rather is described as one of the purposes of marriage – a subtle but important distinction.

Developments in liturgy

We will now turn our attention to the developments in liturgy – and hence belief and the process of doctrinal development – that have occurred since the 1950s in the Anglican context. Before we do so, it is worth explicitly stating what has been implicit through much of this discussion: Cranmer's vision, while indeed highlighting some good purposes of marriage, is nonetheless mostly couched in language that justifies why the Church should have anything to do with this state in the first place. This is in stark contrast to contemporary liturgical provision for marriage, which appears to place a much higher emphasis on marriage being good in and of itself, rather than a 'holy estate' from which goods can come – again, a subtle distinction. While there is much to be welcomed in the more fulsome embrace of marriage in contemporary liturgy, this shift does perhaps help explain why Cranmer's vision of marriage being '*a* holy estate' is so often interpreted in present-day Christian apologetics as '*the* holy estate'. Taking a birds-eye view of Cranmer's liturgy shows just how far this understanding is from his original thinking, and we will address some of the reasons for this when we turn to history.

Common Worship builds on the Cranmerian theme of God's ordination of marriage, suggesting both that God has 'intentions' for it and that it is a 'gift of God in creation' – indeed, there are many similar if not identical themes throughout. Yet early on in the Preface is found some of the distinctiveness of the modern rite – and hence evidence of the development of doctrine:[4]

> It is given that as man and woman grow together in love and trust, they shall be united with one another in heart, body and mind, as Christ is united with his bride, the Church.

It is arguable that this is merely building upon the mutual society and comfort to which Cranmer refers, and of course it relates to the imagery found in his service on Christ and his bride, but the emphasis here is different and for the first time appears to include an explicit mention of what we would commonly term 'romantic love' (an example perhaps of a heterosexual 'redefinition of marriage'!). It would of course be simplistic (and factually inaccurate) to suggest that love per se does not find a place in Cranmer's service. Indeed, the ever-present tendency to reduce all 'love' to romantic love can easily rear its head when analysing what precisely is being said about this sacrament. (Here *Common Worship*'s description of 'maturity in love' is helpful, suggesting that we are not merely talking about romantic love.) Nevertheless, it is certainly the case that romantic love as a driver for marriage is recognized here in a way in which it is markedly absent in the Cranmerian text.

Yet in addition, more generally positive language is found throughout the Preface – sexual union is described in terms of 'delight and tenderness', marriage is described as 'joyful commitment', 'a sign of unity and loyalty' that 'enriches society and strengthens community'. In many ways therefore *Common Worship* builds on the nascent themes found in Cranmer, but if we deny its somewhat different character we will fail to appreciate the associated change in understanding of not only the purposes but also the nature of marriage. It is no longer an institution created to stem sin and to merely provide stability, but an active social good to be celebrated by the Church. As we shall see from our brief discussion of the longer historical view, this is quite a development.

Notable too in the *Common Worship* service is the egalitarian way that the service is presented (with, because it's the Church of England, an inevitable opt out!). Gone are the implicit – indeed, even explicit – references to the *differences* between man and woman, and instead the liturgy emphasizes the similarities and the growing together in one flesh and in a joint journey of faith. While this egalitarianism feels entirely appropriate in the twenty-first-century Church, it is important to note that its implicit presentation of a changing doctrinal understanding is itself a not insignificant change to the historical presentation of this liturgy. Incidentally, this change is not – as we saw earlier – reflected in canon B30, suggesting that whether or not the Church is to embrace equal marriage, work needs to be done on canon B30 to reflect our doctrine as it is *now*.

There is not the time to do justice here to the patriarchal underpinning of marriage, except to note that a mere changing of liturgical language is not enough to fully address this in ecclesial terms. Indeed, while there has been much noise about equal marriage in church, there is a significant group of queer and feminist thinkers and activists who have entirely rejected the idea of marriage as inherently patriarchal and irredeemable, linked to 'traditional' understandings of ownership and male power and hence the very opposite of contemporary understandings about the radical equality of humans each created in the image and likeness of God. Their challenge to us, as catholics, is clear and bifold: first, can we really redeem such an institution, but second – and more complex – how can we argue that an intrinsically patriarchal institution was ever truly sacramental?

These are important challenges that get to the heart of much of our current debates on sexuality and gender. In short, is the egalitarianism and the emphasis on similarity rather than difference found in the *Common Worship* rites merely window dressing in order not to scare the horses, or is it reflective of a genuine development of doctrine? If the latter, have we really considered the implications of this? This is particularly important given the use of Ephesians, Colossians and 1 Peter in Cranmer's reasoning as laid out in the BCP, yet the absence of these sources in *Common Worship* (beyond being among a long list of suggested readings).

Context and social setting

Let us now briefly move away from liturgy and contextualize the Cranmerian and later rites in their social settings. As opposed to what some commentaries on recent marriage debates might suggest, it is a matter of objective fact that the Church's involvement with marriage as an ecclesial institution is a relatively recent innovation, including, importantly, the role of the cleric. In the Western Church it was not until the twelfth century that the Church began to regulate marriages[5] and not until the Council of Trent in the sixteenth century that the need for a cleric to be involved in such a ceremony was formalized (together with witnesses).[6] Before this point the Church was somewhat suspicious of marriage (reflected in part in Cranmer's liturgy), favouring celibacy, although there are examples from the Church Fathers of benedictions said at marriage ceremonies.

It was not until the Clandestine Marriage Act (most popularly known as Lord Hardwicke's Marriage Act) of 1753 that a formal ceremony of marriage was absolutely required in England and Wales, ostensibly to suppress clandestine marriages.[7] Such a ceremony had to be undertaken by an Anglican clergyman in a parish church or chapel of the Church of England in order to be legally binding (with an exemption for Jews and Quakers). Prior to this Act, while marriages had been regulated by different iterations of canon law and the church courts, they had nonetheless retained, to differing degrees, an element of non-ecclesial nature, albeit with a general recognition (which became increasingly formalized) that they were to be undertaken by a Magistrate or Anglican cleric.

The Hardwicke Act meant that marriage mostly became a solely Established ecclesial affair until the Marriage Act of 1836 re-introduced civil marriage and made it possible for other ministers of religion to act as registrars at marriage ceremonies. Of course, this highlights the complexity of calling marriages between 1753 and 1836 primarily ecclesial – they certainly were being undertaken in ecclesial buildings by ministers of the Church of England, but it appears that this was favoured primarily because of the Established nature of the Church of England rather than with any particular theological reasoning. Since 1836 there have been a number of further legal developments but the only one to really impact upon the Church was the Marriage (Same Sex Couples) Act 2013. The resultant quadruple lock further distanced the Church of England from its role as Established Church in the solemnizing of marriages under English law by preventing such marriages from taking place under the jurisdiction of the Church of England.

Beyond the Church of England, and relevant to our conversations as catholic Anglicans, was the development of the sacramental understanding of marriage being undertaken in the Roman Catholic Church. This did not follow a neat, linear process, and relied in its development on the writings of the Fathers and in particular Augustine. Augustine's 'On the Good of Marriage', written in AD 401, appears to be the first exploration of the 'goods' of marriage – offspring (not merely sexual reproduction but nurture and upbringing), fidelity and 'sacrament' or mystery. Augustine's reference to 'sacrament' here needs a little unpacking, but what he is primarily referring to is the indissolubility and permanence of the marital, covenantal bond as a sign of the indissolubility and permanence of the bond between Christ and Christ's Church – a position that continues to be held by the Roman Catholic Church.[8]

It was in 1184 that the first declaration that marriage is a sacrament was made, at the Council of Verona, in a condemnation of the purported heterodox view of the Cathars that marriage and sexual reproduction were evil.[9] From this point forwards the Roman Church's view on marriage is increasingly a positive one, and it is interesting that at the Second Council of Lyon in 1274[10] marriage was described primarily in terms of its impact on the Church rather than its impact on the spiritual development of those who entered into it. The Council of Trent formally outlined the sacraments (referring to the Councils above as well as the Council of Florence in 1439 and the prescribed statement of faith for the Waldensians in 1208),[11] and yet at the same time made clear in Canon X:

> If any one saith, that the marriage state is to be placed above the state of virginity, or of celibacy, and that it is not better and more blessed to remain in virginity, or in celibacy, than to be united in matrimony; let him be anathema.

Before returning to the present day it is worth briefly turning to how Cranmer addresses this idea of marriage being a sacrament in the 39 Articles. In Article 25 he makes clear that marriage is a 'state of life allowed in the Scriptures, but yet ha[s] not like nature of sacraments with Baptism, and the Lord's Supper, for [it does] not [have] any visible sign or ceremony ordained of God'. This is further explored in his Homily 18, where – as we highlighted earlier – he makes clear that marriage is primarily an honourable estate for the salvation of the individuals concerned. It is interesting therefore that *Common Worship* – as we have also met earlier in this chapter – appears somewhat closer to the Second Council of Lyon's understanding of marriage as building up the Church rather than the individual, rather than Cranmer's more individualistic understanding. It is perhaps because of this that its sacramental nature has become more accepted within the wider Church of England – marriage as a communal act being more clearly a sign than if it was merely for the saving of souls from promiscuity and its consequences.

Marriage today

Which bring us back to today and the way that catholic Anglicans might engage with marriage and specifically marriage as a sacrament. Does marriage – should marriage – still have a special or particular place in how we understand human relationships, and if so, why? An institution to which the Church originally paid little attention has over time been discerned to contain grace – both for the couple and for the Church, and I would argue for wider society as well – and yet it is not at all clear that the tension between the different 'estates' of life has been satisfactorily engaged with in contemporary church teaching and practice. What might be described as a 'fetishization of the nuclear family' has been a part of this process, and while marriage may indeed remain an attractive and important 'holy estate' for many within and without the Church, there is an urgent need for us to rethink a positive Christian vision of marriage (rather than a vision of Christian marriage, which is quite a different thing).

This will necessitate us, in the first instance, engaging with questions about our current understandings of the nature and purposes of marriage – both of which might then contribute to our understanding of the 'goods' of marriage. If we are to do this, then we need, for example, to move well beyond discussions of sexual reproduction as being the only meaning of procreation towards a wider engagement with doctrinal developments that engage with marriage as a vehicle for particular social goods that build up the individual *in communion*. At the same time, our focus on the goods of marriage cannot simply pretend away the goods of other estates of living, and it may be that we find these goods to be better thought of as a spectrum of holiness found both within and without the marriage bond. We must ask too how and whether these goods interrelate, and as catholics we must then also ask whether and how these goods relate to the sacramental nature of marriage.

To put it another way: Do we believe that marriage is a sacrament because the Church says it is and therefore we must find what is sacramental within it? Or do we start from first principles and ask whether the traditional understanding of sacramentality – that of covenant and permanence that points to Christ and Christ's Church – remains our understanding of its sacramentality? Indeed, is such sacramental nature found *only* within marriage, and if not, how do we engage with this? Is such a traditional understanding actually sufficient to explain the sacramentality or does it need further engagement on the basis of the development of doctrine? Are we selling an impoverished understanding of marriage if we do not more clearly link the other goods – procreation, mutual society, sanctification – to its sacramentality? To what degree is the metaphor of marriage the best or the only way to point to such a heavenly reality (and, indeed, how do we engage with the somewhat blasé association of human marriage with the marriage feast in heaven alluded to in *Common Worship*)? In other words, and most fundamentally, how does what we call marriage actually relate to the love of Christ for Christ's Church, and how do we think about this in a pastoral way without elevating marriage to being the *only* holy estate? All of these questions appear important and yet have received little engagement.

Yet similarly, to move beyond the abstract, there are also important questions about lived-out pastoral practice in an Established Church. What are we to do with the fact that the sacramentality – at least as currently defined – does not appear to play much, if any, part in a wider public understanding of marriage? To what degree does our current liturgy actually embody it? To what degree is our increasing focus on the importance of marriage for community rather than for the salvation of individual souls helpful, and where might it cause us difficulties?

These are important questions because our inability to engage with them has meant that much of the debate around equal marriage has felt like little more than splashing in the shallow end – we are defending an institution about which we appear to have done far too little deep theological thinking in a changing world and even in a changing doctrinal landscape, albeit one that has changed in an evolutionary way and perhaps almost imperceptibly. How do we link our theological thinking with our pastoral practice – for example in cases of divorce? How does human marriage become something genuinely lived rather than an ideal impossible to attempt?

We have work to do – the work of discernment. We must acknowledge too that this current process of discernment sits within a wider stream of the development of doctrine in which the Church of England is currently engaged and has been engaged in since it first greeted marriage as embodying something of the grace of God. As catholics we need a good story to tell about marriage, which engages with things as they really are and yet is also able to situate human life within the life of God – which the idea of sacraments has always sought to do. What do we think we are doing when we marry people in church or rather when we solemnize what appears to be a deeply human institution that surely does not begin at the exchange of vows? What of sex, love, companionship, procreation, permanence and consensual covenant?

For those of us who believe marriage is a good thing for individuals and society and able to point in some way to the life of God, beginning to ask – and answer – these questions is an urgent task.

Notes

1 The Church of England, 'Section B: Divine Service and the Administration of the Sacraments', https://www.churchofengland.org/about/leadership-and-governance/legal-resources/canons-church-england/section-b, accessed 3.07.2024.

2 Of course, much of Cranmer's marriage liturgy builds on the themes of the Sarum Rite. There is not the space to do this development justice, except to make clear that Cranmer's concept of marriage did not develop in a vacuum.

3 For example, in the language around the blessing offered following a civil marriage: Church of England, 'Wedding Blessings', https://www.churchofengland.org/life-events/your-church-wedding/planning-your-ceremony/wedding-blessings, accessed 3.07.2024.

4 Church of England, 'Marriage', https://www.churchofengland.org/prayer-and-worship/worship-texts-and-resources/common-worship/marriage, accessed 3.07.2024.

5 John Witte, 1997, *From Sacrament to Contract*, Louisville, KY: Presbyterian Publishing, pp. 22–3.

6 The history of this development is covered extensively in Philip L. Reynolds, 2016, *How Marriage Became One of the Sacraments*, Cambridge: Cambridge University Press.

7 Rebecca Probert, 2009, *Marriage Law and Practice in the Long Eighteenth Century: A reassessment*, Cambridge: Cambridge University Press, pp. 6–10). In her book Probert challenges the extent to which the Hardwicke Act made a sharp

contrast with the situation that came before. In any case, the main thrust of our argument – that the Church of England's involvement with marriage was a slow and by no means consistent process – remains.

8 Nicu Dumitraşcu, 2022, *The Fathers on the Bible*, London: Taylor & Francis, pp. 237–8.

9 Herbert Vorgrimler, 1992, *Sacramental Theology*, Collegeville, MN: Liturgical Press, p. 296.

10 John Witte, 2015, *The Western Case for Monogamy over Polygamy*, Cambridge: Cambridge University Press, p. 153.

11 A topic covered in detail in chapter 4 of E. Christian Brugger, 2017, *The Indissolubility of Marriage at the Council of Trent*, Washington DC: The Catholic University of America Press, pp. 90–124.

12

Children and Young People

MTHR SALLY JONES AND FR JACK NOBLE

Introduction

Any conversation about the life (and future) of the Church will eventually come round to the topic of children and young people. This is true for all traditions of the Church of England. Seeing children in church gives us hope for the future and the longevity of our communities. However, the statistics show us a less than promising outlook, with 75% of C of E churches having between 0–5 children on average.[1]

Even when we do have children attending, few of our churches embody the vision of multi-generational worship, and we as clergy and lay ministers frequently forget to treat our young people and children as members of the Church of Christ, often relegating them to a sticky (if colourful) mat at the back of the church or to a draughty parish hall, to be 'entertained' with felt-tip pens and simple and safe stories.

Having acknowledged all this, the question this chapter seeks to ask is: What does catholic youth and children's work look like in the C of E? How does our rich inheritance of sacraments, catechesis and social justice best become God's gift to our youngest disciples?

Children and young people must be allowed to live out their lives sacramentally and to play a full part in the life of the Church. It is our responsibility as shepherds to teach, guide, encourage, invite and welcome them into the ministries to which God is calling them. Jesus preached: 'Let the little children come to me, and do not stop them; for it is to such as these that the kingdom of heaven belongs.'[2]

We hope this chapter will present a fruitful vine, weaving principles and experience with practical tips and inspiration to apply to your context. What is written here comes from a range of experiences and a variety of contexts. There is no 'one size fits all', so take what is useful and leave the rest. It also comes from the lived experience of having launched projects and initiatives that have seen lots of children and young people attend, as well as the regular lived experience of having launched projects and initiatives that very few or even no children and young people attended. This admission is shared in order to encourage you, whatever your ministry and context, that catholic ministry to children and young people is possible however few or many attend and however much or little access your context has to finance and resource.

More than felt-tips and fairy stories

If you talk with a young person or child about their favourite toy/song/film/meal, you'll probably get an enthusiastic and confident answer as they share their love for x or y. These connections are made through regularity and familiarity, things children love. For that matter, speak with an adult about the same aspects of their childhood and you'll probably find the same. We find existential comfort in patterns of ritual and regularity. In good times and bad, and everything in between, they hold us. Traditional prayers (ideally committed to memory over time) and liturgy are (viewed *this* way) not barriers to engagement but an asset. What is more, as catholic Christians we know that worship isn't simply a tool, it is our highest calling.

This is why it is important that children have space in church. However, in too many churches the space that is given to children is out of the way, with poor sight lines to the 'action' of the Sunday Mass, filled with cast-off toys and broken felt-tip pens. This denies our children any sense of awe.

Church for many children can become boring when they are kept away from the main act of worship. Our churches are filled with beauty, from their structure and architecture to decoration, paintings and stained-glass windows, the smell of the incense and burning of wax and the taste of Holy Communion; and we do our children a disservice when we reduce their experience of worship to being out of sight and out of mind.

The saying 'Play is the work of the child' is often attributed to Maria Montessori because she educated according to the teaching of St Thomas Aquinas: 'There are two ways of acquiring knowledge 1) by invention or finding out and 2) by discipline or learning. Invention is the higher mode.'[3] Play and invention is how our children explore the world, in trying on roles and costumes and acting them out, and yet when children come to worship we expect them to act differently. Conventional provision for children in church often leans towards the imparting of knowledge and not the *discovery* of God by our children.

A couple of years ago a council-estate church didn't have any volunteers to lead a Sunday School. Everyone eligible had been there and done that and were tired. But they still wanted to try and give their children a positive, holy and prayerful experience of church. This started with setting up a children's area but they didn't want to fall into the trap that many other churches do. So the church council talked about intentions and purpose for this new area and formed a clear vision, and an agreement that:

1. From this play area the full altar and altar party could be seen, and the children could hear the service happening around them.
2. The *only* things allowed in this area were books and toys that would help the children explore the Bible and the liturgy.

They commissioned a dress-up set of vestments, wooden Communion vessels and a play altar. They bought blocks and bricks for imaginative play, flash cards with items from around the church, a cuddly snake and whale with zip-able mouth, a squishy Jesus, tactile felt prayer beads and a tent for children to read and pray in.

Within weeks of this being established a volunteer came forward who had observed the children playing in church and wanted to help give them some structure. With this volunteer a parallel liturgy was developed as the structure for the new Sunday School. Taking each section of the Eucharist, they created a child-friendly version that could be done at the same time, so that the children could fully participate in the liturgy. This has been dubbed 'Liturgical Play'. Space is given during the notices for the children (and adults) to ask any questions they have about church, the Bible or faith. This started as a way to take the pressure off Sunday School volunteers to find quick answers and to encourage them in saying: 'I don't know, let's find out.' It has become an important part of the ongoing faith journey of the congregation, as children ask questions the adults dare not ask.

It's important to engage young people where they are, and that includes allowing faith to grow *with* children. The Church of England has an abundance of primary school resources but it is sometimes just *too* easy to pull out a favourite colourful picture Bible and a craft, and when children out-grow this method of teaching faith they will need something more. Great resources need to move beyond 'milk' to 'meat', even if it means we take risks and go beyond our glitter glues.[4] Children will often match what we give: so if we're shy and timid to talk about our faith and play things small, so will they. And vice versa: if we model generous and confident invitation, generous worship and prayer, lively intellectual enquiry and openness, so will they. If we keep our children's faith at the level of colourful Bibles, their view of Jesus risks becoming just another fairy story.

Following our young people from childhood into adolescence, imagine a secondary school classroom. The local clergy have managed to obtain a standing invitation into Religion, Ethics and Philosophy GCSE classes for an open Q&A at the end of each term. So often the students are surprised by the radical thoughtfulness and generous reality of the historic orthodox Christian faith as held by the catholic tradition in the Church of England.

Take the complex (and sometimes divisive) question of *identity*. Young people might assume restrictive or even harsh teachings from the church. Instead they are surprised and engaged with the bigger questions Christians want to ask first: 'Who are you?' and 'What are the sources of your identity?' Suddenly our faith opens a conversation (with plenty more than there is room for here) that is both faithful and generous, and deeply rooted in the love of God and God's purposes in our lives.

We are able to give children and young people explicit permission to explore big questions of life and identity within safe spaces. This is a precious gift. Q&As are helpful but so are gifts like reconciliation. The simple and heartfelt confessions heard by a secondary school chaplain felt very healthy for the young people involved, and was a wonderful opportunity to minister the reality of God's grace and the fresh start we receive. Another powerful sacramental encounter was baptism and confirmation in a special educational needs school. Over weeks and weeks, using lots of pictures and 'What do you think this means?' questions, oil, water and other teaching aids, the children were prepared thoroughly, but sensitively, to embrace life with Jesus.

Children's instincts for the catholic faith shouldn't be underestimated. Oliver was ten or eleven when he and his mum started coming to church, and he soon started bringing his friends. Initially the clergy were surprised. But why? Because adults don't evangelize so simply and effectively? Young people and children are natural and honest evangelists, especially if we encourage them a little. More recently, Stanley has brought two of his mates from school to church. One of them has brought his mum, dad and sister. Encouraged 'from the front' to bring friends and family (the clergy having learnt from Oliver), they did, because they like church and they like sharing the things they like.

Are we nearly there yet? In it for the journey

The catholic faith as lived out in the Church of England provides a rich tapestry of stages of faith and life – lifelong catechesis and formation. The stepping stones of the sacraments carry us from baptism through First Holy Communion and Confirmation (be they together or separate), confession and anointing, and even perhaps marriage and/or ordination. It's all there: God's gift to God's beloved children. And many of these gifts come with sincere preparation and a proper party. Lucy Winkett notes that 'church "fun" is quite often not actual fun'.[5] Church fun needs to be real fun. A retired bishop used to say: 'Fewer meetings, more parties.'

Our children and young people deserve real fun as much as they deserve full participation, because they are full members of the church, with an equal stake to adult members of the congregation, and as equal leaders of the church at worship. In some churches a young person acts as Youth Warden, representing the voice of children to the PCC and sharing in the leadership and ministry. Strong lay leadership has always sat alongside the catholic order of bishop, priest and deacon: each strengthening the other in their distinctive vocations.

The sacraments and the daily and weekly round of worship are stepping stones for life. But this is not simply a mindless merry-go-round for us. These are treasures, gifts from God. Furthermore, as well as imparting these gifts, it is good for us to ask: What do we actually *want* for our children and young people?

For some years now the Roman Catholic Jesuit schools in the UK have had a structure called the Jesuit Pupil Profile. In it they list the things that every Jesuit-educated child can be expected to possess by the time they leave school.[6] How refreshing it would be not to track progress by numbers in the service register but rather by the spiritual knowledge and place in the Church universal a young person holds. What treasures can they *expect* to receive from us? To know how to begin learning to pray? To know that they are loved by God? To know that they will be at home in every church in the world? To know that the Sunday Mass is where they belong? To know they are part of a global and universal family that includes the Saints and Blessed Mary as their mother, no matter what happens to their earthly family? To know that the face of every other person is the face of Christ? To know that God has a plan for their life? And to know that like Mary their greatest joy will be to say: 'Be it unto me according to Thy word'?

A great nineteenth-century Anglo-Catholic priest told a colleague catechizing children to teach them not to love the Church of England but to 'love Jesus' and everything else will follow. For our children, we hope for a lifelong relationship that forms them into their *real* selves. This is God's doing, not ours, but we are called to cooperate in God's work. One way we do this is to lead by example and 'show our working'. On its simplest level this might mean saying why we do things in worship. Teaching Masses for a season every couple of years or at the start of a youth group/school term are very good ideas, and can be great fun and very interactive. If we take the Mass seriously, so will our young people.

Increasingly people simply don't *know* that there is this pattern to Christian life. We need to gently, showing our working, explain why being at Mass every Sunday is essential (that is, *esse*: 'life') for us. If you're on holiday, search online and find a Eucharist. Visiting family? Bring them with you. We already hope these things for people; we need to share our hope and *why*, including for our children and young people.

We have already begun to say that this area of ministry is not just about teaching but about *experience*. Being a catholic Christian means seeking unity with our Christian siblings who share the apostolic tradition; to be at home in the belief and worship of the undivided Church through the western Christian tradition. It's not just a matter of holding knowledge and ideas but embracing a relationship and with it the holy habits that will hold us and provide a trellis for life. Church, prayer, Scripture, sacraments: these and other core threads of our life provide the essence of the relationship that is the essence of our lives. As well as teaching the faith we aim to create spaces (in youth clubs, school assemblies, Sunday schools and the rest) in which our children can stand on holy ground, like Moses before the Burning Bush.

In a suburban medieval parish church they hosted 'Nightfire', an all-night sleepover vigil. Turns were taken to watch with the Blessed Sacrament, talks offered, music and worship, hot chocolate, and other activities were available throughout the night (with times to sleep too). It ended with an al fresco Dawn Mass beside a bonfire, followed by bacon butties. Another example from a secondary comprehensive school is a lunchtime 'Faith and Film' club. This involved showing a film (*The Chronicles of Narnia, Harry Potter, The Boy in Striped Pyjamas* etc.) in 25-minute chunks and then discussing how it connected with living as Christians. The aim was to help the children decode the sacred meaning of life within the entertainment they enjoyed. One girl said 'Do you mean films and books and things have meanings behind them?' ... 'Yes!' It was a wonderful Holy Spirit moment. No one had told her that 'The world [including light entertainment] is charged with the grandeur of God.'[7]

Signs and symbols and a place in the world

Children have a natural curiosity, a natural draw to God and a sacramental understanding of the world. Rebecca Nye, who has been working on the topics of children's spirituality for 20 years within the Church of England, argues that 'Spirituality is a common, natural feature of most, probably all, children's lives.'[8] She also notes that the spirituality of children includes an 'initially natural capacity for awareness of the sacred quality to life experiences'.[9] Children so often live in worlds charged with mystery and wonder. Part of our role is to encourage their confidence, be signposts for them to God and feed their wonder and curiosity; to engage, explore, ask questions together.

The rise of Harry Potter, Game of Thrones and so on shows us that children (and all people!) are seemingly hard-wired to seek something beyond ourselves and beyond the obvious. The richness of symbol and sign, the presence of miracles, the lives of the saints and God at work in the world are gifts that simply need revealing and sharing, with confidence and candidness. The liturgy and all that goes with it is a gift for the world, and young people simply need a little help to see that God is here. In this way the liturgy acts as a bedrock in which young people may discover their place in the world – the world as the creation for which we care and the social action to which we're called.

In the exploration for something beyond ourselves we have seen an upsurge in the early twenty-first century in young people exploring, seeking a connection to the natural world and a truth that is older than they can imagine from a source that isn't trying to *sell* them something or reduce them simply to the role of consumer.[10] Scripture is rich in the power given to the natural world, and the catholic tradition maintains this in the incense that we burn, the flowers and herbs we use throughout the year and even in the gems that are used in episcopal rings and in church plate and architecture. The Church's connection with the four seasons, liturgical seasons, the importance of the natural world and our responsibility to be stewards are strengthened through programmes like the Eco Church A Rocha projects, which call and encourage the Church to reconnect herself with the created world.[11]

One urban church, with help from the Eco Ambassadors from the local Church of England Primary School, are planting a garden within the church of flowers and plants that appear in Scripture and those that have ancient associations with the saints.[12] Through this they have been able to explore the ancient understanding of these plants and how they have been used for healing and cleansing rituals. From this, servers have been encouraged to use these plants in the making of their own incense blends, using the knowledge they have gained for use in church, with meaning they have drawn from ancient and modern understanding of these herbs, flowers and resins.

There's also something here about our connection with the environment and the world and connection with the world beyond. This is essential if we are to capture children's 'natural capacity for awareness of the sacred quality to life experienced'.[13] Plants named after the Virgin Mary can help speak immediately to those who seek symbol and natural connection.[14]

Missional outreach and social justice have long been partners in the catholic tradition. We need look no further than the Catholic Movement's work in areas experiencing deprivation and poverty and with people who were treated as outcasts.[15] It is no coincidence that these are the works of mercy found in the teachings of Jesus. Many of our churches will have existing work, or connections with charities who do the work of feeding, clothing, walking alongside, healing, preaching, visiting, but how many of our young people are encouraged in this work? While recognizing the need for robust safeguarding policies, it is possible to encourage our youth to think about the needs of others and enable them to do their part in bringing comfort and justice.

For example, a mid-sized town church encouraged their youth group of 12–16-year-olds to work with a local charity. This charity provided no-questions-asked meals and washing facilities five days a week. To encourage this they were given a tour of the facilities out of hours and given opportunities to question volunteers to understand more about why this charity was needed. The young people went away from this visit on fire to do something to help out. Over the next four years they raised money, produced artwork to brighten the décor, gave gifts for the volunteers and regularly included them in their prayer time.

A sixth former once explained over coffee with the school chaplain about her 'cosmic terror': 'Is this *it*? Am I this small?' ... 'Yes, and yes, and let me explain why that's good news.' The worshipping life of the Church, the story of salvation, as lived out in Scripture, symbol and ritual, the models of the saints and models of everyday discipleship, all give our young people the sense that they are part of something bigger than themselves. This is vital for their spiritual and mental well-being.

There are lots of young saints and saints who did great things for God in their youth. There are also lots of saints who in their 'smallness' showed that there is no such thing as a 'small' life when it is lived for God. However, so much in our world is tailored to be *me* centred. For catholic Christians, God remains the most interesting person in the room.[16] Despite this we are often encouraged to market worship for one group or another along appealing but individual-centred lines. God-centred church (not us-centred church) is at the heart of catholic belief and practice, and is more likely to ignite young people for longer too. The model of the saints can act as signs and symbols for our young people in showing them the way.

Engaging with the world as God's gift and in social action, and discovering our place in relation to God, is a wonderful way to live and to help our children and young people live.

'Fear not'/'Do not be afraid'

Together the phrases 'fear not' and 'do not be afraid' (and the like) appear in the Bible over 300 times, almost one for every day of the year. These most-repeated phrases in Scripture are the perfect mottos for churches looking at their ministry to children and young people. Here are our top three things of which we encourage you not to be afraid!

1. Do not be afraid when they have questions of their own

The Church of England has myriad resources to enable ministry with young children and is a specialist at primary school assemblies and collective worship, but what happens when children grow up and ask challenging questions? When children gain the confidence to ask their own thought-out questions we can be caught off guard. Their questions can seem to come from left field or we can struggle to find an answer to satisfy their curiosity. This is especially true for many lay people who work with children. Do not be afraid!

God and the faith of the Church are big enough to hold such questioning and resource it. When Jesus is found as a young person in the temple, he's not demonstrating his wisdom to the teachers with a series of statements, he is listening to them and asking questions (Luke 2.41–47). We just need to be brave enough to listen openly and ask questions back (after all, Jesus often responds to a question with a question). And sometimes the bravest and most honest thing of all to do and to help our volunteers and leaders do is to say 'I don't know' or 'I don't have an easy answer to that. Let me go and read and pray and we'll talk about that next week. Why don't you read and pray and come back with thoughts too?' We don't need to hold the answer for every question on demand. Rather than giving a poor answer under pressure, demonstrate for your young people an equally curious spirit and thirst for knowledge. The catholic faith we rejoice in with our young people is a spacious and generous home for us to mature in together, not a straitjacket that limits us.

2. Do not be afraid if no one turns up

In one central London parish they founded a new Sunday afternoon Mass in school to reach a different part of the geographical parish. Often only one or two people came. Hold fast, do not be afraid!

Yes, be imaginative with resources, invitation, advertising, format, the recruitment and nurturing of lay leaders, but also do not be afraid. Everything we have is built on the labours of the saints who have gone before us, who often never saw the fruits of their labours. Hold fast, do not be afraid. That goes for sticking with it, and for letting it go and trying something else.

We do all this in the knowledge that whatever grand projects we oversee, strategies we implement, big liturgies we celebrate or anything else that seems important and impactful, praying for our young people (and all our parish) is the most useful thing we'll ever do for them. Don't worry. Silent prayer, daily offices, rosary, the Eucharist – faithfully offering these are the important and helpful things we do. This can be hard to remember among the incessant demands of email inbox pings, school or community chaplaincy commitments and parish life, but do not be afraid: it is true.

3. Do not be afraid of archdeacons and diocesan strategies

There is the anecdote about the village church ashamed to confess to the archdeacon that no children attend church, only to be asked by the archdeacon: 'How many children actually live in the village?'

'Oh, none.'

On the flip side, in another small rural village with an unusually large local Roman Catholic population, the parish church had a youth group of 8 or 10 young members, comprising the entire non-Roman Catholic adolescent population of the parish. The archdeacon's assessment? The vicar needed 'to grow the youth work'!

Both these extremes show the idols we so often construct around this area of ministry. As with every kind of idol, Scripture tells us to be unafraid to dispense with them. Instead, our call is to love young people into holiness; to join the Holy Spirit in nurturing their lifelong discipleship.

And this isn't just wishful thinking. The authenticity versus anxiety axis is key for young people. To be blunt, they will smell *it* a mile off. Be yourself. Be real. Young people have little patience for people who are false and who aren't what they say they are. What's more, any falseness young people detect in us gets transferred on to the God we represent. When young people detect our hypocrisy they assume Jesus to be a hypocrite too.

Conclusion

Success is not an event that looks good on Instagram: in the age of AI and photoshop we can all do that! 'Success' is rather a ministry where each young person or child is given the opportunity to come to a deeper relationship with God.

'Just do it', says the Nike strapline.

'Just do it.' Small is beautiful. One or two or three children. They're worth it. It can be discouraging but keep going if the only thing stopping you is discouragement.

Another 'Just do it' we may all need to hear is in the scary recruitment of volunteers, arranging DBS checks, risk assessments, permission slips, first-aid training, transport and so on. It has got harder (as well as safer, thanks be to God) to do ministry with children and young people. But don't be discouraged. Help can be found from diocesan teams and neighbouring churches. It's worth it! It is our calling after all.

The catholic faith in the Church of England at its best continues to be there for God's children: in schools and colleges, in being taught how to say daily prayers, invited to friendship with saints on earth and in heaven, in priests called to granny's bedside with holy oils, and children serving at the altar on Sundays and feast days, fully playing their part in our liturgy without a sense of being silenced or relegated to the back or downstairs; with our trademark sense of fun and reverence, with the visible Christian witness through clergy and lay ministry in our communities, and the role of seven sacraments as nourishment for a life-long journey of faith into adulthood and beyond. All this helps nurture children who can say with generosity and confidence why they go to church, and suggest 'Why not come along with me?' when friends ask or challenge. Help 'the little children come to me, and do not stop them; for it is to such as these that the kingdom of heaven belongs'.[17]

Notes

1 Ken Eames, 'Statistics for Mission 2022', Church of England Data Services team, https://www.churchofengland.org/sites/default/files/2023-11/statisticsformission2022.pdf, accessed 24.06.2024.

2 Matthew 19.14 NRSV.

3 M. Montessori, 1965, *The Child in the Church*, Melbourne: Hillside Education, p. 91.

4 cf. Hebrews 5.12.

5 L. Winkett, 2021, *Reading the Bible with your Feet*, London: Canterbury Press.

6 https://jesuitinstitute.org/Pages/JesuitPupilProfile.htm, accessed 24.06.2024.

7 G. M. Hopkins, 1995, *God's Grandeur and Other Poems*, New York: Dover Publications.

8 R. Nye, 2009, *Children's Spirituality*, London: Church House Publishing, p. 9.

9 Nye, *Children's Spirituality*, p. 4.

10 C. E. Sanders, 2009, 'Practicing "the Craft": Why Young People are Attracted to Wicca', *Christian Research Institute*, 12 June, https://www.equip.org/articles/practicing-the-craft/, accessed 24.06.2024.

11 https://ecochurch.arocha.org.uk/, accessed 24.06.2024.

12 See A. Dafni and B. Böck, 'Medicinal Plants of the Bible – Revisited', *Journal of Ethnobiology and Ethnomedicine* 15, 57 (2019), https://ethnobiomed.biomedcentral.com/articles/10.1186/s13002-019-0338-8, and M. R. R. Realy, 2015, *A Catholic Gardener's Spiritual Almanac*, Notre Dame, IN: Ave Maria Press, pp. 230–33.

13 Nye, *Children's Spirituality*, p. 4.

14 Realy, *A Catholic Gardener's Spiritual Almanac*, pp. 103–10.

15 See E. Pusey, 1857, *The Councils of the Church from the Council of Jerusalem A.D. 51, to the Council of Constantinople A.D. 381*, Oxford: Parker, pp. 4–5; and G. Rowell, 1983, *The Vision Glorious: Themes and Personalities of the Catholic Revival in Anglicanism*, Oxford: Oxford University Press, pp. 138–9.

16 After E. Underhill, 1930, *Letter to Archbishop Cosmo Gordon Lang*, http://www.anglicanlibrary.org/underhill/UnderhillLettertoArchbishopLangofCanterbury.pdf, accessed 24.06.2024.

17 Matthew 19.14 NRSV.

Sermon

'Mass and Motherhood'

Preached at Evensong and Benediction at
St Peter de Beauvoir Town on 11 May 2024

Mthr Esther Lay

Psalm 104; Deuteronomy 30; 1 John 2.7–17

When I deacon at St Mary Magdalen's in Oxford, the nature of the processional lineup means that I find myself waiting for about a minute at the top of the stairs, staring at a black marble monument from the seventeenth century lauding the virtues of 'the excellent matron Elizabeth Bayle'. After describing the achievements of her husband, the Dean of Salisbury, it goes on to say that 'She was a great instance of prudence in the government of her family, piety in the education of her children, gravity in her conversation, [and] obedience in her behaviour to her husband, with whom she lived in all conjugal affection.'

I started off feeling quite fond of Elizabeth Bayle, and then, over years of being confronted by her many virtues, gradually less fond. Pictures of perfection, after all, can make us sick and wicked. But now I just wonder what she was really like: what formed her in childhood, what sort things – and people – she loved and hated, what music she knew and how she was actually remembered by those who knew her.

I don't need to tell you, whether you've been one or know one, that a big part of being a mother is seeing how much your body can endure and how much it can change, and then wondering who you really are at the end of it, if there can even be an end. (I hope the same is not true of being a spouse; but marriage is a marathon, not a sprint.)

The body of a mother is like a country whose borders are eroded and stretched and tested, from both inside and out. There is generally at least one dark night of the soul, where the physical exertion or pain is too much or the change is too overwhelming, or both. One's identity can seem to be simply melting away.

It was good, therefore, to sing Bach's *B Minor Mass* last night. This might perhaps seem unhelpfully specific but it applies to us all: music, whether listened to or sung, is very good at sparking memory and connecting us with a buried part of ourselves. This is as true of fresh musical discoveries we've never heard before as it is of old favourites: Britten's *Hymn to St Cecilia*, which we heard just now, never ceases to thrill, whether the first or hundredth time.

My children are now four and seven, so those dark times of disassociation and exhaustion are now beginning to recede into vague memory, but one does emerge from the baby years, wonderful though they are, quite changed, and music is a way of reminding yourself that, after all, you are a person with a complex mental life.

The *B Minor Mass* provides a very particular kind of therapy for me, from the rolling seascape of the Sanctus to the priestly meditation and anguish of the Agnus Dei; but for anyone, singing is a marvellous way of recovering a connection to our bodies, especially when they have been through some form of physical trauma, or simply that mental upheaval that accompanies any change.

If ever there was an argument against placing our bodies last, it is Jesus Christ. He tended to the bodies of others during his earthly ministry but perhaps even more significantly, the Resurrection and even the Ascension are fleshy events: if he is our pattern then we know that we are known and loved by God in our entirety, body and soul.

But the Ascension, in whose season we find ourselves, seems almost more difficult to comprehend within a material context than the Resurrection: I can imagine a body coming back to life but a physical body entering heaven? Ascension services that are held outdoors seem to emphasize the need for a good clear launchpad, a clear shot into heaven, though the Gospels don't exactly say that our Lord shot upwards – all that's clear is that he disappeared. Yet still the disciples stood around, staring upwards. Christ's body was as real as theirs. So where had it gone?

It is right and necessary for Catholic Christians to focus on the body, in all its messy difficulty, and right to think of those bodies having a heavenly future. Our bodies' boundaries are important and something we must learn: babies don't know at first that they are separate from their mothers. The Body of Christ expressed as a parish has its boundaries too, walked and prayed around in the ancient Ascension Day tradition of the Beating of the Bounds. But that custom is a bit like tracing a crime-scene outline in chalk. It shows us only what the limits of the person are, what space they take up. It does not even come close to helping us understand how that person lives and loves, prays and sings.

And to sing, as we do now in our evening worship, is to blur the limits of the body by projecting sound into the space around us, making the air vibrate, changing the reality of the room in a way that echoes in miniature that resounding transformation of both Resurrection and Ascension. Our boundaries are meaningless while we sing; we engulf all who hear us. We throw ourselves into heaven, even as we might simultaneously giggle over the first line of our final hymn, which can never be sung at weddings: 'See the conqueror mounts in triumph'.

But the opposite is also true. To sing is to allow the limits of our selves not only to expand but also to collapse inwards. It is to bring God close to us by letting those boundaries dissolve, inviting him into the centre of our very being. His word is suddenly not far off. As we heard in Deuteronomy, 'It is not in heaven, that you should say, "Who will go up for us to heaven, and bring it to us, that we may hear it and do it?" Neither is it beyond the sea … But the word is very near you; it is in your mouth and in your heart, so that you can do it.'

To use our fragile bodies to sing *to* God and *of* God, whether quietly in our homes, loudly in our churches or propelled by an orchestra on a concert stage, is more interesting than just praying twice. It is to suffuse ourselves with God's mystery in Christ, whose body was like ours, who glorified our humanity in his sacrifice and his triumph over death and hell.

Our psalm shows us the proper response to God's glory, which we see in creation – including our own bodies, existing in friendship or celibacy or marriage – and worship in our risen Lord. 'I will sing unto the Lord as long as I live; I will praise my God while I have my being.'

I hope that Elizabeth Bayle, that admirable matron, took time to sing. We will never know what she was really like, but if she sang she did what we do, what even Jesus would have done if he could – and I assume he could – hold a tune: blurring the boundaries between earth and heaven with our breath, placing God's word in our very mouths. Amen.

Index of Names and Subjects

achievement 37
adoration of the Sacrament 21
altarpieces 47–59
Anglo-Catholicism 1–3
Antony of Egypt 146, 150
Aphrahat 147
Aquinas 21, 22–3, 170
ascension 26, 182
asceticism 143–7, 151–2
Aschenbrenner, George 79n8
Attleborough parish church 54
Augustine
 and the Bible 43–4
 and celibacy 146–7
 on marriage 164
 on singing 140

Baden, Joel S. 95n7
baptism 63, 124–35
Basil of Ancyra 148
Basil of Caesarea 146, 149, 150
Bayle, Elizabeth 181
Beckett, Wendy 103
Benedict, rule for monks 65
Betjeman, John 56
Bible 81–94
 in Augustine 43–4
 commentaries on 43–4
 daily reading 90
 exposition 86
 in liturgy 86–90
 see also Scripture

biblical literacy 82–3
biblical studies 83–5, 91
Bodley, G. F. 52
Bouyer, Louis 131
Bower, Stephen Dykes 53, 54
Butler, Josephine 86

catechesis 124–5, 135
celibacy 142–52
Chapman, John 111
Chapp, Larry 129, 132
chastity 143
 vows of 145
children and young people
 169–80
choices 74–8
Christ, as bridegroom 147–8,
 152
Christian ethics 19–30
Church, Richard William 52
Cloud of Unknowing 140
Common Worship
 baptism in 125, 128–9, 133
 Eucharist in 22, 27, 88–9
 marriage in 157, 159, 161–4,
  166
 and Scripture 81
communion of the saints 8–9, 13
communities
 of hermits 146
 monastic 146, 150
community 113–20

Community of the
  Resurrection 64, 117–18,
  142–3
Comper, Ninian 50, 51, 54–7
confirmation 32, 98
consolation 69, 76–7
consumer culture 39
covenant love 15–16
Cranmer, Thomas 158–63, 165
creativity, and communion of
  saints 13
Cyril of Jerusalem 10

Daily Office 43, 64, 87
deaconesses 49–50
Dei Verbum 91–3
dependence 35–45
  on God 7–8
  on Jesus 12–13
  on the whole Church 42
desolation 68, 69, 74–7
discernment 67–79, 167
disciplined life 63
diversity 4
Dix, Gregory 14, 20, 131
Documentary Hypothesis 83–4
Donne, John 139
Douglas, Kelly Brown 58

Easter Vigil 131–2
eating, in the Eucharist 11–12
Ecclestone, Alan 111
Ekserdjian, David 47
Emmaus road 63, 64
Enkratites 144–5
epiclesis 22
eschatological hope 23–4
ethics 19–30
Eucharist 10–18
  commissions Christians 25
  defining activity 44

and ethics 19–30
as feeding on Christ 8–9, 24
First Communion 126–7
as journey 25
proclamation of Scripture 89–90
as supratemporal event 21–4
eucharistic community, social
  vision 13–14
Eustathius of Sebaste 146
evangelism 33
examen 69–72

Farthing, Michael 121–3
Finn, Richard 144
Finney, Nicky 56
First Communion 126–7
fonts 127–9
food and drink, imagery of 12
forgiveness 29, 104, 106
formation 43–4
freedom 35
fun 173
Furlong-Russell, Jeva Soraya 98

Garner, Thomas 52
gathering 27–8
Gilmore, Isabella 49–50
God
  calls us 105–6
  loved by us 140
  loves us 107
good and evil spirits 70–2
Gore, Charles 86
graces 72–4
Gregory Nazianzus 129
Gregory of Nyssa 149
growth in grace 27
Grunewald, Matthias 57–8

Hall, Michael 53
Hannah 99–100, 110–12

INDEX OF NAMES AND SUBJECTS

Hardwicke's Marriage Act 163–4
Hastings, Hubert de Cronin 56
heaven 17, 26
  communal 45
Hebert, A. G. 131
Herbert, George 15, 18
hermits 146
Hirsch, E. D. 93
Holy Spirit
  creativity 13, 18
  and discernment 78
  in Word and Sacrament 20–1, 22, 27
Hughes, Marian Rebecca 142, 152

identity 172
  as Christians 40–2
Ignatius of Loyola 67–79
imaginative contemplation 74, 90
incense 3
independence, personal 35
indifference 73
individualism 44
individuals, in Protestantism 8–9
invitation 32–4
Isenheim altarpiece 57–8
Israel 94

Jacob 93–4
Jerome 146
Jesus
  in art 50
  ascension 26, 182–3
  calls us 74
  crucifixion 14
  healings 45
  Lord's Prayer 103–4
  resurrection appearances 40, 55, 63
Jones, Simon 129, 133

Jubilee Group 10

Kavanagh, Aidan 131
Keiskamma altarpiece 57–8

Larsen, Timothy 85, 86
Lectio Divina 90–1
Leech, Ken 2, 3–4, 6, 10
Levering, Matthew 86–7
Liddon, Henry Parry 52
life
  disciplined 63
  in the present and the eternal 63
listening 119, 177
liturgical year 3
liturgy 161–3
  as formational act 44
  and Scripture 86–90
Lord's Prayer 103–4
love, God's 107–8
Lund, Niels Møller 52

Mckenna, Megan 134
Macquarrie, John 37
Magnificat 41–2, 81
Marian theology 55
marriage 36, 156–67
Mass 59
  see also Eucharist
Maurice, F. D. 131
Mirfield 64, 117
monastic life 109, 117, 150
Montessori, Maria 170
Moore, David 84–5
Morris, May 49–52
motherhood 181–3
Mozley, J. B. 130
music 140–1, 182

new covenant 14–15
Newman, John Henry 85, 142–3

Nye, Rebecca 175

Opus Dei 110
Oxford Movement 1, 48, 85

parenting 35
parish system 41
Paschal Mystery 130–2
pastoral care 6
Paul (saint)
  on Christian community 13
  on worship 11
peace 28–30
Pilgrim course 133
play 170–1
Portsmouth Cathedral 128
poverty, vows of 145
prayer 39, 103–12
  daily office 64
  eucharistic 18
  judgement 100
  leading to solidarity 100–1
  of the saints 8–9, 45, 109
  of thanksgiving 99–100
  see also examen
Pre-Raphaelites 48
Probert, Rebecca 168n7
proclamation, in the Eucharist 89–90
procreation 160
Protestantism 8–9
Pusey, Edward Bouverie 85–6, 129–30, 142–3

Ramsey, Michael 7, 8
reconciliation 29, 117–18
Rees, Martin 63
Reformation 81
religions 11
reservation of the Sacrament 16, 118

revelation 92
Richards, J. M. 56
ritual 11
Rohr, Richard 113

sacraments 44, 115, 140
  and children 170, 173
St Cyprian's, Clarence Gate 54–7
St James's, Piccadilly 58–9
St Paul's Cathedral 52–4
salvation, as dependence 45
Samaritan woman 124–5
Schmemann, Alexander 24–6, 44
Scripture
  nourishes individuals 8–9
  see also Bible
Sellon, Lydia 142
Senn, Frank 87–9
sex and gender 5–6, 93
sexual abstinence 148–9
sexual continence 143–4
Sherwood, Yvonne 84–5
sin 106
singing 65, 140, 182
Siricius 148
solidarity 100–1
Sons and Daughters of the Covenant 145, 147
Southwark Cathedral 50, 58
spiritual direction 72–3
Spiritual Exercises 72–3
spirituality, of children 175
Stancliffe, David 128
Symondson, Anmthony 54
Syriac churches 145

Tatian 145
testimony 98–9, 101
thanksgiving 106–7
Thecla 144, 149
Thomas Aquinas 21, 22–3, 170

INDEX OF NAMES AND SUBJECTS

Tractarians 85
transfiguration 64
transformation
  Christian life 26
  through prayer 100
Triduum 59, 70, 132
True Blood 67–8
Tugwell, Simon 39

Udoh, Unyimeabasi 58–9

Vasey, Michael 133, 134
Vatican Council 91
vestments 3
virginity 143–4, 148

Waddell, Helen 132
Walker, Arthur George 50
The Walking Dead 67–8
war 111
Watts and Company 52

Webb, Philip 49–52
Weil, Simone 42
welcoming 27–8
Wellhausen, Julius 95n7
wells, as image 124–5
wholeness
  in the Church 5–7, 45, 114
  meaning of 'catholic' 10
Wickham, Rob 116
Williams, Charles 62–3
Winkett, Lucy 173
witness 116
word and sacrament 63, 65
worship
  and children 170–2
  congregational co-creation 24
  expectations of 64
  in Paul's letters 11

Yonge, Charlotte 86

www.ingramcontent.com/pod-product-compliance
Lightning Source LLC
LaVergne TN
LVHW041755090825
818074LV00007B/103